TEXAS TRUST LAW:

CASES AND MATERIALS

Third Edition

GERRY W. BEYER

Governor Preston E. Smith Regents Professor of Law
Texas Tech University School of Law

AuthorHouse™
1663 Liberty Drive
Bloomington, IN 47403
www.authorhouse.com
Phone: 1 (800) 839-8640

Published by AuthorHouse 01/12/2017

ISBN: 978-1-5246-5932-5 (sc)
ISBN: 978-1-5246-5931-8 (e)

Print information available on the last page.

PREFACE

This book is designed for courses covering Texas trust law, either alone or as part of a combined Wills & Trusts course. The cases, problems, and questions are drawn extensively from Texas materials and attempt to provide the student with a comprehensive understanding of how trusts are handled in Texas.

When the notation *"read"* is used, the student should immediately read the indicated materials before proceeding. The signal *"see"* indicates that the cited material is highly relevant to the question or statement being made but that, although highly recommended, the source need not be immediately consulted. *"See generally"* indicates background material or material that would be a good place to start researching that particular topic.

All of the cases have been edited, to one extent or another. Omissions are indicated by asterisks and most of the courts' footnotes have been omitted or renumbered without notation.

This book is designed to be used in conjunction with the most current version of TEXAS ESTATE PLANNING STATUTES WITH COMMENTARY which is also published by AuthorHouse. This book is a compilation of the relevant Texas statutes which are referenced in this book. The book also includes commentary entitled *Statutes in Context* to provide background information, explanations, and citations to key cases.

Every attempt was made to ascertain the correctness of the information contained in this book. However, neither AuthorHouse nor the author warrant that this material is without error. Readers should verify all material with the original sources before relying on it. In addition, new cases and legislation make important changes to the law. You may access a list of updates to this work at http://www.ProfessorBeyer.com.

If, as you use this book, you have any suggestions, comments, corrections, or criticisms, I would greatly appreciate your sharing them with me. Please contact me via e-mail at gwb@ProfessorBeyer.com

Gerry W. Beyer

Lubbock, Texas
January 2017

i

SUMMARY OF CONTENTS

TABLE OF CONTENTS

TABLE OF CASES

Principal cases are in all capitals.
Note cases are in regular type.

TABLE OF TRUST CODE SECTIONS

Chapter One

INTRODUCTION[1]

A. BASIC OPERATION

The owner of property may create a trust by transferring that property in a unique fashion. First, the owner must divide the title to the property into legal and equitable interests and, second, the owner must impose fiduciary duties on the holder of the legal title to deal with the property for the benefit of the holder of the equitable title.

1. Splitting of Ownership

a. Legal Interest

Read Trust Code § 111.004(18).

The trustee holds legal title to the trust property. The trustee has all of the responsibilities related to property ownership but receives none of the benefits, except possibly a fee for trustee services. In carrying out ownership responsibilities, a trustee is under a duty to perform as a fiduciary, i.e., the trustee must use reasonable care when dealing with the trust property and maintain the utmost degree of loyalty. If a trustee's conduct falls beneath these standards, the trustee will be personally liable, i.e., subject to civil and perhaps even criminal liability.

b. Equitable or Beneficial Interest

Read Trust Code § 111.004(2).

The beneficiary holds the equitable interest in the trust property. The beneficiary may also be called a donee, grantee, or *cestui que trust*. The beneficiary has the right to enforce the trust. The beneficiary is entitled to the benefits of the trust property as set forth in the trust instrument but typically has little or no control over the trust or the trust property.

---

[1] Adapted from GERRY W. BEYER, TEACHING MATERIALS ON ESTATE PLANNING ch. 2(D) (4th ed. 2013).

Questions

1. Settlor transferred both legal and equitable title to Daughter. Does a valid trust exist?

2. Settlor created a valid trust by transferring legal title to Daughter and equitable title to Son. Thereafter, Daughter transferred legal title to Son. Does a valid trust still exist?

2.   The Settlor

Read Trust Code § 111.004(14).

The settlor is the person who is responsible for the creation of the trust by supplying the initial trust property. The settlor may also be known as the trustor, grantor, or donor. The settlor owned both legal title and equitable title to the property prior to the creation of the trust. The settlor may choose to retain the legal title, the beneficial title, or part of each. Remember that a split of title will not exist unless at least one other person receives some interest, either legal or equitable, in the property.

3.   Trust Property

Read Trust Code §§ 111.004(12) & (17) & 112.005.

A trust is a conveyancing relationship and thus a trust must have trust property. Trust property may be referred to as the trust's principal, corpus, res, or estate. The settlor must have the power to transfer title to the property. Accordingly, if the settlor cannot transfer the settlor's interest in a particular type or item of property, that property may not be held in trust.

4.   Basic Functioning of a Trust

The settlor creates a trust by transferring legal title to an individual or financial institution in which the settlor has confidence and equitable title to an individual or charity deserving of a windfall. As discussed above, the settlor may retain some interest in the trust property, but a split of title must occur for a valid trust to exist.

The instructions contained in the trust instrument and state law control the actions of the trustee. The trustee must manage and invest the property in accordance with these mandates. Additionally, the payments made to or for the benefit of the beneficiary must be consistent with the instructions in the trust instrument.

A trustee's duties end when the trust terminates. Termination occurs either by the trust's own terms or upon depletion of the trust property. If property remains when the trust terminates, the legal title and equitable title are united in the remainder beneficiary.

B.   PURPOSES AND USES OF TRUSTS

Trusts are one of the most powerful, useful, and advantageous tools available to the modern estate planner. This section discusses some of the reasons you may decide to recommend a trust to your clients.

1.   Provides for and Protects Trust Beneficiaries

The settlor's desire to provide for and protect someone is probably the most common reason for choosing to use a trust. Although a donor could make a quick, convenient, and uncomplicated outright gift, there are many situations in which such outright gifts would not effectuate the donor's true intent.

a. Minors

Minors lack legal capacity to manage property and usually have insufficient maturity to do so as well. Thus, a trust allows a settlor to make a gift for the benefit of the minor without giving the minor control over the property. A trust is also more flexible and allows a settlor to have greater control over how the property is used when contrasted with other methods such as a transfer to a guardian or conservator of the minor's estate or to a custodian under the Uniform Transfers to Minors Act.

b. Individuals Who Lack Management Skills

A person may lack the skills necessary to properly manage the trust property. This deficiency could be the result of mental or physical incompetence or a lack of experience in the rigors of making prudent investment decisions. For example, persons who suddenly obtain a large amount of money, such as actors, professional athletes, lottery winners, or personal injury plaintiffs, tend to deplete this "windfall" rapidly because they have never learned how to manage their money wisely. By putting the money under the control of a trustee with investment experience, the settlor increases the chances that the beneficiary's interests are served for a longer period of time.

c. Spendthrifts

Some individuals may be competent to manage property but are prone to use it in an excessive or frivolous manner. By using a carefully drafted trust, a settlor can protect the trust property from the beneficiary and the beneficiary's creditors.

d. Persons Susceptible to Influence

When a person suddenly acquires a significant amount of property, that person may be under pressure from family, friends, investment advisors, and many others to let them share the windfall. A trust can make it virtually impossible for the beneficiary to transfer trust property to these people.

2. Provides Flexibility of Asset Distribution

An outright gift, either inter vivos or testamentary, gives the donee total control over the way the property is used. With a trust, the settlor can restrict the beneficiary's control over the property in any manner the settlor desires so long as the restrictions are not illegal or in violation of public policy. This flexibility allows the settlor to determine how the trustee distributes trust benefits, such as by spreading the benefits over time, giving the trustee discretion as to whom receives distributions and in what amount, requiring the beneficiary to meet certain criteria to receive or continue receiving benefits, or limiting the purposes for which trust property may be used, e.g., health care or education.

3. Protects Against Settlor's Incompetence

Once a person is declared incompetent due to illness, injury, or other cause, the person cannot manage property. The court then needs to appoint a guardian of the estate or conservator to manage the property. This process may cause the person considerable embarrassment and there is no guarantee the incompetent person will be happy with the guardian's decisions. Guardianships are also inconvenient and costly.

Trusts can be used to avoid the need for a guardian. The settlor may create a trust and maintain considerable control over the trust property by, for example, actually serving as trustee, retaining the power to revoke the trust, and even keeping a beneficial life interest. However, upon incompetency, the settlor's designated successor trustee would take over the administration of the trust property in accordance with the directions expressed by the settlor in the trust instrument.

An alternative method to protect property and avoid the need for a guardian in the event of incompetency is to have the client execute a durable power of attorney for property management.

4. Allows Professional Management of Property

The settlor may create a trust to obtain the services of a professional asset manager. Trustees, such as banks and trust companies, may have more expertise and experience with various types of investments than most individuals. Professional trustees also have greater investment opportunities. For example, a bank may combine funds from several trusts into one common trust fund to take advantage of opportunities that require a large investment and to diversify, thus reducing the damage to the value of a particular trust when one investment turns sour.

However, you must consider the effect of trust fees when discussing the selection of a trustee with the client. The value of the trust property and its potential for income should be high enough to insure that the benefit from professional management outweighs the cost of that management.

5. Avoids Probate

Property in an inter vivos trust is not part of the probate estate upon the settlor's death. The property remaining in the trust when the settlor dies is administered and distributed according to the terms of the trust instead of passing under a will or by intestate succession. Advantages to avoiding probate include providing for the property to reach the hands of the beneficiaries quickly, avoiding gaps in management, and evading probate publicity. These advantages, however, do not apply to testamentary trusts since they do not avoid probate.

6. Provides Tax Benefits

Another popular reason for utilizing trusts is tax avoidance. Income taxes can be saved by shifting income earning property to a person in a lower tax bracket. Additionally, gift taxes may be avoided by structuring the transfers to a trust to fall within the annual exclusion from the federal gift tax. Likewise, if a trust is properly constructed, the trust property will not be treated as part of the settlor's estate and estate taxes are reduced.

Notes and Questions

1. Despite these benefits, a trust may not be the best tool to accomplish the client's intent. For example, assume your client's main goal is to plan for disability. Although a properly drafted trust would do the job, it will entail additional time and money to establish the trust and transfer title to the property to the trust. Perhaps a durable power of attorney for property management which can be prepared quickly and economically is all the client needs. Thus, like any estate planning technique, you must evaluate

the benefits and disadvantages of a trust before making your recommendation.

2. Some attorneys heavily hype inter vivos trusts as an estate planning panacea to the general public through the use of newspaper and other media advertisements and estate planning "seminars." Although a trust is an extremely useful technique, a person should not create a trust until the person carefully balances the benefits against the trust's creation, administration, and transfer costs.

3. Several states are attempting to stop the sale of living trusts by non-lawyers. Illinois' Attorney General Roland Burris stated, "Living trusts in the hands of unscrupulous con artists are one of the fastest growing areas of fraud against senior citizens." David N. Anderson, *Living Trust Fraud Bill is Approved,* ISBA BAR NEWS, June 21, 1993, at 1. How do you think purveyors of inter vivos trusts are hurting their clients?

4. To protect the public from exaggerated claims of the benefits of a living trust, some states have taken steps to regulate how attorneys advertise them. For example, in November 1997, Texas prohibited attorneys from making the following statements about trusts created during the settlor's lifetime because they are potentially misleading and may create unjustified expectations:[2]

- Living trusts will always save the client money.
- The use of a living trust in and of itself will reduce or eliminate estate taxes otherwise payable as a result of the client's death.
- Estate tax savings can be achieved only by use of a living trust.
- The use of a living trust will achieve estate tax savings that cannot be achieved using a will.
- The probate process is always lengthy and complicated.
- The probate process should always be avoided.
- The use of a living trust will reduce the total expenses incurred compared to expenses incurred using other estate planning devices intended to address the same basic function.
- The use of a living trust avoids lengthy delays experienced in the use of other estate planning devices intended to

---

[2]Interpretive Comment No. 22: Advertisement of Living Trusts, as reported in 61 TEX. B.J. 71 (1998).

address the same basic function.

- Lawyers use will-writing as a loss leader.

C. TEXAS TRUST LEGISLATION

There are three major "eras" of trust legislation in Texas.

1. Before 1943

Before 1943, there was only sparse codification of Texas trust law. Additionally, there was not much case law regarding express trusts and what existed was often conflicting.

2. Texas Trust Act

As the use of trusts as an estate planning technique began to grow, it became apparent that more substantial guidance was needed. Accordingly, the Texas State Bar appointed a committee to study the Texas law of trusts. As a result of this committee's work, the Texas Trust Act was introduced and it subsequently passed the legislature with only minor changes. See R. Dean Moorhead, *The Texas Trust Act*, 22 TEX. L. REV. 123 (1944). The Act took effect on April 19, 1943.

The Act provided a fairly detailed scheme for the creation and administration of trusts. The Act's major thrust, however, was not to control the details of all trusts but rather to fill in the gaps when a trust instrument did not provide how a specific situation was to be handled. Except for a very small number of restrictions, the settlor remained the master of his or her trust.

The Act served Texas well and, with occasional amendments, remained effective until December 31, 1983, a span of over forty years.

3. Texas Trust Code

The Texas Trust Code had its origin ten years before its enactment. In 1973, the Real Estate, Probate, and Trust Law Section of the State Bar of Texas established the Trust Code Committee to study the Texas Trust Act and propose revisions. The Committee found that although the Act was fundamentally sound, new statutory provisions were needed because of the increasing complexity of trust law as well as changes in economic and social conditions. See STATE BAR OF TEXAS, GUIDE TO THE TEXAS TRUST CODE (1983).

As a result of ten years of extremely hard work, the Committee formulated a comprehensive Texas Trust Code detailing the creation, administration, and enforcement of express trusts. The Code consolidated much of the existing trust law, both statutory and common, added provisions to address issues not covered by the Act, and established a framework to facilitate the making of amendments and additions. The Code retained a great deal of the Texas Trust Act with enhancements from the Restatement (Second) of Trusts.

The Code was introduced in the 68th Legislature and, after a few amendments, was passed. It is interesting to note that before the Trust code was passed, the Legislature adopted the Property Code which contained a non-substantive re-writing of the Act. Thereafter, those provisions of the Property Code were amended by the Texas Trust Code.

The Texas Trust Code took effect on January 1, 1984 and is found in Title 9B of the Texas Property Code. It applies to all trusts created after the effective date as well as to all transactions occurring after the effective date relating to trusts created before the effective date. *Read* Trust Code § 111.006. The Code and the Act are treated as one continuous statute, that is, the Code is an "amendment" to the Act. *Read* Trust Code § 111.002(b).

The Code is amended on a regular basis and frequently incorporates concepts borrowed from the Uniform Trust Code. (Note that the Texas Trust Code was one of the statutes the drafters of the UTC used as a starting point for their work.)

4. Other Trust Legislation

In addition to the Texas Trust Code, there are many other statutory provisions concerning trusts scattered throughout the Texas statutes. Below is a *non-exclusive* list of some of the areas covered by these statutes.

- Effect of divorce of settlor and beneficiary (Est. Code §§ 123.051-123.055).
- Pension trusts (Prop. Code §§ 121.001-121.005).
- Employees' trusts (Prop. Code §§ 121.051-121.058).
- Trusts for minors' property when property recovered in suits by next friends (Prop. Code § 141.005).
- Trust bank accounts (Est. Code §§ 113.001-113.210).
- Attorney General's involvement with charitable trusts (Prop. Code §§ 123.001-123.006).
- Reformation of trusts that violate the Rule Against Perpetuities (Prop. Code § 5.043).

- Criminal penalties for breach of trust (Penal Code § 32.45).
- Foreign corporations as trustees (Est. Code §§ 505.001-505.006).
- Pour over wills (Est. Code § 254.001).
- Trustees as beneficiaries of life insurance policies (Ins. Code §§ 1104.021-1104.022).
- Child support (Fam. Code § 154.005).

Chapter Two

TRUST CREATION

This chapter analyzes the requirements for a valid *express trust*, that is, a trust created based on the expressed intent of the settlor. It is important to make a distinction between two categories of express trusts. First, the *private trust*, that is, a trust created for non-charitable beneficiaries, and second, the *charitable trust* which the settlor establishes for charitable purposes. The requirements are basically the same for both private and charitable trusts. However, some of the validity requirements are different for charitable trusts.

Other types of trusts are discussed in Chapter 5, such as *resulting trusts* which arise by operation of law when the facts and circumstances show that a person had the intent to hold equitable title to property although legal title is in the hands of another and *constructive trusts* which courts impose as an equitable remedy to prevent unjust enrichment.

The fundamental requirements for a valid express trust are summarized below:

- **Trust Intent** — The settlor must intend to split legal and equitable title and impose fiduciary duties on the holder of legal title (trustee) for the benefit of the holder of equitable title (beneficiary).

- **Capacity** — The settlor must have the capacity to make a conveyance of property in trust form.

- **Statute of Frauds Compliance** — In certain situations, the settlor's trust intent must be documented by a written instrument.

- **Purpose** — The purpose of the trust must not be illegal or against public policy.

- **Property** — The settlor must place property into the trust and the trust must continue to hold property.

- **Trustee** — A trustee must ultimately hold legal title and be obligated to deal with the property for the benefit of the beneficiaries. However, the court will appoint a trustee if necessary to assure the trust's creation or continued existence.

- **Beneficiary** — The trust needs a beneficiary to hold the equitable title to the property. The settlor may either retain equitable title and become a beneficiary or transfer it to a third party.

- **Rule Against Perpetuities Compliance** — The duration of a private trust cannot exceed the period permitted by the Rule Against Perpetuities.

A. TRUST INTENT

Trust intent is the threshold factor in determining whether or not a conveyance of property is sufficient to create an express trust. If the transferor does not manifest trust intent, no trust is created and the court will not intervene to create a trust. *Read* Trust Code § 112.002.

A transferor of property has trust intent if the transferor (1) divides title to the property into legal and equitable components, and (2) imposes enforceable fiduciary duties on the holder of legal title to deal with the property for the benefit of the equitable title holder. *Read* Trust Code § 111.004(4).

1.   Ascertaining the Settlor's Intent

PERFECT UNION LODGE NO. 10 v. INTERFIRST BANK OF SAN ANTONIO

Texas Supreme Court, 1988
748 S.W.2d 218

ROBERTSON, Justice.

This is a suit to construe the will of an attorney, A.H. Lumpkin. The pertinent provisions of his will are as follows:

IV.

I give, devise and bequeath to my beloved wife, Cornelia Lumpkin, all property of every kind and character I may own at my death, including real, personal and mixed, wheresoever situated, except the foregoing property *given to her absolutely, for and during her natural life, to have the use and benefit thereof during her said natural life.*

This bequest, however, to my said wife is in lieu of her community interest in our homestead comprised of approximately 133 acres on the Hausman Road, out of the Perry Davis Survey in Bexar County, Texas* * *

V.

Subject to the foregoing life estate devised to my wife, Cornelia Lumpkin, or in case she dies before I do, *I give, devise and bequeath the hereinbefore described homestead in Bexar County, Texas and the 40 acres of land in Dimmit County, Texas, and all the rest and residue of my property, real, personal and mixed, wheresoever situated, to Perfect Union Lodge No. 10 A.F. & A.M. of San Antonio, Texas, in fee simple* * * *

VII.

I hereby nominate, constitute and appoint Charles W. Barrow and Travis M. Moursund *Independent Executors* of this my Last Will and Testament, and direct that no bond or security be required of them as such, and that no action be taken with reference to my estate other than the probating of this my Will and the filing of an inventory, appraisement and list of claims of my estate as may be required by law.

* * *

My said *Executors* shall handle my estate during the life of my wife, Cornelia Lumpkin, and as long thereafter as may be reasonably necessary to carry out the terms of this my Will.

To the end that my said Independent Executors shall have full power and authority to handle and settle my said estate without the necessity of court orders, I hereby confer upon them all such powers as are given to Trustees under and by virtue of the provisions of the Texas Trust Act (Article 7425b, Vernon's Civil Statutes of the State of Texas Annotated) as the same exists at the date of this my Will, regardless of whether such Act may hereafter be repealed or amended, as fully as though its provisions were written in this my Will; provided further that *my said Independent Executors* may also exercise any additional powers conferred on Trustees by any subsequent amendment of such Act, it being my intention that *my Executors appointed by me in this my Will shall have full and complete power to manage, sell, mortgage, invest and reinvest and handle my estate as to such Executors may seem best and proper without the necessity of court orders.* (emphasis added).

The probate court concluded that the will created a testamentary trust with Cornelia Lumpkin as income beneficiary. The executor of the estate,

Travis Moursund[1] was named trustee. Pursuant to section 113.110 of the Texas Property Code, the court further ordered the trustee to sell certain real property which it found had been underproductive since 1975. The proceeds were to be distributed between Cornelia Lumpkin and Perfect Union Lodge according to section 113.110(a). The court of appeals affirmed the trial court judgment, 713 S.W.2d 391. We affirm the judgments of these courts.

The cardinal rule for construing a will requires that the testator's intent be ascertained by looking to the provisions of the instrument as a whole, as set forth within the four corners of the instrument. The court shall effectuate that intent as far as legally possible. *Stewart v. Selder*, 473 S.W.2d 3, 7 (Tex. 1971); *Sellers v. Powers*, 426 S.W.2d 533, 536 (Tex. 1968). The will should be construed so as to give effect to every part of it, if the language is reasonably susceptible of that construction. *Republic National Bank of Dallas v. Fredericks*, 155 Tex. 79, 83, 283 S.W.2d 39, 43 (1955). However, the court will not redraft the will or add provisions under the guise of construction in order to effectuate some presumed intent of the testator. *Shriner's Hospital for Crippled Children v. Stahl*, 610 S.W.2d 147, 151 (Tex. 1980); *Huffman v. Huffman*, 161 Tex. 267, 273, 339 S.W.2d 885, 888 (1960).

The requisites of an express trust are provided by the Texas Trust Code (TEX. PROP. CODE ANN. §§ 101.001-115.017 (Vernon 1984)); however, the new trust code provides that the Texas Trust Act (repealed 1984) will govern the creation of trusts entered into while the Act was in effect. TEX. PROP. CODE ANN. § 110.006(2) (Vernon 1984). Under the Act, a testamentary trust is created through "[a] transfer by will by the owner of property to another person or persons as trustee for a third person or persons* * *" Texas Trust Act, ch. 148, § 7, 1943 Tex. Gen. Laws 232, 234, *repealed and codified* TEX. PROP. CODE ANN. § 112.001(3) (Vernon 1984). Implicit in this statutory definition is the requirement of a trustee with administrative powers and fiduciary duties. *Nolana Development Ass'n v. Corsi*, 682 S.W.2d 246, 248 (Tex. 1984). Even more fundamental than this, it is well established that the legal and equitable estates must be separated; the former being vested in the trustee and the latter in the beneficiary. * * *. This separation of the legal and equitable estates in the trust property is the basic hallmark of the trust entity.

Technical words of expression, however, are not essential for the creation of a trust. To create a trust by a written instrument, the beneficiary, the *res*, and the trust purpose must be identified. It is not

---

[1]Charles Barrow resigned as executor in 1978.

absolutely necessary that legal title be granted to the trustee in specific terms. Therefore, a trust by implication may arise, notwithstanding the testator's failure to convey legal title to the trustee, when the intent to create a trust appears reasonably clear from the terms of the will, construed in light of the surrounding circumstances. *Dulin v. Moore*, 96 Tex. 135, 139, 70 S.W. 742, 743 (1902) * * *.

In *Dulin v. Moore*, this court construed a will in which the testator, after devising real property in fee simple, provided that another person would be "trustee to receive and control the property" during the lives of the devisees. The court recognized the issue as being whether the testator intended to confer mere "naked powers" upon the trustee or to invest him with legal title for the purposes of the trust. The court concluded that "although the will contains no words which expressly convey legal title to Dulin, the intention that he should take the legal title is as clearly manifested as if express terms had been employed." *Dulin*, 96 Tex. at 139, 70 S.W. at 743.

Similarly, in *Heironimus v. Tate*, the court construed a will in which there were no express words giving the executor legal title to any property. The will bequeathed property to two beneficiaries but further provided that the executors had discretion in making distributions to the beneficiaries during their lives, and upon their deaths the remainder passed to their lineal descendants. The court concluded that a trust had been created with legal title vested in the executors. *Heironimus*, 355 S.W.2d at 80.

As in *Dulin* and *Heironimus*, we must construe a will which lacks specific language conferring legal title upon the executors. From the provisions of the will as a whole, A.H. Lumpkin's intent to create a testamentary trust can be ascertained. By its terms, Lumpkin devised all the residue of his estate to his wife for her life, with the remainder to Perfect Union Lodge. He clearly intended to separate the management and control of his residual estate from the beneficial interest conferred upon his wife. The provision in paragraph VII that "my said executors shall handle my estate during the life of my wife" indicates that Lumpkin intended to provide for more than a mere settlement of his business affairs and distribution of assets. Furthermore, the provision, granting the executors the powers found under the Trust Act, authorized Moursund to exercise greater control over the property than was necessary for administration of the estate. We hold that Lumpkin's will created a testamentary trust for the life of his wife, which would terminate upon her death.

[discussion of issues regarding jurisdiction, underproductive property, and mootness omitted]

The judgment of the court of appeals is affirmed.

SPEARS, J., not sitting.

RAY, J., dissented, joined by PHILLIPS, C.J., and WALLACE, J.

RAY, Justice, dissenting.

I respectfully dissent. It is fundamental for the creation of a trust that the legal estate must be vested in the trustee and the equitable estate vested in the beneficiary. *Cutrer v. Cutrer*, 334 S.W.2d 599, 605 (Tex. Civ. App.—San Antonio 1960) *aff'd*, 162 Tex. 166, 345 S.W.2d 513 (1961). This will contains no language expressing the testator's intention that the legal estate vest in the executors or that a trust be created. I would reverse the judgment of the courts below.

Paragraphs IV and V evidence the testator's intent to devise to his wife a life estate in all the rest and residue of his estate, with the remainder in fee simple to Perfect Union Lodge. The majority relies on the last two clauses in paragraph VII to hold that a trust was created because the testator granted the executors powers under the Texas Trust Act during the life of his wife. However, no transfer of the legal estate to the executors was effectuated by these administrative provisions. I would hold that the will's dispositive provisions, which state that the nature and quantum of the estate vested in the wife, should control over the will's purely administrative provisions establishing the executors' powers and duties.

This case is controlled by the ruling in *Beckham v. Beckham*, 227 S.W. 940 (Tex. Comm'n App. 1921, judgm't adopted) in which the testator made an absolute bequest of all of her property to her children, followed by a provision stating:

> I hereby authorize and empower my said executor to take possession of any and all property belonging to my estate; to sell and convey same; to invest any money that may come into his hands in such way as he shall deem proper; and to execute all the deeds of conveyance, acquittances and receipts necessary and proper to be executed in order to carry out the object of this instrument.

To determine whether the testator intended to create a trust empowering the executor to administer the estate until the children reached their majority, the court considered the following: (1) that the will expressly stated, "my said executor"; (2) that the additional powers conferred were not inconsistent with the duties of the executor; and, (3) that there was no language indicating an intent to create a trust. The court held that no trust was created because no clear intent appeared from the will. *See also Time Securities v. West*, 324 S.W.2d 583, 585-86 (Tex. Civ. App.—San Antonio 1959, writ ref'd n.r.e.).

This is a self-made will of an attorney who practiced law in Texas for over 50 years and it is apparent by his reference to the Texas Trust Act that he was cognizant of the requisites for the creation of a testamentary trust, but he specifically excluded designating the executors as trustees. It is logical to assume that the terms used in Lumpkin's will were used correctly and intentionally unless the context of the will showed a clear intention to the contrary. *Mitchell v. Mitchell*, 151 Tex. 1, 244 S.W.2d 803, 806 (1951).

The majority erroneously relies on cases inapposite to the instant case, *McMurray v. Stanley*, 69 Tex. 227, 6 S.W. 412 (1887) and *Gonzalez v. Gonzalez*, 457 S.W.2d 440 (Tex. Civ. App.—Corpus Christi 1970, writ ref'd n.r.e.), which held that the legal estate was separated from the equitable estate. In *McMurray*, the testator devised the residue of her estate to her husband and provided that he would have full control and the right to use and dispose of the estate as he desired, but any property remaining at the husband's death would pass to the testator's nieces. The court held that the testator's will established a trust in which her husband was trustee for the benefit of the remainders, her nieces. The legal estate had already vested in the husband and the equitable estate was vested in the beneficiaries subject to being defeated by the husband's right to dispose of or consume the property during his lifetime, thus allowing a trust to come into existence. Compared with the instant case, the legal estate never vested in the executors, nor was there evidence of this intent. The legal estate was vested in Mrs. Lumpkin. Similarly, in *Gonzalez*, the testator devised his estate to his wife and seven minor children in eight equal parts. The court found that the obligations imposed upon the wife to maintain and improve the property created a trust for the benefit of the wife and children, with the wife as trustee. As in *McMurray*, the legal estate had already vested in the wife before she was denominated trustee.

The majority fallaciously relies on *Dulin v. Moore*, 96 Tex. 135, 70 S.W. 742 (1902); and *Parton v. Baugh*, 265 S.W. 250 (Tex. Civ. App.— Dallas 1924, no writ) because the wills: (1) create express trusts; (2) appoint named trustees to hold the property as trustees; and (3) vest legal title in the trustee. Additionally, in *Heironimus v. Tate*, 355 S.W.2d 76 (Tex. Civ. App.—Austin 1962, writ ref'd n.r.e.), the court held that a trust was created because the will vested the legal estate in the executors and gave them full power of attorney to control and distribute the trust. Finally, *Najvar v. Vasek*, 564 S.W.2d 202 (Tex. Civ. App.—Corpus Christi 1978, writ ref'd n.r.e.) is not in point because the court held that no trust was created.

In conclusion, this court should follow *Beckham* and hold that the will of A.H. Lumpkin did not vest the legal estate in the residue of his property in his executors. The purely administrative powers created in the executors authorized an independent administration, thereby obviating probate formalities and were designed to aid in the orderly distribution of the residuary estate. *Chadwick v. Bristow*, 146 Tex. 481, 208 S.W.2d 888, 892 (1948).

I would hold that the will of A.H. Lumpkin did not authorize the appointment of the executors to serve as trustees of his estate and would thus reverse the judgment of the court of appeals and remand this cause to the trial court for further proceedings.

PHILLIPS, C.J., and WALLACE, J., join in this dissent.

ON MOTION FOR REHEARING

WALLACE, Justice, dissenting.

[dissenting opinion regarding underproductive property omitted]

TOMLINSON v. TOMLINSON

Court of Appeals of Texas – Corpus Christi 1998
960 S.W.2d 337
pet. denied

CHAVEZ, Justice.

The trial court granted the cross-motion for summary judgment of appellee, Toni Annette Tomlinson. We reverse and remand for proceedings consistent with this opinion.

Facts

The relevant facts underlying this opinion are essentially uncontroverted. Richard Tomlinson ("Richard"), deceased, was a participant in the Walter Rossler Company Profit Sharing Plan and Trust ("Rossler Plan"). During Richard's marriage to appellee, she was the designated beneficiary of Richard's death benefits under the Rossler Plan. On December 21, 1993, Richard executed a new beneficiary designation, removing appellee (then his ex-wife) as the beneficiary of his Rossler Plan death benefits. Richard died on April 3, 1995.

The December 21, 1993 beneficiary designation was completed by Richard as follows:

Designated beneficiary: Richard Lee Tomlinson II, Rileigh William Tomlinson, Trustee Lynn Tomlinson.

Richard Lee Tomlinson II and Rileigh William Tomlinson were Richard's minor sons; their mother is appellee. Lynn Tomlinson, who is also the appellant, was Richard's brother.

Aside from the language quoted above, the record contains no other trust instrument. The crux of the instant dispute is, therefore, as follows: Appellant contends that the quoted language created a trust of which he is the trustee, whereas appellee contends that the quoted language fails to create a valid trust by reason of vagueness. Appellee contends, based on her argument that no trust was created, that she is entitled to receive Richard's death benefit on behalf of their minor children as named beneficiaries, based a contractual clause in the Rossler Plan.

The trial court entered its order granting appellee's cross-motion for summary judgment on April 29, 1996. The order recites the court's finding that "although Richard Tomlinson may have intended to create a trust which would name Lynn Tomlinson as trustee, such trust is not effective for the failure to provide any terms or instructions regarding the operation of any trust." This appeal ensued.

Discussion

As a starting point, we note that a trust may be created by a property owner's inter vivos transfer of his property to another person as a trustee for third persons (i.e., trust beneficiaries). TEX. PROP. CODE ANN. § 112.001(2) (Vernon 1995). The property transferable to a trustee includes "contract rights, including a contractual right to receive death benefits as designated beneficiary under a policy of insurance, contract, employee's trust, retirement account, or other arrangement." TEX. PROP. CODE ANN. § 111.004(12) (Vernon 1995); see also TEX. PROP. CODE ANN. § 121.052(a) (Vernon 1995) ("Payment of Death Benefit to Trustee"). However, "[a] trust is created only if the settlor manifests an intention to create a trust." TEX. PROP. CODE ANN. § 112.002 (Vernon 1995).

There exist no particular forms or words required to create a trust, if there exists reasonable certainty as to a putative trust's property, object and beneficiaries. * * * By using the term "trustee" in the December 21, 1993 beneficiary designation, we believe that Richard manifested his intention to create a trust. The trust's property was to be the benefits paid in the event of his death pursuant to the Rossler Plan. The beneficiaries of said trust were to be Richard's minor sons, and the object of the trust was, clearly, the maintenance of his sons' welfare.

Appellee contends that no trust was created because no specific duties as trustee were devolved to appellant in the December 21, 1993 beneficiary designation. We disagree. By statute, a trustee shall administer a trust according to (1) its terms and (2) Texas Property Code, Title 9, Subtitle B. TEX. PROP. CODE ANN. § 113.051 (Vernon 1995).

Although the December 21, 1993 beneficiary designation lacks specific detail, all necessary details are supplied by Texas Property Code, Title 9, Subtitle B. See, e.g., TEX. PROP. CODE ANN. §§ 113.002 ("General Powers"), 113.006 ("General Authority to Manage and Invest Trust Property"), 113.021 ("Distribution to Minor or Incapacitated Beneficiary"), 113.024 ("Implied Powers"), 113.056 ("Standard for Trust Management and Investment"), 114.001 ("Liability of Trustee to Beneficiary") (Vernon 1995).

Appellee has cited the case of City of Wichita Falls v. Kemp Public Library Bd. of Trustees, 593 S.W.2d 834, 836 (Tex. Civ. App.--Fort Worth 1980, writ ref'd n.r.e.), which states as follows:

> A declaration of trust must be reasonably certain in its material terms. This includes identification of the property covered by the trust, the beneficiaries or persons in whose behalf the trust is created and the manner in which the trust is to be performed. If any of these elements are vague, general or equivocal, the trust will fail for want of certainty.

City of Wichita Falls, 593 S.W.2d at 836. However, the foregoing language is dictum.

The court in City of Wichita Falls was faced with a situation wherein a charitable donor had not expressed any desires regarding the creation of a trust. Id. That makes City of Wichita Falls distinguishable from the case at bar, because Richard expressed his desire to create a trust by specifically naming his brother as "trustee." In the present case, and consistent with Richard's express intention, the Texas Property Code supplies necessary trust terms.

By statute and common law, a wide measure of discretion is accorded to a trustee in the prudent operation of a trust. TEX. PROP. CODE ANN. §§ 113.002, 113.006, 113.024 (Vernon 1995); see also, Heironimus v. Tate, 355 S.W.2d 76, 79 (Tex. Civ. App.--Austin 1962, writ ref'd n.r.e.) ("The amount which a beneficiary is entitled to receive may be left to the discretion of the trustee."); Taysum v. El Paso Nat. Bank, 256 S.W.2d 172, 176 (Tex. Civ. App.--El Paso 1952, writ ref'd) ("There seems to be no question that the testator, or settlor of a trust, may leave the trustee a wide discretion as to the mode of realizing the end sought."). Accordingly, we determine that the trust instrument was not so vague as to invalidate the settlor's intentions. We hold that a trust was created.

Notes and Questions

1. Steve transferred $10,000 to Thomas stating, "Invest this money for my Son, Brad. Give Brad the income every year on his birthday until

he reaches age thirty. Then give him the $10,000." If asked, Steve would define "trust" as having confidence in someone who is honest, "legal title" as the official name of a book in the Library of Congress records, "equitable title" as the formal name of horses used at professional racing tracks, and "trustee" as a special type of tea served at Starbucks. Did Steve have the intent necessary to create a trust?

2.   Susan transferred $10,000 to Teresa stating, "I am creating a trust of this money. You are the trustee and thus have full power to use any and all of this money for any purpose that you wish." Did Susan have the intent necessary to create a trust?

3.   Steve included the following dispositive language in his valid will, "I give Thomas $10,000 with the hope that he will use this money for the educational expenses of his son, Brad." Did Steve have the intent necessary to create a trust?

4.   Susan told Teresa, "Tomorrow morning, I am going to give you $10,000 in trust for you to use for the benefit of your children. In addition, if I ever buy stock in Acme Corporation, I will give those shares to you in trust for your children as well." Does Susan have the intent which is necessary to create a trust?

5   Steve transferred his vacation home and surrounding land to Thomas and signed a written instrument instructing Thomas to hold the land in trust for Brad and to deed the land to Brad on his twenty-fifth birthday. Brad was eighteen years old when this happened. Brad is now twenty-four years old and has no knowledge that Thomas is supposed to be holding the property for his benefit. Did Steve have the intent to create a trust? *See* Trust Code § 111.0035(c).

6.   *See* Examples & Explanations § 19.1.1.

2.   Statute of Uses[2]

Read Trust Code § 112.032.

The historical origin of the two components of trust intent, the split of title and the imposition of duties, is derived from the common law history of trusts. The common law precursor to a trust was called a *use*. Before the fifteenth century, uses were not enforceable and thus a "beneficiary" had no rights and had to hope that the "trustee" would fulfill a merely honorary obligation. This situation changed in the 1400s as uses started to be

---

[2]Portions of this section adapted from Examples & Explanations § 19.1.2.

enforceable as equitable estates in property. By the 1500s, uses were common and were, from the government's point of view, often abused. Property owners were employing uses to avoid their duties of property ownership under the feudal land ownership system, especially financial obligations such as paying money (today called taxes) to the monarch (now the Internal Revenue Service), to hinder creditors and others with claims against the property, and to provide benefits for various religious organizations contrary to the Crown's wishes.

The English Parliament enacted the Statute of Uses[3] in 1536 to end these abuses. The statute *executed the use* which meant that the beneficiary's equitable interest in real property was turned into a legal interest as well. Because this had the effect of eliminating the legal interest which the trustee formerly held, the beneficiary was now the owner of all title, both legal and equitable, and was fully responsible for all of the burdens of property ownership. Had the Statute of Uses been carried out exactly as written, trusts as we know them would not exist.

An important exception to the Statute of Uses developed for the *active trust*. An active trust is an arrangement where the trustee's holding of property is not merely nominal in an attempt to gain some untoward benefit, but where the trustee actually needs legal title to the property to perform a power or duty relating to the property for the beneficiary's benefit. This exception provides the basis for modern trust law and the two-pronged trust intent requirement.

3.   Split of Title and Merger

Any separation of legal and equitable title coupled with the imposition of fiduciary duties on the holder of the legal title is sufficient to satisfy the split of title requirement for a valid trust.

Read Trust Code § 112.034.

Notes & Questions

1.   Examine each of the following situations and determine whether there is a sufficient split of title to create a trust.

    a.   Steven transfers legal title to Thomas and equitable title to Brenda.

---

[3] 27 Hen. 8, ch. 10 (1536).

      b.   Steven retains legal title and transfers equitable title to Brenda.

      c.   Steven transfers legal title to Thomas and retains equitable title.

      d.   Steven transfers both legal and equitable title to Thomas.

      e.   Steven transfers legal title to Thomas and equitable title to both Thomas and Brenda.

      f.   Steven transfers legal title to both Thomas and Brenda and equitable title to Brenda.

      g.   Steven transfers legal title to both Thomas and Brenda and equitable title to both Thomas and Brenda as well.

2.   If all legal and equitable title becomes reunited in one person, *merger* occurs and the trust will cease to exist. In the normal course of events, this is what happens when the trust terminates and the trustee distributes the property to the remainder beneficiaries. However, merger could occur earlier either because of circumstances the settlor did not anticipate or because the trustee and beneficiary are working together to terminate the trust. Note that Trust Code § 112.034(c) prevents merger in some trusts containing spendthrift provisions.

3.   Settlor created a valid trust naming Tom and Teresa as trustees. On January 10, 2006, Tom and Teresa conveyed all of their legal title to Bruce, the only beneficiary of the trust. What are the ramifications of the trustees' conduct?

4.   Settlor created a valid trust naming Bruce and Brenda as beneficiaries. On January 10, 2006, they conveyed all of their equitable interests to Tom, the trustee. What are the ramifications of the beneficiaries' conduct?

5.   Settlor created a valid trust naming Tom as the trustee and Bruce as the beneficiary. On January 10, 2006, both Tom and Bruce conveyed their interests to Sarah. What are the ramifications of their conduct?

6.   *See* Examples & Explanations § 19.1.3.

4. Distinguishing Trusts from Other Legal Relationships

You must be able to distinguish trusts from other legal relationships which may, at first glance, appear trust-like in nature either because they involve a split of legal and equitable title or because a person is subject to fiduciary duties in favor of another. Correctly making this distinction is of utmost importance because the law governing trusts is often considerably different from the law controlling other relationships. For example, a plaintiff may find the statute of limitations for bringing an action based on breach of trust to be longer than the limitations period for an action grounded in contract or tort.

SARAH v. PRIMARILY PRIMATES, INC.

255 S.W.3d 132
Texas Appeals – San Antonio, 2008
pet. denied

Opinion By KAREN ANGELINI, Justice.

Appellants appeal from the trial court's order dismissing their case for lack of standing. On appeal, they argue that (1) an agreed order between them and Appellee Primarily Primates, Inc. entered into during the pendency of the underlying lawsuit gave them standing, and (2) they have standing pursuant to section 112.037 of the Texas Trust Code, which allows the creation of trusts to provide for the care of animals. We affirm the trial court's order dismissing the case for lack of standing.

Background

In January 2006, Primarily Primates, Inc. ("PPI") and Ohio State University entered into an agreement whereby Ohio State "transfer[ed] nine chimpanzees and three new world monkeys utilized in research at its Chimpanzee Center ('the Chimps and Monkeys')" to PPI, and PPI in turn agreed "to accept ownership of the Chimps and Monkeys and to provide for their lifetime care." The agreement lists the following as PPI's responsibilities:

(1) PPI agrees to accept ownership of the Chimps and Monkeys and to provide for their lifetime care in a humane environment that complies with all relevant state and federal regulations. PPI will not breed the Chimps and Monkeys, will not use them in research projects of any kind, and will not euthanize any of them except for humane reasons relating to a health condition.

(2) PPI will construct facilities for the housing of the Chimps and Monkeys in accordance with the specifications set forth in Attachment A.

(3) PPI will provide personnel and other assistance in connection with the shipment of the Chimps and Monkeys to PPI, in accordance with the Shipment Schedule set forth in

Attachment B. The Parties will mutually agree on a shipping date.

(4) PPI will construct a temporary enclosure to house the Chimps and Monkeys pending completion of a permanent facility. PPI acknowledges receipt of $14,944.00 from Ohio State to cover the cost of constructing the temporary enclosure.

The agreement also lists the following as Ohio State's responsibilities:

(1) Ohio State will pay facility construction costs in the total amount of $236,483.00 as set forth in Attachment A. This amount will be paid upon execution of this Agreement.

(2) Ohio State will provide personnel and other assistance in connection with the shipment of the Chimps and Monkeys to PPI, and will pay the shipping costs in accordance with the Shipping Schedule set forth in Attachment B.

(3) Ohio State will provide an endowment to PPI in the amount of $8,000 per chimpanzee for a total of $72,000. A check for this amount, payable to Primarily Primates, Inc. will be delivered no later than 60 days after the Point of Transfer. Ohio State is not required to pay an endowment for the New World Monkeys.

The agreement, under a section titled "Ownership," also discusses that Ohio State "warrants that it is the owner of all rights, title and interest in the Chimps and Monkeys" and "transfers all rights, title and interest in the Chimps and Monkeys to PPI." In return, PPI "agrees to accept such transfer" effective at the "Point of Transfer." Further, according to the agreement, if "a lawsuit is initiated against Ohio State or PPI after the Point of Transfer challenging Ohio State's ownership," "its authority to transfer ownership," or "the validity of the ownership rights conveyed to PPI under this Agreement," then ownership of the Chimps and Monkeys will revert to Ohio State, but Ohio State will be responsible for all legal fees.

The agreement also provides that it "shall be governed by and construed in accordance with the laws of the State of Ohio" and that "[e]ither party may, at any time, and for any reason, terminate this Agreement by giving 7 days written notice to the other party."

In February of 2006, the primates were shipped from Ohio to PPI's facilities in Texas. Shortly after their arrival, two of them died, and a third escaped from a cage.

On April 27, 2006, attorneys purporting to act on behalf of "Sarah, Harper, Emma, Keeli, Ivy, Sheba, Darrell, Rain, and Ulysses" (the surviving primates) filed suit against PPI, alleging breach of contract. In the alternative, they brought a declaratory judgment action, asking the trial court to declare that "the contract [between PPI and Ohio State] is void because it violates Texas law." They also sought "removal from PPI and transfer to an appropriate sanctuary that will provide them with appropriate care as is described in the contract." Additionally, "[i]n the alternative, and in the unlikely event that the court does not order specific performance," they requested the "creation" of a trust and "an award of damages in the amount of $236,483.00 (the full contract price) to be held in trust and applied towards the acquisition of shelter and care at a suitable facility." They attached a copy of the contract to their petition.

On May 4, 2006, they filed a "Second Amended Original Petition," adding Henry Melvyn Richardson, Stephany Harris, and Klaree Boose, "people interested in Plaintiffs' welfare," as plaintiffs. This amended petition retained the same claims as the original one: breach of contract, declaratory judgment, and "recognition" (instead of "creation") of a trust.

In response to the lawsuit, PPI filed a motion to dismiss for lack of standing. After several hearings, the trial court dismissed the case for lack of standing. "Sarah, Harper, Emma, Keeli, Ivy, Sheba, Darrell, Rain, and Ulysses" (the surviving primates), along with Henry Melvyn Richardson, Stephany Harris, and Klaree Boose (the interested persons), filed a notice of appeal, seeking review of the trial court's order.

Discussion

A. Did the agreed order to appoint a master in chancery give appellants standing? * * *

We * * * hold that the agreed order to appoint a master in chancery did not confer standing upon appellants.

B. Do appellants have standing pursuant to section 112.037 of the Texas Trust Code?

A party must have standing to bring a lawsuit. *Coastal Liquids Transp., L.P. v. Harris County Appraisal Dist.*, 46 S.W.3d 880, 884 (Tex.2001). "Standing" is a party's justiciable interest in the suit. *Nootsie, Ltd. v. Williamson County Appraisal Dist.*, 925 S.W.2d 659, 661-62 (Tex.1996). The test for standing requires that there be a real controversy between the parties that will actually be determined by the judicial declaration sought. *Austin Nursing Ctr., Inc. v. Lovato*, 171 S.W.3d 845, 849 (Tex.2005). A plaintiff has standing when it is personally aggrieved, regardless of whether it is acting with legal authority. *Nootsie*, 925 S.W.2d at 661. If a party lacks standing, a trial court lacks subject-matter jurisdiction to hear the case. *Lovato*, 171 S.W.3d at 849. Thus, standing cannot be waived and can be raised for the first time on appeal. *Id.* And, whether a court has subject-matter jurisdiction is a question of law. *Tex. Dep't of Parks & Wildlife v. Miranda*, 133 S.W.3d 217, 226 (Tex.2004). * * *

2. Did the contract between PPI and Ohio State create a trust to provide for the care of the primates?

The contract between PPI and Ohio State clearly states that it will be governed by Ohio law: "This Agreement shall be governed by and construed in accordance with the laws of the State of Ohio." PPI argues that because Ohio law did not recognize the creation of a trust to provide for the care of an animal at the time PPI and Ohio State entered into the contract, the contract cannot be construed as creating a trust. In response, appellants argue that "PPI's choice of law theory ... is a matter of affirmative defense, which has no impact on subject matter jurisdiction," and that PPI waived this affirmative defense by failing to plead it. Thus, they argue that we must look to Texas law in considering whether the contract created a trust to provide for the care of the primates. Because we hold that the contract did not create a trust under Texas law, we need not decide whether Ohio law should apply.

Section 112.037 of the Texas Trust Code allows a trust to "be created to provide for the care of an animal alive during the settlor's lifetime." Tex. Prop. Code Ann. § 112.037(a) (Vernon 2007). Such a trust terminates on the death of the animal and may be enforced by a person appointed in the terms of the trust or, if a person is not appointed, by a person appointed by the court. See *id.* § 112.037(a)-(b). However, although section 112.037 allows the creation of a trust to provide for the care of an animal, that does not necessarily mean that every contract relating to animals creates such a trust. Thus, we must consider whether the contract between PPI and Ohio State created a trust. Pursuant to the Texas Trust Code, there are many methods of creating an express trust. A trust may be created by:

> (1) a property owner's declaration that the owner holds the property as trustee for another person;

> (2) a property owner's inter vivos transfer of the property to another person as trustee for the transferor or a third person;

> (3) a property owner's testamentary transfer to another person as trustee for a third person;

> (4) an appointment under a power of appointment to another person as trustee for the donee of the power or for a third person; or

> (5) a promise to another person whose rights under the promise are to be held in trust for a third person.

Tex. Prop. Code Ann. § 112.001 (Vernon 2007).

In arguing that the contract does not create a trust, PPI first emphasizes that the only types of trusts governed by the Texas Trust Code are express trusts-not resulting trusts, constructive trusts, business trusts, or deeds of trust. See *id.* § 111.003 ("For purposes of this subtitle, a 'trust' is an express trust only and does not include: (1) a resulting trust; (2) a constructive trust; (3) a business trust; or (4) a security instrument such as a deed of trust, mortgage, or security interest as defined by the Business & Commerce Code."). PPI then argues that the contract between Ohio State and PPI does not create an express trust; instead, it transfers title of the primates in fee from Ohio State to PPI.

"A trust is created only if the settlor manifests an intention to create a trust." *Id.* § 112.002. According to PPI, the contract here does not manifest such an intention; it does not indicate that PPI or Ohio State intended to create a trust. For example, an express trust requires a person be named as trustee. See *id.* § 112.001; *Perfect Union Lodge No. 10 v. Interfirst Bank*, 748 S.W.2d 218, 220 (Tex.1988) (explaining that implicit in the statutory definition of trust "is the requirement of a trustee with administrative powers and fiduciary duties"); *Humane Soc'y v. Austin Nat'l Bank*, 531 S.W.2d 574, 577 (Tex.1975) ("An express devise of property to another as trustee for named beneficiaries is required for creation of an express trust."). PPI emphasizes that the contract here does not name anyone as trustee for the primates. Indeed, the word "trustee" does not appear anywhere in the contract. PPI further points out that the contract also does not mention the terms "trust," "beneficiaries," "settlor," "grantor," or "donor." According to PPI, if it and Ohio State had intended for their agreement to create a trust, then the agreement would have included these terms. Instead, the contract uses terms like "transfer" and "ownership" to describe their agreement. For example, the contract states that Ohio State is "the owner of all rights, title and interest in the Chimps and Monkeys" and that it "hereby transfers all rights, title and interest in the Chimps and Monkeys to PPI and PPI agrees to accept such transfer, effective when the PPI veterinarian and the Ohio State veterinarian mutually agree that the Chimps and Monkeys have recovered from all pre-shipment procedures and are ready for actual shipment ('the Point of Transfer')." According to PPI, the use of these terms "plainly indicate that the agreement is a bilateral contract under which Ohio State transferred ownership of the chimpanzees and monkeys to PPI and PPI agreed to house and care for them."

In their reply brief, appellants make clear that they are arguing that the contract between PPI and Ohio State created an express trust. An "express trust" is "a fiduciary relationship with respect to property which arises as a manifestation by the settlor of an intention to create the relationship and which subjects the person holding title to the property to equitable duties to deal with the property for the benefit of another person." *Id.* § 111.004 (Vernon Supp.2007). Although acknowledging that the contract does not contain the terms "trust" or "trustee," appellants emphasize that such technical words of expression are not necessary to create a trust relationship. They argue that all that is required is that the beneficiary, the res, and the trust purpose be reasonably clear based on the entire instrument when construed in light of the circumstances surrounding its execution. According to appellants, here, the contract provides for Ohio State funds to be transferred to PPI "with the intent that the funds be used exclusively for the animals' benefit" and that "PPI accepted the trust property and agreed to be bound to provide the animals with lifetime care." Thus, appellants argue that the "material terms and the trust purpose are clear in light of the circumstances surrounding the execution of the agreement."

It is true that technical words of expression are not essential for the creation of a trust. *Perfect Union*, 748 S.W.2d at 220. A trust is a method used to transfer property. *Jameson v. Bain*, 693 S.W.2d 676, 680 (Tex. App.-San Antonio 1985, no writ). Thus, the trustee holds legal title and possession for the benefit of the beneficiaries. *Faulkner v. Bost*, 137 S.W.3d 254, 258 (Tex.App.-Tyler 2004, no pet.). "To create a trust by a written instrument, the beneficiary, the res, and the trust purpose must be identified." *Perfect Union*, 748 S.W.2d at 220. "It is not absolutely necessary that legal title be granted to the trustee in specific terms." *Id.* "Therefore, a trust by implication may arise, notwithstanding the testator's failure to convey legal title to the trustee, when the intent to create a trust appears reasonably clear from the terms of the will, construed in light of the surrounding circumstances." *Id.* (emphasis added).

For example, in *Dulin v. Moore*, 96 Tex. 135, 137, 70 S.W. 742, 742 (1902), the supreme court construed a will in which the testator, after devising real property in fee simple, provided that another person would be "trustee to receive and control the property" during the lives of the devisees. "The court recognized the issue as being whether the testator intended to confer mere 'naked powers' upon the trustee or to invest him with legal title for the purposes of the trust." *Perfect Union*, 748 S.W.2d at 221 (explaining *Dulin's* reasoning). The court concluded that "although the will contains no words which expressly convey legal title to *Dulin*, the intention that he should take the legal title is as clearly manifested as if express terms had been employed." *Dulin*, 96 Tex. at 139, 70 S.W. at 743.

Similarly, in *Heironimus v. Tate*, 355 S.W.2d 76 (Tex. Civ. App.-Austin 1962, writ ref'd n.r.e.), the Austin Court of Appeals construed a will in which there were no express words giving the executor legal title to any property. "The will bequeathed property to two beneficiaries but further provided that the executors had discretion in making distributions to the beneficiaries during their lives, and upon their deaths the remainder passed to their lineal descendants." *Perfect Union*, 748 S.W.2d at 221 (explaining *Heironimus*). "The court concluded that a trust had been created with legal title vested in the executors." *Id.* (citing *Heironimus*, 355 S.W.2d at 80).

In *Perfect Union Lodge No. 10 v. Interfirst Bank*, 748 S.W.2d at 221, the supreme court noted that "[a]s in *Dulin* and *Heironimus*, we must construe a will which lacks specific language conferring legal title upon the executors." The court concluded that "[f]rom the provisions of the will as a whole, A.H. Lumpkin's intent to create a testamentary trust can be ascertained." *Id.* The will "devised all the residue of [Lumpkin's] estate to his wife for her life, with the remainder to Perfect Union Lodge." *Id.* It then provided that "my said executors shall handle my estate during the life of my wife." *Id.* According to the court, this language indicated that "Lumpkin intended to provide for more than a mere settlement of his business affairs and distribution of assets." *Id.* Furthermore, the court reasoned that "the provision granting the executors the powers found under the Trust Act authorized Moursund to exercise greater control over the property than was necessary for administration of the estate." *Id.* Therefore, pursuant to the language of the will, the court reasoned that Lumpkin "clearly intended to separate the management and control of his residual estate from the beneficial interest conferred upon his wife." *Id.* Thus, the court held that the will "created a testamentary trust for the life of his wife, which would terminate upon her death." *Id.*

Unlike the facts presented in *Dulin, Heironimus*, and *Perfect Union Lodge*, there is no clear intent in the contract between PPI and Ohio State to create a trust to provide for the care of the primates. While appellants emphasize that pursuant to the contract Ohio State transferred funds to PPI with the intent that the funds would be used for the primates' benefit and that PPI agreed to provide for their lifetime care, the contract also states that PPI agrees to accept "ownership" of the primates, that Ohio State "warrants that it is the owner of all rights, title and interest " in the primates, that Ohio State " transfers all rights, title, and interest" in the primates to PPI and that PPI agrees to accept "such transfer, effective" at "the Point of Transfer," and that if a lawsuit is initiated against Ohio State or PPI after "the Point of Transfer" challenging Ohio State's ownership of the primates, its authority to transfer ownership to PPI or the validity of the " ownership rights conveyed to PPI " under the contract, then "ownership" of the primates "shall revert to Ohio State." After reviewing the language used in the contract, we see no intention by Ohio State to create a trust; therefore, we hold that the contract between Ohio State and PPI did not create a trust to provide for the care of the primates.

Conclusion

Because the contract between Ohio State and PPI did not create a trust to provide for the care of the primates, appellants have no standing under section 112.037 of the Texas Trust Code to bring their claims. We, therefore, affirm the trial court's order dismissing the cause for lack of standing.

Notes & Questions

1.   Paul gave Arthur written authority to sell some of Paul's property located in another state and to remit the proceeds back to Paul. Did Paul create a trust?

2.   Adam and Brooke were neighbors. Adam borrowed a stepladder from Brooke to install a ceiling fan in Adam's living room. Brooke gave Adam her dog to feed and care for while Brooke went on vacation. Brooke lent Adam her notebook computer for one month in exchange for Adam's promise to buy her a new battery for the computer. Did any of these transactions create a trust?

3.   Oscar conveyed real property to George as follows, "To George and his heirs but if tobacco products are sold on the premises, then I or my heirs may reenter and terminate the estate." Did Oscar create a trust?

4.   Aunt transferred $10,000 to Sister as custodian for Niece (Sister's daughter) naming Sister as custodian under the Texas Uniform Transfers to Minors Act. Did Aunt create a trust? *See* Prop. Code ch. 141.

5.   David agreed to transfer $5,000 to Cindy in exchange for Cindy's promise to repay the money with interest at a specified future date. Did David create a trust?

6.   Terry's valid will contained the following devise, "I leave all my real property located in Lubbock County, Texas to Juanita Gomez provided she pays $25,000 to Sean Edwards." Did this provision of Terry's will create a trust?

7.   For an undiagnosed reason, Eve became reality challenged and was no longer able to manage her property. Eve's mother petitioned the local probate court and was appointed as the guardian of Eve's vast holdings. Has a trust relationship been established?

8.   Erwin was appointed by the probate court as the personal representative of his father's estate. Has a trust relationship been established?

9.   Father gave Son the power to appoint particular items of Father's property to Grandson. Did Father create a trust?

10. Pauline could not afford to purchase her dream house and thus she obtained a loan from Bank. Bank, however, was not satisfied with Pauline's mere promise to repay the loan and thus demanded collateral for the loan. She granted Bank a mortgage in her dream house as well as a security interest in her expensive sport utility vehicle. Did any of Pauline's transactions create a trust? *Read* Trust Code § 111.003(4).

11. *See* Examples & Explanations § 19.1.4.

B. METHODS OF TRUST CREATION

The settlor may create a trust while the settlor is alive or delay the time of creation until the settlor's death by including trust gifts in the settlor's will.

1. Inter Vivos Trusts

A trust which the settlor creates to take effect while the settlor is still alive is referred to as an *inter vivos trust* or a *living trust*. The two basic methods a settlor may use to create an inter vivos trust are distinguished by the identity of the person who holds legal title to the trust property.

In a *declaration* (or *self-declaration*) of trust, the settlor declares him- or herself to be the trustee of specific property and then transfers some or all of that property's equitable title to one or more beneficiaries. The settlor retains the legal title and is subject to self-imposed fiduciary duties. *Read* Trust Code § 112.001(1).

In a *transfer* or *conveyance* in trust, the settlor transfers legal title to another person as trustee and imposes fiduciary duties on that person. The settlor may retain some or all of the equitable title or transfer all of the equitable title to other persons. *Read* Trust Code § 112.001(2).

2. Testamentary Trusts

A settlor can create a trust to take effect upon the settlor's death by including a gift in trust in the settlor's will. *Read* Trust Code § 112.001(3). The split of title and the imposition of duties does not occur until the settlor dies. This type of trust is called a *testamentary trust*. A precondition to the validity of a testamentary trust is for the will itself to be valid. If the will fails, any testamentary trust contained in that will is also ineffective. After the will is established, the trust is examined to determine its validity. The trust is not automatically valid just because the will is valid.

3. Relevance of Consideration

Because a trust is a type of gratuitous property transfer, rather than a contractual arrangement, the beneficiary does not need to give consideration to the settlor for the transfer. *Read* Trust Code § 112.003. Do not be confused when a written document creating a trust is carelessly referred to as a "trust agreement" rather than a "trust instrument." The term "agreement" in this context does not connote an agreement of any kind, contractual or otherwise, between the settlor and the beneficiary.

Notes & Questions

1. Settlor established a valid irrevocable trust for Daughter on September 10, 2010. The trust property consisted of $250,000 worth of investment securities. Settlor served as the trustee of this trust. The trust provided for payments of trust income to Daughter on the first of every month. Daughter never thanked Settlor for the October, November, and December payments. During the holiday season, Daughter did not call or visit Settlor and did not even send Settlor a holiday card. Settlor was furious at Daughter for her ungrateful conduct. Settlor then made a New Year's resolution never to be taken advantage of again and did not make the January 1, 2017 payment to Daughter. May Settlor invalidate the trust on the basis that Daughter did not give any consideration for the creation of the trust?

2. On February 1, 2017, Settlor told Son, "You have been a good son to me and I love you very much. Tomorrow, I am going to create a trust for your benefit containing my cotton and oil land in Midland, Texas." Son gave Settlor a big hug and stated, "Thank you Dad. You're the greatest. I love you, too." Groundhog Day came and went without Settlor creating the trust. May Son force Settlor to create this trust? *Read* Trust Code § 112.003.

3. If the settlor transfers only promises to a trust, those promises need to be enforceable contracts to give the promises value as trust property. If the trust consists merely of unenforceable promises, the trust fails for lack of property.

4. *See* Examples & Explanations § 19.2.3.

C. STATUTE OF FRAUDS

Under certain circumstances, a trust must be evidenced by a writing before the beneficiary has the right to enforce the trust. English law did not require trusts to be supported by a writing until Parliament enacted the

Statute of Frauds in 1677. 29 Chas. II, ch. 3 (1677). Section seven provided that all trusts of real property must be "manifested and proved" by a writing signed by the settlor. This writing could be either inter vivos or testamentary. Most states base their Statute of Frauds on this statute. Thus, the general rule in the United States is that trusts of real property must be evidenced by a written instrument. The precise details of this requirement vary among the states.

The policy underlying the requirement that certain trusts be evidenced by a writing is to protect a transferee who actually received an outright conveyance from having those rights infringed upon by someone claiming that the transfer was actually one in trust. Thus, an alleged trustee will use the lack of a writing to raise the Statute of Frauds as a defense to a plaintiff who is trying to deprive the alleged trustee of that person's rights as the donee of an outright gift.

Read Trust Code § 112.004.

The writing must contain (1) evidence of the terms of the trust (e.g., identity of the beneficiaries, the property, and how that property is to be used) and (2) the signature of the settlor or the settlor's authorized agent (see Government Code § 311.005(6) defining "signed").

The normal requirements are relaxed in some situations for trusts containing personal property. Trust Code § 112.004(1) explains when an oral trust may be enforceable and § 112.004(2) provides when a writing which does not meet the standard requirements may be sufficient.

Courts may enforce an oral trust of real property if the trustee partially performs. In other words, if the alleged trustee acts, at least temporarily, as if a trust exists, the trustee may be estopped from denying the existence of a trust at a later time and claiming the property as the donee of an outright gift. For example, if the trustee permits the beneficiary to possess the land or make valuable improvements to that land, the trustee may be prohibited from later asserting that a trust did not exist.

AYERS v. MITCHELL

Court of Appeals of Texas—Texarkana 2005
167 S.W.3d 924
no pet.

Opinion by Justice ROSS.

Roy A. Ayers and his wife, Lorayne, deposited funds in an account at a bank where they, along with two of their children, Gail Mitchell and Larry Ayers, were signatories on the account. Mitchell eventually gained sole control over the funds. Roy testified that he demanded a return of the funds. When Mitchell refused, Roy filed suit against her, alleging, among other things, breach of contract, conversion, breach of fiduciary duty, and fraud. Roy also sued for "a declaratory judgment that all monies in issue are owned by Roy A. Ayers and should be returned to Roy A. Ayers." Mitchell counterclaimed, seeking a declaratory judgment as to the existence of a trust, terms of the trust, and her status as trustee. The funds at issue were ultimately deposited in the registry of the court.

The case was tried to the court and resulted in a judgment that Roy take nothing by his suit, that the funds at issue were held in an irrevocable trust for the benefit of Roy, and that Mitchell was the sole trustee of that trust. The court filed findings of fact and conclusions of law in support of its judgment. Roy appeals, challenging the material findings and conclusions made by the court. Because we hold the trial court erred in finding the existence of a valid trust, we reverse and render judgment that Roy is entitled to have the funds returned to him. We remand to the trial court the question of Roy's reasonable and necessary attorney's fees.

Background

In 1998, Roy and Lorayne became concerned about their future health and living care needs. According to Mitchell's testimony, her parents asked her to take charge of their life savings to provide for their future healthcare needs. She said that her parents wanted to "shelter [these funds] ... from Medicaid." So, on December 18, 1998, Roy and Lorayne created a savings account at a bank in Winnsboro, depositing approximately $48,000.00. There were four signatories on the account: Roy, Lorayne, Mitchell, and Larry. Mitchell's social security number was shown on the account, and she paid the taxes on the income from the account. Mitchell testified Roy instructed her to keep her siblings from misusing any of this money. Mitchell's siblings are: Larry, Marsha Kull, and Paul Ayers.

Lorayne died sometime after the creation of the savings account. In January 2003, Roy had surgery to amputate one of his legs. Following Roy's surgery, Mitchell and Kull broached the subject of Roy living in a nursing home. Larry was opposed to this idea and took Roy home to live with him. Larry testified he "gutted" his home and did significant remodeling to make the home accessible for Roy. There was also testimony that Larry isolated Roy from the rest of the family. Larry, a single person, hired care providers to come into the house to help with Roy's needs and with the cooking and other household chores. One caregiver testified it was her understanding from the other caregivers that Roy was not to be left alone with other members of the family. Jeff Ayers, Larry's son, testified Larry told him not to associate with Mitchell or Kull, or any of their children. Jeff also testified that Larry had coached Roy on how to answer questions in court.

In June 2003, Mitchell became aware that Larry had been writing checks of increasing value on Roy's checking account (not the account the subject of this suit). Mitchell then removed the funds in question from the savings account and opened a new account, with herself and Kull as signatories. Kull's name was removed from the account, at her request, leaving Mitchell as the only signatory. Mitchell testified she viewed herself as trustee of these funds and felt responsible to protect the money and see to it that the money was used for Roy's reasonable medical needs and for his "comfortable living expenses."

Trial Court's Findings and Conclusions

In its written findings of fact, the trial court found, among other things, that the bank account in question did not reflect that Mitchell was a trustee; that Roy and Lorayne intended that Mitchell hold the account subject to their requirements for comfortable living and medical needs; that Roy, Lorayne, Mitchell, and Larry were permitted to withdraw from the account; that Larry exerted undue influence over Roy; that the only withdrawal from the account made by Mitchell was for the construction of a bridge requested by Roy; that Roy was disoriented on the day of trial; that Roy was unable to care for himself; that Roy and Lorayne intended to completely divest themselves of any legal interests in the account in question; that Roy never made a demand on Mitchell for return of the account before filing suit; and that Roy and Lorayne intended for Mitchell to have complete control over the account subject only to their needs for healthcare and comfortable living.

In its conclusions of law, the trial court concluded that Mitchell is the trustee of the funds in the account in question; that the trust was intended to be irrevocable; that the trust became irrevocable on the death of Lorayne; that Roy is in need of a guardian; that, should any of the trust fund remain after the death of Roy, the trust terminates and the funds shall be paid out equally to the children of Roy and Lorayne; and that Roy and Lorayne intended to and did divest themselves of any interest in the trust fund except as beneficiaries thereof.

Roy's Contentions

Roy contends the evidence established as a matter of law that Roy revoked the trust, and that failing to so find was against the great weight and preponderance of the evidence. He also contends the evidence established that Roy and Lorayne intended Larry and Mitchell to be joint trustees, and failing to so find was likewise against the great weight and preponderance of the evidence. Roy further contends the trial court erred in enforcing an oral trust and in ordering the trust res be divided equally among Roy's children following his death. Finally, Roy contends the trial court should have awarded him attorney's fees.

* * *

Evidence of Oral Trust Not Legally Sufficient

We begin our analysis with Roy's contention the trial court erred in enforcing an oral trust. In general, a trust must be in writing to be enforceable. Tex. Prop. Code Ann. § 112.004 (Vernon 1995). That statute requires a trust in either real or personal property to be created with a written document. However, a trust in personal property may be created, and the trust enforced, where there is a) a transfer of the trust property; b) to a trustee; c) who is neither settlor; d) nor beneficiary; e) if the transferor expresses at the time or before the transfer his or her intent to create a trust. Tex. Prop. Code Ann. § 112.004(1). A trust meeting these requirements need not be in writing.

Mitchell contends, and the trial court found, that Roy, as settlor, transferred the funds in question to her as trustee. The Texas Property Code defines "beneficiary" as "a person for whose benefit property is held in trust, regardless of the nature of the interest." Tex. Prop. Code Ann. § 111.004 (Vernon Supp. 2004-2005). Mitchell does not contend, and the evidence does not show, that Mitchell is a beneficiary of the alleged trust. The evidence does show that, at the time or before the bank account in question was created, Roy made statements to Mitchell consistent with creating a trust. Fatal to Mitchell's contention that an oral trust was established, however, is the absence of a complete transfer of the alleged trust property.

As it pertains to trusts, the Texas Property Code does not contain a definition of "transfer." See Tex. Prop. Code Ann. § 111.004. However, in a case construing, in part, certain bank savings accounts opened by the account holder "in trust" for others, the Texas Supreme Court held that such trusts are governed in general by the rules applicable to gifts and explained that:

The principal difference between such a trust and a gift lies in the fact that in the case of a gift the thing given passes to the donee, while in the case of a voluntary trust only the equitable or beneficial title passes to the cestui qui trust. In each case the equitable title must pass immediately and unconditionally and the transfer thereof must be so complete that the donee might maintain an action for the conversion of the property. Absent a completed gift of the equitable title, no trust is created, for an imperfect gift will not be enforced as a trust merely because of its imperfection.

"But the peculiarity with respect to these so-called 'savings bank trusts' is that the courts require that the declarant shall express his intent to create a trust more clearly and by a larger number of acts than in the case of an ordinary trust. The deposit of money in a bank under a trust title is considered equivocal. Men frequently deposit money under a trust title from other motives than that of creating a trust."

Fleck v. Baldwin, 141 Tex. 340, 172 S.W.2d 975, 978 (1943) (holding insufficient evidence of trust creation, particularly, lack of evidence of original owner's intent to yield control over funds in question).

More recently, the Eastland Court of Appeals held that the intent of the donor is the principal issue in determining whether a gift has been made. Hayes v. Rinehart, 65 S.W.3d 286, 289 (Tex. App.-Eastland 2001, no pet.). That case was one brought by the testator's son seeking, in part, a determination that funds in a certificate of deposit (CD) account in the name of the testator's daughter were property of the estate, not a gift to the daughter. Part of the court's consideration in upholding the trial court's finding that there was no transfer of the funds by gift was the fact that the testator had used money from another CD account to purchase a pickup truck after also placing that CD account in the daughter's name. Id. Significantly, the court also noted that the testator had, similar to the instant case, placed the CD account in his daughter's name to be eligible for Medicare and Medicaid benefits. Id.

In another case, a mother put a CD in her name and in the name of her children, and the children asserted that this act constituted a gift as a matter of law. In rejecting the children's contention, the Dallas Court of Appeals held that, for a gift to be effective, delivery must divest the donor of all dominion and control over the gift. McConathy v. McConathy, No. 05- 95- 01036-CV, 1997 WL 145172, *3-4 (Tex. App.-Dallas Apr. 1, 1997, pet. denied), 1997 Tex. App. LEXIS 1592, at *9-11 (not designated for publication). The court, noting that the mother, as a joint account holder of the CD, had the authority to dispose of the CD without the children's consent, further stated:

[The mother's] placing [the children's] names on the CD did not divest her of all dominion and control over the CD or immediately and unconditionally vest [the children] with ownership of the CD. Thus, [the mother's] action of having [the children's] names placed on the CD account with her own name did not establish present donative intent and delivery as a matter of law.

Id. 1997 WL 145172 at *4, at *11.

Applying these principles applicable to gifts, we hold that, to have a "transfer of the trust property to a trustee," as contemplated by Section 112.004(1), the transfer must divest the trustor of all dominion and control over the trust res.

In the instant case, there is evidence that, at or before the time the funds in question were placed in the savings account, Roy and Lorayne instructed Mitchell to take charge of such funds to provide for their future healthcare needs. Further, Roy's niece, Irene Ayers (daughter of Roy's brother) testified Roy told her that Mitchell was in charge of Roy's finances. However, the evidence further shows that neither Roy nor Lorayne ever divested themselves of all dominion and control over these funds. They both remained as signatories on the account where the funds were located. As such, they expressed their intent to retain control over such funds. It is axiomatic that, when an order to pay from an account has been signed by an authorized signer on the account, the order is to be paid. See Tex. Bus. & Com. Code Ann. § 4.401(a) (Vernon 2002) (bank may charge account for amount of item "properly payable") and § 4.402(b) (Vernon 2002) (bank that refuses to pay item "properly payable" may be liable for wrongful dishonor). Roy and Lorayne remaining as signatories on the account defeats any claim that the funds in that account were transferred away from them.

Roy's continued control over the account is also shown by Mitchell's own testimony that her father instructed her to deduct $2,425.00 from the account to reimburse Mitchell for the cost of a bridge she had built on Roy's property. Roy's authorization of this expenditure shows his continued control over these funds and is inconsistent with the view that a complete transfer of those funds away from himself ever took place. Roy's continued control of the funds is also shown by evidence that he made one or more loans to Larry from those funds.

The undisputed evidence shows that Roy had control over these funds until Mitchell moved them, without Roy's knowledge or consent, into an account where she had sole control. We hold, as a matter of law, there was never a "transfer of the trust property to a trustee" as contemplated by Section 112.004(1). In the absence of a writing representing the creation of a trust, and in the further absence of a complete transfer of the funds, we hold that, as a matter of law, no valid trust was created. Accordingly, we sustain Roy's point that the trial court erred in enforcing an oral trust.

Any Trust Created Was Revocable

Notwithstanding our conclusion that no valid trust was created, we will address Roy's contention that the evidence established, as a matter of law, that Roy revoked any trust created and that the trial court's failure to so find was against the great weight and preponderance of the evidence. Even if a valid trust had been created, we hold that, as a matter of law, any such trust was revocable and that it was revoked by Roy.

The trial court found the alleged trust to be irrevocable. That finding, however, is not supported by the evidence and is contrary to law. Trusts created under Texas law are revocable, unless made specifically irrevocable. Westerfeld v. Huckaby, 462 S.W.2d 324, 327 (Tex. Civ. App.-Houston [1st Dist.] 1970), aff'd, 474 S.W.2d 189 (Tex. 1971). The irrevocability of a trust must appear from the terms and language of the instrument creating the trust. Tex. Prop. Code Ann. § 112.051(a) (Vernon 1995). Otherwise, the trust is revocable. See Tex. Prop. Code Ann. § 112.051(a), (b) (Vernon 1995). Here, there was no written document establishing the trust and stating its purposes, duration, or whether it was revocable. The alleged oral trust was, as a matter of law, revocable.

* * *

We also hold that, as a matter of law, Roy revoked any such trust. * * *

Summary and Conclusion

Because we hold that no valid trust was created in this case and that, even if such trust was created, it was, as a matter of law, a revocable trust and was revoked, we find it unnecessary to address Roy's other points of error.

We reverse and render judgment that Roy owns all the funds in issue and that such funds should be immediately returned to him. We remand to the trial court the determination of Roy's reasonable and necessary attorney's fees under Section 37.009 of the Texas Civil Practice and Remedies Code.

Notes and Questions

1. Violating the Statute of Frauds merely makes the trust unenforceable (voidable) rather than void. Accordingly, the trustee may carry out the terms of a trust which does not comply with the Statute of Frauds although no one could have forced the trustee to do so.

However, if an alleged trustee files for bankruptcy, the bankruptcy trustee (a person appointed to represent the bankrupt person's unsecured creditors; not a trustee of an express trust) has "the benefit of any defense available to the debtor as against any entity * * * including statutes of limitation, statutes of frauds, usury, and other personal defenses." 11 U.S.C.A. § 558. Thus, the bankruptcy trustee may raise the Statute of Frauds defense even over the alleged trustee's objection. This statute makes sense from a policy perspective. If the bankruptcy trustee did not have this authority, everyone who files for bankruptcy would claim that they hold their real property subject to oral trusts for the benefit of others thereby keeping the property out of the hands of their creditors.

2.   See Trust Code § 112.051(c) which requires a trust revocation, modification, or amendment to be in writing if the settlor created the trust in writing.

3.   An *acknowledgment* is a notarized statement that the settlor willingly executed the trust as an act of the settlor's own free will. Although an acknowledgment is not a prerequisite to a valid trust, an instrument normally must be acknowledged before it can be filed in the public records. See Prop. Code § 12.001. Trust instruments that involve real property often must be filed in the deed records to establish the chain of title to the property. Thus, prudent practice is to have the settlor acknowledge all inter vivos trust instruments.

4.   The existence and terms of a trust may be proven with competent evidence when the original has been lost or destroyed. For example, in *Gause v. Gause*, 496 S.W.3d 913 (Tex. App.—Austin 2016, no pet. h.), the settlor created an inter vivos trust in the 1940's but the trust instrument disappeared shortly after the settlor's death in 1998. The settlor's wife, a primary beneficiary of the trust, claimed that a non-beneficiary child intentionally destroyed or lost the trust instrument. In 2000, this non-beneficiary child convinced her mother (the settlor's wife) who was then in poor health to convey the trust property to her for a nominal consideration. A few months later, the settlor's wife successfully sued her daughter to cancel the deed. Then, in 2002, the settlor's wife conveyed all of the trust property to another of the non-beneficiary children. In 2007, one of the beneficiary children successfully sued to set aside this conveyance and the settlor's wife appealed.

The Austin Court of Appeals affirmed rejecting the settlor's wife's claim that the trial court erred in determining the existence and terms of the trust based on parol evidence. The court explained that a trust instrument is not rendered ineffectively merely because it is lost or destroyed if there is sufficient evidence to prove its contents. In this case, the settlor's wife swore to the terms of the trust when she successfully set aside her 2000 deed. The court also determined that Trust Code § 112.004's statute of frauds requirement of a written and signed document "does not remove trust instruments from the operation of general rules relating to the proof of lost documents." *Gause* at 917. In addition, the court explained that judicial estoppel prevents the settlor's wife from now claiming she had no memory of trust when she earlier gave detailed sworn testimony about the trust and its contents.

5.   *See* Examples & Explanations § 19.4.

D. RULE AGAINST PERPETUITIES

Article I, § 26 of the Texas Constitution adopts the common law version of the Rule Against Perpetuities, that is, "a future interest not destructible by the owner of a prior interest cannot be valid unless it becomes vested at a date not more remote than twenty-one years after lives in being at the creation of such interest, plus the period of gestation. Any future interest so limited that it retains its indestructible and contingent character until a more remote time is invalid." Interpretive Commentary to Article I, § 21.

Read Trust Code § 112.036. This section makes it clear that the Rule Against Perpetuities applies to all noncharitable trusts. However, the court must reform or construe transfers that violate the Rule under Prop. Code § 5.043 to carry out the general intent and specific directives of the grantor to the extent possible without violating the Rule. The court may apply the equitable doctrine of cy pres in this process.

KETTLER v. ATKINSON

Texas Supreme Court 1964
383 S.W.2d 557

SMITH, Justice.

Mercantile National Bank at Dallas, named as Executor and Trustee in the holographic will of Bernice E. Atkinson, now deceased, dated May 9, 1959, filed this action for declaratory relief and construction of the will and the trust or trusts created by the will, pursuant to Article 2524-1, Sec. 2 of Vernon's Annotated Civil Statutes and Article 7425b-24, Vernon's Annotated Civil Statutes, known as the Texas Trust Act. The petition named as defendants Doris Marie Kettler, Jeane Bernice Shaw and husband, Charles Shaw; Katherine Jeane Kettler, Lynn Elsa Fisher, and Jeane Lynne Shaw, Thelma Marie Atkinson, Walter Wells Atkinson, Lynn Shirk Atkinson, April Atkinson, Judy Atkinson and Heidi Atkinson, all residents of the State of California; the Salvation Army, a charitable organization with State headquarters in Dallas, Dallas County, Texas, and the State of Texas.

Mrs. Atkinson was a resident of the State of California at the time of her death on December 24, 1959, and her holographic will was admitted to probate in the Superior Court of the State of California in and for the County of Los Angeles, on February 17, 1960. Doris Marie Kettler and Jeane Bernice Shaw were appointed administratrices with will annexed.

The will contains two trust provisions. The trust[4] upon Texas Real Estate, hereinafter referred to as the Ranch-Trust, is the one with which this court is primarily concerned. * * *

The trial court, without the aid of a jury, held that the Ranch-Trust provisions of the will were void; that no residuary trust was established by the will, and that title to the ranch passed by intestate succession to the defendants, Doris Marie Kettler and Jeane Bernice Shaw, the only children of Bernice E. Atkinson, deceased. All others were denied interest in the ranch.

In Salvation Army, The State of Texas, and the defendant, Thelma Marie Atkinson, perfected an appeal to the Court of Civil Appeals. That court agreed with the trial court's holding that the Ranch-Trust violated the rule against perpetuities and was void, and affirmed the judgment of the trial court on that phase of the case. The Salvation Army and the State of Texas have assigned such action as error to this court in their application for writ of error. Thelma Marie Atkinson has filed a conditional application.

Although the Court of Civil Appeals held the Ranch-Trust was void, nevertheless, the Court in considering the provisions of the other trust[5] set

---

[4]'I want my ranch (3300 acres) in Kinney County to be set up in a perpetual trust. I specify that it must never be sold. The income to be divided equally between my direct blood heirs as long as there is a blood heir of mine living-and Mr. Lynn S. Atkinson and his sister Mrs. Thelma Marie Atkinson as long as they live-When the time comes that there are no blood heirs of mine from the issue of my own children-their children-I want the income from the ranch to be divided equally between any blood issue of 1. Walter Wells Atkinson, 1522 North Orland, San Gabriel, California and 2. Lynn Shirk Atkinson, 1522 North Orland, San Gabriel, California. The income is to be continued and divided between all direct blood issue of Lynn Shirk Atkinson and Walter Wells Atkinson until their direct blood issue has run out completely. When the time comes that there is no direct blood issue living of my two daughters Doris M. Kettler and Jeane Bernice Shaw and no remaining direct blood issue from Walter Wells Atkinson and Lynn Shirk Atkinson-I want the income from the ranch to go to The Salvation Army. If the Salvation Army should be dissolved or disbanded-I want the ranch to be given to the State of Texas.'

[5]'I want all of my financial assets placed in-Trust with the Mercantile National Bank at Dallas. I name the Mercantile National Bank at Dallas, as my sold executor.

'My financial assets consist of 3566 shares of Mercantile National Bank at Dallas. 60 Shares of First National Bank in Dallas. 110 Shares Merchants Discount Co., Winnsboro, Texas, 400 Shares of Revlon Inc. 200 Shares Texas Gulf Sulphur, 3500 in cash in Security First National Bank of Los Angeles, Larchmont Blvd., Branch. $10,891 in cash in my brokerage account-with E. F. Hutton and Company-Wilshire Branch Salesman Mr. Tod Barrington, 4155 Wilshire Blvd., Los Angeles 5. 7 Shares National Securities-a 3300 acre ranch 18 miles South of Del Rio, Texas-the ranch is in kinney County, Texas.'

up in the will, wherein the Testatrix provided that she wanted all the income from her estate divided equally between her two daughters, Doris Marie Kettler and Jeane Bernice Shaw and her former husband, Lynn S. Atkinson held that (1) Mrs. Kettler should recover a life estate in 1/3 of the ranch with remainder to her children; (2) Mrs. Shaw, a life estate in 1/3 of the ranch with remainder to her children; and (3) Thelma Atkinson, sister of Lynn S. Atkinson, deceased, should recover a life estate in 1/3 of the ranch with remainder in fee to the children of Mrs. Kettler and Mrs. Shaw. The Salvation Army and the State of Texas were denied a recovery of an interest in the ranch property.

Mrs. Kettler and Mrs. Shaw, in their motion for rehearing in the Court of Civil Appeals, and in their application for writ of error, assert that the Texas courts do not have jurisdiction to construe the provisions of a California will relating to the income from the ranch property; that the trust, under which the Court of Civil Appeals held that Thelma Marie Atkinson was entitled to a life estate, was void because such trust contained no provision for its termination, and that it did not provide for the distribution or final vesting of the corpus; and, that the 'gift of income for life from a trust estate consisting of both real estate and dividend paying stocks' did not create a vested legal life estate on realty in the income donee.

The Kettler-Shaw application was granted. The other applications were granted because of the action of this court in granting the Kettler-Shaw writ. Since the granting of the writ, all parties, with the exception of the Salvation Army and the State of Texas, have filed in the Superior Court of the State of California, where the matter of the Estate of Bernice E. Atkinson, deceased, is pending, an agreement, effective March 10, 1964, to settle, adjust and compromise, as between themselves, 'their respective rights, claims, demands or interest arising out of any relationship whatsoever with or any will of the said Bernice E. Atkinson, deceased,' subject to the approval of the Superior Court.

On April 27, 1964, the Superior Court formally issued its order approving the agreement, and an authenticated copy of such order has been filed with the Clerk of this court.

In view of the settlement agreement and the approval of the Superior Court of California, it is unnecessary for this court to decide the law questions presented in the Kettler-Shaw application for writ of error which affect the rights of the petitioner-respondent, Thelma Marie Atkinson.

We come now to a consideration of the issues presented as between the Petitioners, Kettler and Shaw, and the Petitioners-Respondents, the Salvation Army and the State of Texas. We have concluded to affirm the trial court on these issues. At this point, we perhaps should note that the

Attorney General of Texas is acting both as attorney for the State of Texas, a contingent remainderman, and on behalf of the interests of the general public in the trust for the benefit of the Salvation Army.

It is apparent from the pleadings filed by the Mercantile National Bank of Dallas, hereinafter referred to as the Bank, that this declaratory judgment suit was deemed necessary because a controversy had arisen as to the proper construction of the holographic will of Mrs. Bernice E. Atkinson, deceased, and because of the necessity to determine the rights of the parties, and the title to the Ranch property situated in Kinney County, Texas. The pleadings state that the bank had been advised by its counsel that 'such will is in all probability void as being in violation of the rule against perpetuities stated in Article I, Section 26 of the Constitution of the State of Texas (Vernon's Ann. St.).' The Bank further alleged that '(b)ecause of the uncertainty as to the validity and meaning of such will, Plaintiff is not in a position to determine whether or not it desires to act and until uncertainties are resolved, Plaintiff does not have a basis upon which to make its determination.'

The Bank called upon the trial court to adjudicate and determine three questions:

'(a) Are the provisions creating the trust and naming Plaintiff as Trustee with respect to the real property located in Kinney County, Texas, more fully described above, valid or is such trust void as contrary to the rule against perpetuities?

'(b) If such trust is void as being in violation of the rule against perpetuities who are the proper heirs of Bernice E. Atkinson with respect to the real property located in Kinney County, Texas?

'(c) If the trust created by the will of Bernice E. Atkinson, deceased, is valid in connection with the real property located in Kinney County, Texas, who are the beneficiaries of such trust and what are the rights and duties of Plaintiff as Trustee under such trust?'

In view of our holding on question (a) and the settlement agreement, it is unnecessary for this court to pass upon questions (b) and (c).

The Salvation Army and the State of Texas have taken the position throughout that the proper construction to be placed on that portion of the holographic will relating to the Kinney County Ranch is that Mrs. Atkinson intended that there be a series of life estates to be followed by a charitable trust, and that a charitable perpetual trust in favor of the Salvation Army vested in it at the time of the death of Mrs. Atkinson, the contention being that it is well settled that a perpetual trust may legally be created for charitable purposes. The Salvation Army and the State further contend that the Ranch-Trust created a charitable trust, and, that such trust is immune from the rule against perpetuities. In making such contention, however, they apparently recognize the rule that a gift to charity which is preceded by a gift given in trust for noncharitable purposes will be upheld if, and only if, the gift to charity must vest, if at all, within the period of the rule against perpetuities. The gift over is valid if it is from the outset a vested gift. * * *

The scope of the rule against perpetuities is not the question. All parties recognize it to be well settled that the 'rule against perpetuities renders invalid any will which attempts to create any estate or future interest which by possibility may not become vested within a life or lives in being at the time of the testator's death and twenty-one years thereafter, and when necessary the period of gestation.' Henderson v. Moore, 144 Tex. 398, 190 S.W.2d 800 (1945), and cited cases.

The purpose of the rule is to prevent the taking of the subject matter of the perpetuity out of commerce or trade for the prohibited period. As this court said in Singer v. Singer, 150 Tex. 115, 237 S.W.2d 600 (1951):

"A perpetuity has been defined as a limitation which takes the subject matter of the perpetuity out of commerce for a period of time greater than a life or lives in being, and 21 years thereafter, plus the ordinary period of gestation."

We cannot agree with the Salvation Army and the State of Texas that the will of the Testatrix, Bernice E. Atkinson, does not violate the rule against perpetuities. The will is unambiguous; it created and established two separate trusts, a general trust and a separate trust for the ranch. The Texas Ranch does not go into the general trust, even though it is listed as a part of her 'financial assets.' The will clearly (1) makes a disposition of the income from her estate, and (2) makes separate provision for the ranch. The Ranch-Trust is a trust separate and distinct from the general trust. Therefore the terms and provisions of the general trust which make disposition of the income from the entire estate are not to be considered as affecting the ranch property. It is clear that under the provisions of the Ranch-Trust quoted above, the land was never to be sold, the income was to go to her direct blood issue or blood relatives. Clearly, the trust is a perpetual noncharitable trust, and only when blood issue or blood relatives run out would the income go to the Salvation Army, and later to the State.

The Salvation Army and the State, in their briefs and in oral argument, in effect, concede that their burden is to secure a holding by this court that the will is ambiguous. It is argued that the terms used in the will, such as, 'direct blood heirs,' 'blood heir,' 'blood heirs,' 'issue,' 'blood issue' and 'direct blood issue,' be construed to mean 'children.' By construing the terms used in the will to mean 'children,' it is argued that the Ranch-Trust is a valid, charitable trust, preceded only by a series of successive vested life estates. Thus, the Salvation Army contends that it has discharged its burden and has brought its case within the rule announced in Scott on Trusts, Section 401.7, supra.

The Salvation Army and the State of Texas contend that because Mrs. Atkinson, in other parts of the will, used the term 'blood issue,' etc., as meaning 'children,' it can be inferred that she intended the term to mean 'children' in the paragraph of the will creating the Ranch-Trust

This court is not disposed to rewrite the will of the testatrix, Mrs. Atkinson, and thereby create ambiguities. We decline to resort to the substitution of words for the words of the testatrix to accomplish such purpose. In ascertaining the intention of the testatrix, we must give effect to the words selected by her. Salvation Army of Texas v. Ford et al., Tex. Civ. App., 256 S.W.2d 953 (1953) no writ history. The intention of the testatrix so far as the ranch property is concerned is clearly expressed, therefore, we do not get to the rule which authorized the Court to adopt a construction of a will which will avert intestacy.

Under the terms of the will which reads:

'(W)hen the time comes that there is no direct blood issue living of my two daughters Doris M. Kettler and Jeanne Bernice Shaw and no remaining direct blood issue from Walter Wells Atkinson and Lynn Shirk Atkinson, * * *.'

The testatrix clearly meant that the income from the ranch property was not to go to the Salvation Army until the happening of a named event which possibly would not occur within a life or lives in being at the time of the testator's death and twenty-one years thereafter. Obviously, the Ranch-Trust provided for in the will violates Section 26, Article 1 of the Texas Constitution.

The judgments of the trial court and the Court of Civil Appeals holding that the Ranch-Trust provisions of the will are void are affirmed. However, in view of the settlement agreement entered into between all parties, except the Salvation Army and the State of Texas, the cause is remanded to the trial court with instructions to enter judgment in accordance with the settlement agreement and this opinion.

Notes and Questions

1. *Time of Trust Creation Example.* Settlor indicated that the trust is to begin when "the first person walks on Mars." Assuming the rest of this trust is valid, will this provision cause the trust to violate the Rule Against

Perpetuities? Yes, Settlor's trust violates the Rule. A trust to begin upon a contingent event must start within the period specified by the Rule Against Perpetuities. At this point in time, we cannot determine with certainty whether someone will, or will not, walk on the surface of Mars within the perpetuities period. Accordingly, both the vesting of the legal interest in the trustee and the equitable interest in the beneficiary are contingent on an event that is not certain to occur, or not occur, by the expiration of the perpetuities period and thus, at common law, both interests would fail.

2. *Beneficiaries During Existence of Trust Example.* Settlor created a trust containing the following provision, "The trustee shall pay the income of the trust to Brenda for twenty-five years. At the end of twenty-five years, the trustee shall pay the income to my then living descendants. Upon the death of the last of these descendants, the trustee shall deliver all remaining trust property to Ralph." Assuming the rest of this trust is valid, will this provision cause the trust to violate the Rule Against Perpetuities? Yes, Settlor's trust violates the Rule. All beneficial interests during the existence of a trust must vest within the perpetuities period. If Brenda were to die within the first four years of the trust, we could not ascertain in whom the beneficial interest would vest until after the expiration of the twenty-one year period. Remember, the trust gave Brenda the income interest for twenty-five years. Her interest does not end upon her death. Instead, her right to the income for the balance of the twenty-five years would pass to her heirs or beneficiaries. We cannot determine the identity of Settlor's "then living" descendants until this period expires. At common law, this delay is beyond the permitted twenty-one years and thus the trust violates the Rule Against Perpetuities.

Settlor could have avoided this problem by limiting Brenda's interest to her life. For example, Settlor could have provided that: "The trustee shall pay the income of the trust to Brenda for twenty-five years or life, whichever period is shorter. The trustee shall then pay the income to my then living descendants. Upon the death of the last of these descendants, the trustee shall deliver all remaining trust property to Ralph." In this case, the interests in Settlor's descendants can be ascertained immediately upon Brenda's death. Vesting is always certain to occur within the period because the interests in Settlor's descendants vest immediately upon the death of Brenda, the life in being. In fact, none of the "extra" twenty-one years is even touched in this arrangement.

3. *Remainder Beneficiaries Upon Trust Termination Example.* Settlor created a trust containing the following provision: "The trustee shall pay the income of this trust for twenty-five years to Brenda or, if she dies before the end of twenty-five years, to her closest family members by consanguinity. At the end of the twenty-five years, the trust terminates and the trustee shall pay all remaining trust property to my then-living

descendants." Assuming the rest of this trust is valid, will this provision cause the trust to violate the Rule Against Perpetuities? Yes, Settlor's trust violates the Rule. All remainder interests in a trust must vest within the perpetuities period. Under this trust, the identity of the recipients of the remainder interest cannot be ascertained until the expiration of the twenty-five year period thus exceeding the twenty-one years allowed by the Rule Against Perpetuities. Remember, if any possible fact pattern violates the Rule, the Rule is violated. In this case, all lives in being could die within the first four years of the trust thus causing the remainder interests to vest beyond the perpetuities period.

4. To lessen the impact of a Rule Against Perpetuities violation, a trust should include a *savings clause* which specifies exactly what is to happen to the trust property if a court determines that the settlor violated the Rule.

5. *See* Examples & Explanations § 19.9.

E. TRUST PURPOSES

Read Trust Code § 112.031.

The settlor may create a trust for any purpose as long as that purpose is not illegal. In addition, the terms of the trust may not require the trustee to commit an act that is criminal, tortious, or contrary to public policy.

Courts have used two main approaches in evaluating the legality of a trust purpose. The first analysis concentrates on the settlor's intent and the effect of the trust's existence on the behavior of other persons. Under the intent approach, a trust is illegal if the existence of the trust could induce another person to commit a crime even if the trustee does not have to perform an illegal act. This is the majority approach in the United States and appears to be the one adopted by § 112.031 by its use of the word "purpose." The second approach focuses on how the trust property is actually used, rather than on the motives of the settlor.

HUNT v. CARROLL

Texas Civil Appeals – Beaumont 1941
157 S.W.2d 429
aff'd on other grounds, 168 S.W.2d 238 (Tex. Comm. App. 1943)

WALKER, Chief Justice.

This suit was instituted in county court of Colorado county by appellee, Mrs. Laura Belle Carroll, joined by her husband, Hulen R. Carroll, Jr., under the provisions of Articles 3433, 3434, 3435, R.C.S.1925, praying for judgment annulling and suspending the provisions of the last will and testament of Horace H. Hunt, executed on the 4th day of May, 1937. The testator died in Colorado county on May 31, 1938, and his will was duly admitted to probate. This suit was instituted by appellees as a proceeding in the probate of the will. We here give the will in haec verba:

"Last Will and Testament of Horace H. Hunt.

"The State of Texas,
County of Colorado;

Know All Men by These Presents:

"That I, Horace H. Hunt, of Columbus, Colorado County, Texas, being of sound mind and memory and in good health but knowing the uncertainty of life and the certainty of death, and being desirous of making disposition of the property with which it has pleased God to endow me and which I may possess at my death, do make and publish this my last Will and Testament, hereby revoking and cancelling any and all other wills which I may heretofore have made.

"First: I desire that at my death I shall be decently buried without unnecessary parade or ostentation.

"Second: I desire and direct that my just and legal debts be paid, if there by any, as soon after my death as practicable and as good business judgment would require.

"Third: Having learned from long experience and many adversities, that money is hard to get, harder to save and easy to get rid of and believing that too much of it is a damage rather than a help to the inexperienced, and believing also that it is a husband's duty and privilege to provide for his wife and family through his own labor; and desiring to protect my daughter, Laura Belle, who is my only child, against future contingencies and adversities, I do, with deep love for her, make the following provisions for her and for such child or children as she may have.

"Fourth: So long as the present marriage of my said daughter may continue, no part of my estate or income thereof after my death shall be paid to her; but in event she should become a widow within ten years from date hereof, then and in that event so long as she does not remarry her present husband she shall receive for the support of herself and of any children she may have the sum of $250.00 (two hundred, fifty & no/100 dollars) per month, that is, the total sum of $250.00 per month to be paid to her to be spent by her and in any manner she may see fit for herself and children and without being accountable to any one as to how she may spend it or dispose of it, said payments when once begun to be paid on or about the fifteenth of each month thereafter, payable out of the income--(Page 2)--from my estate; but if the income be insufficient at that time to meet such payments, then a sufficient amount shall be taken from the accumulated funds to make up such payments of two hundred and fifty dollars per month.

"Fifth: In event any effort should be made by the said beneficiary, my beloved daughter, to break this will or to dispose of her prospective interest or benefits under this will by an attempted mortgage or sale, she shall thereby automatically forfeit any and all of her rights hereunder so far as said two hundred and fifty dollar per month payments are concerned, and in lieu thereof she shall receive only the some of one hundred dollars per month. I make this provision for, in my opinion, the protection of my said beneficiary, as I have observed in my contacts with the world that high-powered salesmen, confidence men and other crooks will some times persuade a beneficiary of an estate or of an interest in an estate (where the benefit is payable in installments) to sell such interest or benefits or rights under a will for a lump sum and at considerable sacrifice of its real worth, thereby defeating the purpose and will of a testator to make provision for the future protection of his loved ones. I hereby expressly forbid the sale or mortgage of any part of my estate or of any benefit hereunder, except as may hereafter be specifically authorized by me.

"Sixth: If at any time prior to her receiving any of the above mentioned benefits under this will, my daughter should become seriously ill or in need of special medical attention and in the opinion of my executor or administrator it is necessary that she have aid from the estate, my said executor or administrator is authorized to expend such sum or sums as he in his own opinion may deem necessary, reasonable and proper for the benefit of her health, such expenditures (if any) not to be deducted from any payments which may thereafter become due her under this will.

"Seventh: In event my said daughter should die without issue or should she precede her present husband in death or--(Page 3)--if for any reason she fails to become entitled to benefits under this will, then and in such event my estate shall be divided as follows, towit, one third to my brother, Ben B. Hunt, one third to my brother, Warren Wood Hunt and one third to my sister, Mrs. Henry M. Hefley. Except, however, if my said daughter should die with issue, that is, should she leave a child or children, it is my will and I here direct that my executor or administrator look after the care and education of said child or children, using his own discretion and judgment as to their needs and education and as to the amount or amounts to be expended therefor and he shall not be required to account to any one for his manner of carrying out this provision, and it shall be at his own discretion as to whether he deems it proper to go to any expense whatever in this connection, it being my intention to leave it exclusively up to him as to whether anything whatever be expended in this connection and if so then as to the amount or amounts which shall be expended for said child or children.

"Eighth: If at the end of twenty years from date hereof my said daughter is still living she shall thereupon be entitled to receive my entire estate as it may then exist. But if she should die prior to the end of twenty years from this date and leave a child or children surviving her, such child or children (each) after completing its education as provided for in paragraph 'Seventh' above, shall receive the sum of fifty dollars per month until it attains the age of thirty years, as long as it is engaged in a legitimate occupation, and upon attaining thirty years of age it shall be entitled to receive its proportionate part of the estate but if it should die without issue prior to attaining thirty years of age its portion of the estate then remaining shall go to its brother (brothers) and sister (sisters), if any there be at that time but if there be none then its portion of the estate shall go to my brothers and sister above mentioned or to their heirs.

"Ninth: I hereby appoint my brother, Ben B. Hunt, as--(Page 4-- Executor without bond of this my last will and testament, to carry out the terms and conditions of this will, and I direct that there be no court or probate procedure of any kind save the probating of this will and the return of an inventory and appraisement of the estate I shall die possessed of; and my brother, Ben B. Hunt, my said executor, is hereby authorized to dispose of all or any part of my estate after my death as in his judgment may be wise or expedient for the best interests of the estate and upon such terms and conditions as he may deem expedient and in keeping with good business judgment, and to collect all revenues, pay all taxes due & do all other things necessary or proper in the management & control of my Estate. It is also my will that if for any reason my brother,

Ben B. Hunt, cannot serve as executor of this will or if for any reason he does not desire to do so, he is hereby authorized and empowered to designate and authorize a trust company to act in his stead and place as executor of this will.

"Witness my hand this the 4th day of May, A. D. 1937.

"Horace H. Hunt.

"This is to certify that the Testator, Horace H. Hunt, signed the foregoing will this day in our presence, we each signing our names below, as subscribing witness, at his request in his presence and in the presence of each other.

"L. Altman   Witnesses."
"Vick Paulos

Appellees alleged, generally, the following grounds for annulling the will of Horace H. Hunt, as admitted to probate: (1) that the will is void because it is conflicting and unintelligible; (2) that it is contrary to public policy and void because it was intended to bring about a divorce; (3) that its provisions are contrary to the rule against perpetuities; and (4) that the independent executor named in the will (a brother of testator) may, in certain events, personally receive a share of the estate under Items 7 and 8, which disqualifies him to perform faithfully the duties incumbent on him under Item 7, regarding the education of testator's grandchildren. Ben B. Hunt was named in this proceeding as the proper party to be served; he was duly served, and he duly filed his answer. In probate court the will was sustained as against all objections urged by appellees, but on their appeal to the district court of Colorado county, judgment was entered on September 23, 1940, granting them the relief prayed for, that is, judgment was entered suspending and annulling in all respects the last will and testament of Horace H. Hunt, as admitted to probate. The appeal was prosecuted to the Galveston Court of Civil Appeals, and is on our docket by order of transfer by the Supreme Court.

In entering judgment annulling and suspending the will, the trial court gave weight to the following collateral facts: Appellee, Laura Belle Carroll, was the only child of the testator, Horace H. Hunt. She was born December 29, 1917; her mother died when she was a young child; her father never remarried. Her husband, Hulen R. Carroll, Jr., is her first cousin, and three years her senior. Laura Belle and Hulen were secretly married in January, 1937, and their marriage was not discovered until April, 1937. Up to the date judgment was entered herein, two children were born to this marriage; the first, November 4, 1937, and the second,

July 31, 1939. Before his marriage to Laura Belle, Hulen had been married and divorced; he has no profession but a general academic education; his parents are not people of means; at the time of the execution of the will and of the death of the testator, he was working as a "roughneck" for the Humble Oil & Refining Company. The testator left two brothers, Ben B. Hunt, named by him as his executor, and Warren Wood Hunt, both in middle age. He also left two sisters, Mrs. Hefley, of Cameron, named in the will as a beneficiary, and Hulen's mother, not named as a beneficiary. Ben qualified as executor and has continuously acted as such; he estimated the value of the testator's estate at forty or fifty thousand dollars, consisting primarily of producing oil royalties in eastern Texas.

The court did not err in overruling appellant's plea in abatement, on the ground that this proceeding to annul was improperly filed, with the same number, in the proceedings probating the will. * * *

The brothers and sisters of the testator were not necessary parties to this proceeding to annul and suspend the will of Horace H. Hunt, as admitted to probate. * * *

The last will and testament of Horace H. Hunt is not so conflicting in its provisions as to be void. This proposition is based upon the conflict between Item 4: "So long as the present marriage of my said daughter may continue, no part of my estate or income thereof after my death shall be paid to her," and Item 8: "If at the end of twenty years from date hereof my said daughter is still living, she shall thereupon be entitled to receive my entire estate as it may then exist." The conflict between items 4 and 8 does not render the will void. In Martin v. Dial, Tex. Com. App., 57 S.W.2d 75, 79, 89 A.L.R. 571, the court said:

> "With this direct conflict we should be compelled to give effect to the provision of the fifth clause, as it appears later in the will. It is the general rule that where there is an irreconcilable conflict between two clauses of a will, the later clause will prevail as being the latest expression of the testator's intent." See, also, 44 Tex. Jur. 714.

* * *

Construed in the light of these general rules, we conclude that the will is not unintelligible, but that the testator provided the following plan for the distribution of his estate: (1) At the end of twenty years from the date of the will, if his daughter is living she will receive the entire estate, as it might then exist, free of all control by the executor; but during the first twenty years if she remains the wife of Hulen she will receive no part of the estate, except by Item 6. (2) In the event she should become a widow within ten years from the date of the will, and if by divorce, she should not remarry Hulen, she would receive $250 per month for her support. (3) In the event she should become a widow during the second ten-year period from the date of the will, no provision is made for her support, except by Item 6. (4) If, after receiving the estate, the daughter should die without leaving surviving children, the estate would go to the brothers and sister of the testator named in the will. (5) If the daughter should die prior to twenty years from the date of the will, survived by children, the estate would go to the children in equal shares, subject to control by the executor, on the conditions named in the will; the executor's authority in this respect is clear and unambiguous. (6) As each child reaches the age of thirty years, if it inherits, it will receive title and possession of its proportionate share of the estate. If a child should survive its mother and should die without children of its own, and before reaching the age of thirty years, its share of the estate would go in equal shares to its surviving brothers and sisters. In the event all the children surviving the daughter should die before attaining the age of thirty years without leaving surviving children, the estate would go to the testator's brothers and sister named in the will. (7) If the daughter should die without leaving children surviving her, the estate, as it then exists, would go to the testator's named brothers and sister in equal shares. The intention of the testator in all other respects requires no construction.

Having determined the intention of the testator and his general plan for the distribution of his estate, the next inquiry is whether the will as thus construed contravenes the public policy of the state or the rule against perpetuities. On this issue, appellees' first point is that the will is void because it manifests a clear intent to induce Laura Belle to divorce Hulen, and that it is subject to no other construction. The testator did not expressly declare that intention. The preamble to the will manifested a lawful intention; that it was the duty of Hulen to support his wife, that money was hard to get and harder to save, and that it was his intention to protect his daughter against future contingencies and adversities; he declared in his will a deep love for his daughter. The law left to him the right to dispose of his estate in the manner best suited in his judgment to accomplish these express purposes. While it is clear from the terms of the will that the testator did not want his property to be controlled directly or indirectly by his daughter's husband; the undisputed facts give the reason for his decision in that respect, Hulen was improvident; he had been married and divorced; he had married his daughter in a secret marriage which was concealed for about three months. As against a construction that the testator was trying to induce his daughter to divorce her husband, the will is subject to the construction that it was his intention to provide for her support should he divorce her. A legitimate purpose on the part of the testator is apparent on the face of the will, more apparent on a reasonable construction of its terms than the purpose to induce his daughter to divorce her husband; that is, it was the intention of the testator not to induce a divorce, but to provide for the support of his daughter in the event of a divorce, which is a valid provision. Hood v. St. Louis Union Trust Co., 334 Mo. 404, 66 S.W.2d 837. On this construction the will is valid. Ellis v. Birkhead, 30 Tex. Civ. App. 529, 71 S.W. 31.

[Rule Against Perpetuities discussion omitted.]

It is our order that the judgment of the lower court be reversed and this cause remanded with instructions that judgment be entered denying appellees the relief prayed for.

Reversed and remanded with instructions.

STEWART v. REPUBLICBANK, DALLAS, N.A.

Texas Appeals – Fort Worth 1985
698 S.W.2d 786
writ ref'd n.r.e.

HILL, Justice.

Margaret Boulboulle Stewart appeals from the trial court's judgment construing her father's will in favor of her four nieces, Diane Kirby Briggs, Linda Kirby Keyser, Carolyn Ann Kirby, and Mary Catherine Kirby, in a declaratory judgment action brought by RepublicBank, Dallas, N.A., trustee under the will of J.E. Boulboulle, deceased. She presents twenty-two grounds of error.

We affirm, because we find that provisions of the will which seek to disinherit the four nieces because of the appointment of third persons as their guardians are void as against public policy.

J.E. Boulboulle executed his last will and testament on February 24, 1970, naming RepublicBank, Dallas, N.A. as executor and trustee. He devised certain property to his surviving wife, Mildred, and placed the residue of the estate in trust, with Mildred to receive the income as long as she lived. Upon Mildred's death, the trust was to be divided into two equal shares. One share went to fund the "Margaret Stewart Trust," a trust in which Mr. Boulboulle's daughter, Margaret, would receive the income, with the principal to be distributed to her at specified ages.

The other share went to fund the "Mildred Ramirez Children Trust." This share was to be divided into four equal shares for Mr. Boulboulle's grandchildren, the children of Mildred Ramirez, a daughter who had died prior to the making of the will. The grandchildren were to receive income and distribution at various ages.

On May 1, 1970, Mr. Boulboulle executed a codicil in which he added the following condition to the will:

If either Robert or Marjorie Kirby are named and appointed and do actually act as either the Guardian of the person or the Guardian of the Estate of any of the beneficiaries taking under the said Mildred Ramirez Children Trust then, and in that event, all funds and all property held in trust for said beneficiary shall revert and become a part of the MARGARET STEWART TRUST and shall be distributed pursuant to the provisions thereof.

Subsequently, the Kirbys were appointed by a probate court as guardians of the person of the children. They took care of the needs of the children while their father was incapacitated and eventually the Kirbys formally adopted the Ramirez children.

By point of error number eight, Stewart urges that the trial court erred in holding that the codicil, as construed to effect a forfeiture, is void as against public policy.

Ordinarily, a testator has a legal right to devise his property as he sees fit and to prescribe the terms upon which his bounty should be enjoyed. State v. Rubion, 158 Tex. 43, 308 S.W.2d 4, 8 (1957). This right is subject to limitation by law or public policy. * * *

There is no Texas case which determines whether such a provision as contained in the codicil is void as against public policy. The Supreme Court of Michigan has held in a case involving forfeiture due to a will contest, that where the contest is made in the name of a minor through a guardian appointed by the probate court, that such a clause is invalid as against public policy, Farr v. Whitefield, 322 Mich. 275, 33 N.W.2d 791 (1948); see also Bryant v. Thompson, 59 Hun. 545, 14 N.Y.S. 28 (1891).

These courts held that such a codicil is void as to infants because it is against public policy since it seeks to deprive the courts of the powers and duties imposed on them by law for the protection of infants. We find this rationale to be equally persuasive as applied to the codicil we have before us since it also seeks to forfeit the estates of minor children because of an action taken by the probate court in their best interest.

In the case of Lewis v. Green, 389 So. 2d 235 (Fla. App.--5th Dist. 1980), the Florida appeals court held invalid as against public policy a provision in a will which required a minor to be placed in charge of the will's trustees or forfeit all but $3,000 of her inheritance. In its ruling the court said, "Doris' surviving parent had the right to name a personal guardian for her child, or if she did not do so, a court, acting in the child's 'best interest' had this responsibility. The condition in the will appears invalid because it violates public policy." Id. at 243.

Stewart relies on the cases of National Bank of Commerce v. Greenberg, 195 Tenn. 217, 258 S.W.2d 765 (1953); Jenkins v. First Nat. Bank in Dallas, 107 F.2d 764 (5th Cir. 1939); Ellis v. Birkhead, 30 Tex. Civ. App. 529, 71 S.W. 31 (Tex. Civ. App. 1902, writ ref'd) and Hunt v. Carroll, 157 S.W.2d 429 (Tex. Civ. App.--Beaumont 1941), aff'd on other grounds, 140 Tex. 424, 168 S.W.2d 238 (1943).

The case of Ellis v. Birkhead involved a will which provided that the bequests to the testator's daughter were conditional upon the death of her husband or upon divorce from him. The appellees sought to cancel the will, alleging that it was void on the ground of public policy in that it tended to incite the wife to murder and to destroy the marital relation. This court upheld the will, saying that the conditions could have been for the valid purpose of seeing to it that the wife was cared for in the absence of a husband or to protect the assets from her husband. In that case the beneficiary was not to receive the bequest unless she lost her husband, either through death or divorce. The testator provided for her in the event she should be confronted with those events.

In the case at bar, the gift to the appellees was conditional upon the Kirbys not being appointed and acting as their guardian. It made no effort to provide for the children in the event they were left without a guardian once the Kirbys had been appointed and acted as a guardian. Further, if the desire of the testator had been to favor the other daughter in the event that the appellees were well taken care of, it would be more reasonable that he would have provided that the forfeiture would occur in the event that anyone was appointed as guardian. Another distinguishing factor is that the bequests in Ellis were not conditioned upon the action of a court calling for the court's discretion on behalf of children. The case of Hunt v. Carroll presents basically the same fact situation as Ellis v. Birkhead, with a similar result.

The case of Jenkins v. First National Bank of Dallas, is also similar to that of Ellis v. Birkhead. That case involved a grandfather who left money in trust for his grandson. The will provided that while the grandson was under twenty-one years of age he could not receive any of the income in trust if he were living with or in legal custody of his father. The father contested the provision on the ground that it was void as to public policy and tended to separate father and son. The court noted that no forfeiture was made and noted that the delay while the child was being cared for by his father was for a legitimate purpose. The court held that the provision of the trust did not compel an inference of wrongful purpose. Like the Ellis case and unlike the case at bar, the court's finding of lawful purpose was supported by the fact that the beneficiary would receive the bequest in the event that the person supporting the beneficiary was unable to continue supporting him. The will in this case makes no such provision.

Additionally, although an action of a trial court in determining the custody of the Jenkins' grandchild could have delayed his receipt of the bequest until his maturity, it could not have caused a forfeiture.

The case of National Bank of Commerce v. Greenberg, a Tennessee Supreme Court case, involved a trust in favor of the testator's granddaughter. The grandfather's will provided for a forfeiture of the granddaughter's interest in the event she were adopted and her name changed before she was eighteen. The court held that such a provision was not void as against public policy. We do not agree, and we choose to adopt the reasoning of the courts in Farr v. Whitefield, 33 N.W.2d at 791, and Bryant v. Thompson, 14 N.Y.S. at 28, for the reason that such a provision would seek to deprive the courts of the power imposed on them for the protection of infants. We overrule point of error number eight.

We find that because of our holding with respect to point of error number eight, it is unnecessary for us to consider the remaining points of error.

The judgment is affirmed.

ASHWORTH, J., dissents.

ASHWORTH, Justice, dissenting.

I respectfully dissent.

I subscribe to the holding and reasoning of the Supreme Court of Tennessee in National Bank of Commerce v. Greenberg, 195 Tenn. 217, 258 S.W.2d 765 (1953), which has been rejected by the majority.

Notes and Questions

1.   Settlors often desire to create trusts that limit benefits to persons of a particular religion, sex, race, or national origin. The validity and enforceability of any discriminatory trust provision is problematic. These provisions are contrary to modern law which prohibits discrimination on these and other grounds.

Under traditional analysis, a private person may discriminate as he or she wishes but a court cannot lend its power and authority to the enforcement of discriminatory provisions. The equal protection clause of the Fourteenth Amendment to the United States Constitution prohibits the use of state action to carry out an individual's desire to discriminate.

In recent years, there has been a tremendous increase in litigation regarding this type of provision, especially if the restrictions are for a "good" cause, such as the education of individuals from a certain minority group. The decisions reflect that the law is still in a state of flux regarding the enforcement of discriminatory provisions. Some courts refuse to enforce the discriminatory restrictions treating the trust as essentially public because of the special benefits the law grants to charitable trusts and the enforcement assistance the state attorney general's office provides.

After the court concludes that a restriction is illegal, the court may either eliminate that restriction or declare the entire trust invalid. In making this decision, the courts attempt to determine what the settlor would have wanted, that is, if the settlor knew the discriminatory provision would not be enforced, would the settlor have expanded the class of beneficiaries or permitted the trust to fail. On the other hand, some courts treat the judicial involvement in such trusts as relatively de minimus, cite the public benefit of providing benefits to members of certain classes, especially if that class had been previously subject to discrimination, and hold that these provisions are valid.

See *Powers v First Nat'l Bank*, 161 S.W.2d 273 (Tex. 1942) (religious purposes) and *Coffee v. William Marsh Rice Univ.*, 408 S .W. 2d 269 (Tex. Civ. App.—Houston 1966, writ ref'd n.r.e.) (approval of lower court's action in exercising its equitable power to authorize a deviation from terms of trust established by donor so as to allow charging of tuition and acceptance of qualified applicants without regard to color).

2.   A creditor may set aside a transfer the settlor makes to a trust if that transfer meets the requirements set forth in the Texas version of the Uniform Fraudulent Transfer Act. *See* Bus. & Com. Code ch. 24. This Act frequently comes into play when a donor makes an outright gift or creates a trust which would otherwise restrict the ability of an existing or future creditor to get paid from the transferred property. Note that a disclaimer under Property Code § 240.051(b)(2) or (c)(2) will not be considered as fraudulent even if the disclaiming beneficiary's intent is to keep the property away from the beneficiary's creditors (definition of "transfer" in § 24.002(12)).

3.   Courts have several options available to them when they decide that a settlor created a trust for an illegal purpose. The appropriate remedy depends on the reason for the illegality. If the complaining party is a defrauded creditor, the usual remedy is to allow the creditor to set aside the conveyance to the trust to the extent of the creditor's claim. The trust remains effective with regard to property in excess of the creditor's claim.

In other situations, courts have the choice of two remedies. First, the court could undo the transfer and permit the settlor to regain the legal and equitable title to the property by application of resulting trust principles. If the settlor is deceased, the settlor's successors in interest (heirs, if intestate; beneficiaries, if testate) could claim the property. Courts use this remedy when the settlor has no moral culpability and public policy is not adverse to allowing the settlor to regain the property.

Second, the court could refuse to enforce the rights of the purported holder of equitable title which consequently permits the trustee to be treated as the outright owner of the property (the trustee already had legal title and now no one can enforce the trust). Courts are likely to select this remedy when the settlor has moral culpability and it would be against public policy to allow the settlor to regain the property because the settlor and others similarly situated would have no reason to refrain from attempting to create trusts with illegal purposes.

4. *See* Examples & Explanations § 19.5.

F. THE SETTLOR

The settlor creates a trust by splitting the title of property into legal and equitable interests and by imposing fiduciary duties on the holder of legal title. The settlor is sometimes referred to by other terms such as the trustor, grantor, or donor. *Read* Trust Code § 111.004(14).

The settlor must have the capacity to convey property to create a trust. This requirement does not impose any different standard on the settlor as the settlor would face in an outright, non-trust, transfer of the same property. If the settlor can convey property, the settlor may elect to convey that property by splitting the legal and equitable title and creating a trust. Thus, the capacity required to create an inter vivos trust is usually the same as the capacity to make an outright gift and the capacity necessary to create a testamentary trust is the same as the capacity to execute a will (*see* Est. Code § 251.001). *Read* Trust Code § 112.007.

Notes and Questions

1. In *Cooper v. Cochran*, 288 S.W.3d 522 (Tex. App.—Dallas 2009, no pet.), both the trial and appellate courts agreed that an inter vivos trust was invalid because the settlor was induced to enter into the trust because of fraud, duress, and undue influence. With regard to the fraud claim, the evidence showed that the settlor placed property into the trust for the beneficiary in exchange for the beneficiary's (grandson's) promise to take care of the settlor (grandmother). Further, the evidence showed that the beneficiary never intended to take of the settlor.

Regarding the duress and undue influence assertions, the evidence revealed that the beneficiary told the settlor that "she would never see the light of day" and that he would "put her in an insane asylum" if she did not sign the trust. This, coupled with the fact that the settlor was elderly, living alone, and needed assistance, was sufficient evidence to support the trial court's finding of duress and undue influence.

2. Does the settlor owe fiduciary duties to the beneficiaries? *See Alpert v. Riley,* 274 S.W.3d 277, 292 (Tex. App.—Houston [1st Dist.] 2008, pet. denied) ("[a] trust settlor has no fiduciary obligation to a trust beneficiary once [a] trust is created, and control of the trust assets is vested with the trustee.").

WESTERFELD v. HUCKABY

Texas Supreme Court, 1971
474 S.W.2d 189

POPE, Justice.

Maurice Westerfeld, Temporary Administrator of the Estate of Virginia B. Miller, instituted suit against Arthur L. Huckaby to recover title and possession of two lots located in Houston, Texas, and for judgment declaring of no force and effect two trust instruments and two quitclaim deeds executed by Virginia B. Miller. In a trial before the court, judgment was rendered in favor of defendant Huckaby and the court of civil appeals affirmed. 462 S.W.2d 324. We affirm the judgments of the courts below.

On November 7, 1966, Virginia B. Miller executed two declarations of trust, each describing a separate lot in Houston. Virginia B. Miller also executed and recorded two separate quitclaim deeds by which she quitclaimed to herself as trustee and to her successor trustee the same lots covered by the declarations of trust. The settlor died on February 24, 1968. One of the declarations of trust, and one of the deeds, omitting the settlor's signature and acknowledgment, will be set forth in full. The others are substantially the same.

The Declaration of Trust:

WHEREAS, I, Virginia B. Miller of the City of Houston, County of Harris, State of Texas am the owner of certain real property located at 1203 and 1209 Matthews, also, 1220 Andrews Streets in the said City of Houston, State of Texas which property is described more fully in the Deed conveying it from Frankie Watkins to Virginia B. Miller, as "that certain piece or parcel of land with buildings thereon standing, located in said Houston, being Lot no. four (4), in Block eighteen (18) of the Castanine Addition to the City of Houston, South Side of Buffalo Bayou.

NOW, THEREFORE, know all men by these presents, that I do hereby acknowledge that I hold and will hold said real property and all right, title and interest in and to said property and all furniture, fixtures and real and personal property therein, In Trust

1. For the use and benefit of Arthur L. Huckaby—whose address is 1717 Dowling Street Houston, Harris County, Texas.

Upon my death, my Successor Trustee is hereby directed fortwith [sic] to transfer said property and all right, title and interest in and to said property unto the beneficiary absolutely and terminate this trust.

2. I reserve unto myself the power and right (1) to place a mortgage or other lien upon the property, (2) to collect any rental or other income which may accrue from the trust property and, in my sole discretion as trustee, either to accumulate such income as an addition to the trust assets being held or pay such income to myself as an individual.

3. I reserve unto myself the power and right at any time during my lifetime to amend or revoke in whole or in part the trust hereby created without the necessity of obtaining the consent of the beneficiary and without giving notice to the beneficiary. The sale or other disposition by me of the whole or any part of the property held hereunder shall   constitute as to such whole or part a revocation of this trust.

4. The death during my lifetime, or the beneficiary designated hereunder shall revoke such designation; I reserve the right to designate a new beneficiary. Should I for any reason fail to designate such new beneficiary, this trust shall terminate upon my death and the trust property shall revert to my estate.

5. In the event of my death or legal incapacity, I hereby nominate and appoint as SUCCESSOR TRUSTEE: Arthur L. Huckaby—1717 Dowling Street Houston Harris County, Texas to be Successor Trustee.

6. This Declaration of Trust shall extend to and be binding upon the heirs, executors, administrators and assigns of the undersigned and upon the Successors to the Trustee.

The Quitclaim Deed:

KNOW ALL MEN BY THESE PRESENTS, that I, Virginia B. Miller in conformity with the terms of a certain Declaration of Trust executed by me under the date of 7 November, 1966, do by these presents release and forever quitclaim to myself as Trustee under the terms of Such Declaration of Trust, and to my successors as Trustee under the terms such Declaration of Trust, all right, title, interest, claim and demand whatsoever which I as Releasor have or ought to have in or to the property located at:

Houston Harris County, Texas, known and described as Lot four (4), in Block eighteen (18) of the Castanine Addition SSS BB.

To have and to Hold the premises, with all the appurtenances, as such Trustee forever, and I declare and agree that neither as an individual nor my heirs or assigns shall have or make any claim or demand upon such property.

We granted the writ in this case upon points which urge that the extensive powers which the settlor reserved to herself made the trust declarations void, because they were illusory and testamentary in character and imposed no enforceable fiduciary duties upon anyone. Certainly paragraphs 2 and 3 of the trust declarations constitute broad reservations of power in the settlor. However, the court of civil appeals correctly held that an application of the illusory trust doctrine, as enunciated in Land v. Marshall, 426 S.W.2d 841 (Tex. 1968), is limited to instances in which a non-consenting spouse's property is used to fund a trust. Land v. Marshall dealt with a problem created by our community property protection of the wife's distributive share. We therefore could not look solely to the husband's reservation of powers over his own property but had to bring additional policy considerations to bear. Adopting the illusory trust doctrine, we held that the trust failed as to the wife's property. It was only after reaching this conclusion that we could invalidate the whole trust. Since the invalidating of one-half of the trust corpus was held to disrupt the trustor's plan, the entire trust scheme was aborted. The Marshall trust did not fail because the husband reserved too much control over his own property * * *

In Land v. Marshall we cited a number of cases upholding the validity of trusts even though the settlor had retained extensive powers of control. 426 S.W.2d at 848 * * *

Our question is whether Virginia B. Miller, dealing with her own property, could create valid trusts even though she reserved in herself broad beneficial rights, as well as the right to revoke the trusts and the right to control or manage the acts of the trustee. The trusts were not fatally defective by reason of her power to revoke them, because [of § 112.051 of the Texas Trust Code.] * * * The [T]rust [Code in § 112.001] also permits the settlor to hold property as trustee for another, or for himself and another. * * *

If we should follow the rule advanced by the 1935 Restatement of Trusts, * * * we would strike down the Miller trusts. Since that earlier statement, however, there has been such a wide use of inter vivos trusts for a variety of reasons and such a marked shift in judicial decisions that the 1959 edition of the Restatement of Trusts has adopted a different rule as the better and the prevailing rule:

> Sec. 57. Disposition Inter Vivos Where Settlor Reserves Power to Revoke, Modify or Control.
>
> Where an interest in the trust property is created in a beneficiary other than the settlor, the disposition is not testamentary and invalid for failure to comply with the requirements of the Statute of Wills merely because the settlor reserves a beneficial life interest or because he reserves in addition a power to revoke the trust in whole or in part, and a power to modify the trust, and a power to control the trustee as to the administration of the trust.
>
> Comment b: Where settlor reserves power of control. Where the owner of property transfers it inter vivos to another person in trust, the fact that he reserves not only a power to revoke and modify the trust but also power to control the trustee as to the administration of the trust does not make the disposition testamentary and invalid for failure to comply with the requirements of the Statute of Wills.

Comment "h" of the same section recognizes that the trustee of a revocable inter vivos trust can be the settlor alone:

> Declaration of trust. The rule stated in this Section is applicable not only where the owner of property transfers it to another as trustee, but also where he declares himself trustee of the property. The disposition is not testamentary and invalid for failure to comply with the requirements of the Statute of Wills merely because the settlor-trustee reserves a beneficial life interest and power to revoke and modify the trust. The fact that as trustee he controls the administration of the trust does not invalidate it.

Professor Bogert expresses the view that a majority of the cases now upholds the validity of an inter vivos trust even though the settlor reserves a life estate combined with many powers of management, and that the settlor may retain the powers to alter, revoke and take capital as well as the powers to direct and manage. According to Bogert, the beneficiary receives a defeasible interest at the time of the execution of the instrument; the accumulation of reserved powers only subjects the interest of the beneficiary to a greater possibility of defeasance. G. Bogert, Trusts and Trustees § 104 at 536-542 (2d ed. 1965). See Schmidt v. Schmidt, 261

S.W.2d 892 (Tex. Civ. App. 1953, writ ref.). Professor Scott says, "The trend of the modern authorities is to uphold an inter vivos trust no matter how extensive may be the powers over the administration of the trust reserved by the settlor." 1 A. Scott, The Law of Trusts § 57.2 at 485 (3d ed. 1967).

The fifth paragraph of the trust declarations is significant in expressing the settlor's scheme for her trusts. She stated in that provision, "I hereby nominate and appoint as successor trustee: Arthur L. Huckaby * * *" In addition, she provided that the successor trustee's powers and duties would arise "[i]n the event of my death or legal incapacity * * *" The word, "hereby," means "by this, or the present, declaration, action, document, etc.,; by means of this; as a result of this * * *" Random House Dictionary of the English Language (1967). It indicates an act in praesenti. 39 C.J.S., Hereby at 892 (1944). Consequently, it is clear that Virginia Miller intended the trust to take effect immediately. The settlor gave further evidence of her intent to make her trust plan presently operative. After designating Arthur L. Huckaby as her successor trustee, she conveyed her property, in the same instrument, to herself as trustee and also to the successor trustee. See 1 A. Scott, The Law of Trusts § 26.2 (3d ed. 1967).

The settlor's plan was a good one. She would retain control during her competency, and, when she was no longer capable of tending to her property, one who was charged with fiduciary duties would assume the duty of caring for the property during the remainder of her life. She thus made present arrangements for any period of disability during her lifetime. This plan was operative prior to her death, not after or upon her death.

By her sixth paragraph the settlor provided that the declaration would be binding upon her heirs, executors, administrators and assigns as well as the successor trustee. She did not, however, grant to the successor trustee the broad powers which she reserved to herself as settlor. During her lifetime, the successor trustee would be charged with the duties owing by a trustee to the life beneficiary, who would be Virginia B. Miller. The successor trustee would, during the lifetime of the incompetent beneficiary, possess the powers and be subjected to the duties imposed by Art. 7425b-25, Vern. Ann. Tex. Civ. Stats. See Restatement (Second) of Trusts §§ 169-185 (1959). We are unable to say, therefore, that the trust declaration accomplished nothing until the event of the settlor's death.

A document which can stand as a trust is not rendered invalid because it avoids the need for a will. Good reasons often exist for a presently operative trust in preference to a will, which cannot be operative until death and which can accomplish nothing during lifetime. "If an owner of property can find a means of disposing of it inter vivos that will render a will unnecessary for the accomplishment of his practical purposes, he has a

right to employ it. The fact that the motive of a transfer is to obtain the practical advantages of a will without making one is immaterial." National Shawmut Bank of Boston v. Joy, 315 Mass. 457, 471, 53 N.E.2d 113, 122 (1944). A settlor's business or property may be of such character that it cannot endure even a short period of suspension of operations between death and probate. *See Notes*, Use of Inter Vivos Trusts in Agricultural Estate Planning, 55 Iowa L. Rev. 1328 (1970). A settlor may wish to avoid the expense of administration, attorney fees or executor's fees. A settlor may, as did Virginia B. Miller, desire some fiduciary to take over the management of the trust corpus in the likely event of incompetency by reason of sickness or age. The reasons one might have for making a transition during lifetime are varied. Living trusts often afford better management, greater protection, more privacy and considerable economy.
* * *

We affirm the judgments of the courts below.

Dissenting opinion by STEAKLEY, J., in which WALKER, GREENHILL and DANIEL, JJ., join.

STEAKLEY, Justice (dissenting).

I am unable to join in judicially sanctioning a device which, to my mind, is no more, in substance, than a contrived use of the trust principle to effect a testamentary disposition during lifetime. In my view, the instruments executed by Virginia B. Miller were patently designed for distribution of her properties at death, and the transfers purportedly effected were not genuinely effective prior to her death. I recognize, of course, that a person may dispose of property while living by means of effective inter vivos transactions. But there can be no inter vivos trust when the legal and equitable ownership continues to rest in the settlor. This is the circumstance here when the instruments employed by Virginia B. Miller are viewed in their true effect. In the trust acknowledgments to herself, she expressly retained the plenary power and right to mortgage or otherwise encumber the properties; to receive and enjoy all income therefrom by reason of the reservation to herself as trustee of the right to accumulate the income or pay it to herself as an individual; to amend or revoke the trusts in whole or in part; and to designate a new beneficiary. She provided further that the sale or other disposition by her of the whole or any part of the properties would constitute a revocation of the trusts and that the death of the named beneficiary during her lifetime would revoke the designation. As trustee she did no more than hold the properties in name as such; she had no significant acts to perform, or responsibilities to discharge or discretion to exercise. *See* McMurray v. Stanley, 69 Tex. 227, 6 S.W. 412 (Tex. Sup. 1887). There was nothing she could do as trustee that would constitute a breach of a fiduciary duty to anyone, including her death beneficiary. *See* Restatement (Second) of Trusts § 2 and § 25 (1959). Huckaby as the named beneficiary would enjoy a use and benefit only upon her death and then only if, prior thereto, a new beneficiary was not named, or the declarations were not revoked, or the properties were not sold or otherwise consumed.

The quitclaim deeds by which a present transfer was sought to be effected were operative only in conformity with and pursuant to the declarations of trust. Under the living trusts, Virginia B. Miller was settlor, beneficiary and trustee. The cumulative effect of the powers and rights retained by her is such that there was no separation of the legal and equitable interests in the properties during her lifetime. She retained beneficial ownership notwithstanding the seeming conveyances, and each transaction was a ceremony without present substance, an act that was meaningless in effect and hence a nullity. See Annot., 32 A.L.R.2d 1270 (1953).

The majority professes to find a presently operative trust plan in the naked designation of Huckaby as successor trustee in event of legal incapacity. It says that this "indicates an act in praesenti." But two features of the successor trustee designation are quite obvious: the contingency upon which it rests may never occur; and there are no directions to the successor trustee indicative of the wishes of the so-called settlor in the administration of the trust should she become incompetent. This is too frail to constitute a lifetime disposition and too slender a thread with which to validate and hold together the otherwise ineffective inter vivos transactions.

The device under review is comparable in effect to a living trust where one person is named sole beneficiary and sole trustee. The assets are held free of any trust under these circumstances. It is as stated in the Restatement (Second) of Trusts § 99, comment 5 (1959):

[T]here are no duties running from himself to himself, and no rights against himself. He is in a position where he can dispose of the property as freely as any owner can do, since there is no one who can maintain a proceeding against him to prevent him from so doing, and if he transfers the property there is no one who can make him accountable for the proceeds or can reach the property in the hands of the transferee * * *

I am not unmindful of the provision in the Texas Trust [Code § 112.001] that an owner of property may declare in writing that he holds it as trustee for another person; and that revocable declarations of trusts are recognized as valid under the law of our State. But as pointed out by Professor Johanson, the statutes do not reach the issue of whether a trust will be recognized if the settlor-trustee reserves broad controls exercisable either in his capacity as settlor or as trustee. Johanson, Revocable Trusts and Community Property: The Substantive Problems, 47 Tex. L. Rev. 537 footnote 71 at 556 (1969). Clearly, the provisions of the Texas Trust Act are not a mandate for validation of all arrangements in such form, and judicial sanction should not be given to an arrangement without substance or effect as an inter vivos transfer.

I would declare the instruments of no force and effect * * *

Notes and Questions

1.   *Read* Trust Code §§ 112.033 & 112.051.

2.   *Westerfeld* was a 5-4 decision of the Texas Supreme Court. Which side do you favor and why?

3.   What impact does Trust Code § 112.033 have on the *Westerfeld* holding?

4.   The use of the *Westerfeld* type of trust gained public attention in Norman Dacey's books HOW TO AVOID PROBATE (1966) and HOW TO AVOID PROBATE II (1983). He suggests that all of one's property be placed in trust to avoid the necessity of the estate going through the probate system. Is his advice sound? Why or why not? *See* Allan Howeth, *How to Avoid Probate — An Answer from Texas*, 29 TEX. B.J. 897 (1966).

5.   *See generally* Theodore Lustig, *Living Trusts in Texas—Are They Being Over-Promoted or Under-Used?*, 56 TEX. B.J. 762 (1993).

6.   *See* Examples & Explanations § 19.3.

G. TRUST PROPERTY

A trust is a method of holding title to property. Consequently, the existence of property is essential for the initial creation and continued existence of a trust. No trust exists until it has property and a trust terminates when no property remains. *Read* Trust Code § 112.005.

Any type of property (e.g., real, personal, tangible, intangible, legal, equitable, chose in action, claim, contract right, etc.) may be held in trust. *Read* Trust Code § 111.004(12) (defining "property") and § 111.004(17) (defining "trust property").

If a person cannot transfer the property, such as property belonging to another person, property that has valid restrictions on its transfer, or the expectancy to inherit from someone who is still alive, then that property cannot support a trust.

Legal title to the trust property must reach the hands of the trustee. It is not enough for the settlor to sign a trust instrument, own assets that would make good trust property, and intend for that property to be in the trust. The settlor must consummate this intent by actually transferring or delivering the property.

BIRK v. FIRST WICHITA NATIONAL BANK OF WICHITA FALLS

Texas Civil Appeals— Fort Worth 1961
352 S.W.2d 781
writ ref'd n.r.e.

BOYD, Justice.

In 1936 C. Birk died testate, devising the bulk of his estate to his wife and his four children share and share alike, appointing the First National Bank of Wichita Falls (now The First Wichita National Bank) executor, granting the bank five years in which to carry out the provisions of his will, and, with the consent of a majority of the beneficiaries, an additional period not to exceed three years, and directing the bank to make semiannual distributions of available funds to the beneficiaries. The term was so extended.

Mrs. Birk and the four children, on November 15, 1943, executed a written operative trust agreement and allowed the properties devised by C. Birk to remain in the hands of the bank and Ralph A. Birk, one of the sons, as trustees, for a period of five years with a provision for extensions. The bank was to handle and manage the properties without the joinder of Ralph A. Birk except in certain instances. On August 15, 1950, the trust instrument was amended so as to make applicable the provisions of the Texas Trust Act. By extensions of the term of the trust agreement it was in force at the time of Mrs. Birk's death.

On January 17, 1958, the four children, each "acting severally as to his interest", executed a written instrument extending the term of the trust for a period of fifteen years, with a provision for further extensions until a majority of the original beneficiaries should request a termination of the trust and a final distribution of the assets; the trust was to continue with the same accounting procedures, powers and duties as theretofore followed or set out in instruments executed by the signers, and "distribution of all cash, less reasonable reserves, to be made semi-annually to the undersigned beneficiaries, or their estates, in equal shares".

This instrument of January 17, 1958, also contained the following paragraph: "And we severally GRANT, SELL, CONVEY and DELIVER unto such Trustees, to continue in Trust, all of our mother's interest in such Trust, Including all portions of such interest which we may later acquire under her Will or as her heirs at law, same to form a part of the C. Birk Trust Estate and be handled and distributed agreeable with this and all other instruments relating to the C. Birk Estate."

Mrs. Birk died testate on January 29, 1958, devising "* * * all of the real estate I own, or have any interest of any kind in, except my home where I now reside * * *" to C.E. Birk. The realty in the trust estate consisted principally of 2,820.435 acres of land, which had been devised by C. Birk to his wife and his four children share and share alike. A clause in Mrs. Birk's will devised the residue, after certain other bequests, to the four children share and share alike.

Until the time of this law suit, the bank continued to make semi-annual distributions of available funds, except that it held in suspense the accruals since her death from what had been Mrs. Birk's one-fifth interest, which at the time this suit was filed amounted to $18,000.00.

C.E. Birk sued the trustees and the other three children to recover the $18,000.00 which had accrued to such one-fifth interest; prayed that the ownership of the Mrs. Birk interest in the trust estate be established as against all adverse claims; and that the trustees respect his distributive rights thereunder. C.E. Birk claimed such one-fifth interest under his mother's will.

The trustees and the other defendants denied that Mrs. Birk owned any real estate at the time of her death and contended that her interest in the trust estate was personalty and vested in all four children equally under the residuary clause of her will; at least, they claimed that the distributable funds constituted personalty; but if it be realty, and, by the other terms of said will passed to C.E. Birk, it was conveyed by him through the instrument of January 17, 1958, to the trustees, and became a part of the "C Birk Trust Estate", and is subject to be distributed as other accruals and properties, that is, equally to the four children.

Trial was to the court and resulted in a judgment for the defendants, and C.E. Birk has appealed.

Appellant contended in the trial court, and here contends by thorough brief and oral argument, that Mrs. Birk's interest in the trust properties was an interest in land, and passed to him by the specific devise of the will; and that the instrument of January 17, 1958, was ineffectual to alienate his title, and that the estate would be "* * * handled and distributed agreeable with this and all other instruments relating to the C. Birk Estate", by the distributions being made, not in equal portions, but according to the ownership and interests of the children.

It is a close point, but we have concluded that the judgment should be affirmed. Without determining whether Mrs. Birk's interest in the trust lands was realty or personalty, and therefore whether it was devised to appellant specifically or passed to the four children under the residuary clause, it is our opinion that by the instrument of January 17, 1958, appellant conveyed whatever interest came to him from his mother's one-fifth interest to the C. Birk Trust Estate, and agreed that the distributions should be made equally to the four children.

When the instrument of January 17 was executed, none of the children knew the contents of their mother's will or whether she had made or would make a will. None could know whether he would be loser or gainer by executing the instrument of January 17. Each had a hope, which in law is an expectancy. An expectancy may be conveyed. *Humble Oil & Refining Co. v. Luckel*, Tex. Civ. App., 171 S.W.2d 902, error refused w.o.m. The January 17 instrument granted, sold, conveyed and delivered to the trustees the Mrs. Birk one-fifth of the trust property. This seems to have been a complete alienation* * * And a deed will be construed to confer upon the grantee the greatest estate which the terms of the instrument will permit* * * If there is any doubt as to the meaning of the language of a deed it will be resolved against the grantor* * * There need be no consideration to support a conveyance in trust* * * It is immaterial in what order clauses appear in a deed* * * It will be presumed that there was meant to be equality in the conveyance* * *

We think it is neither unreasonable nor unusual for children to agree to share equally in their parent's estate, even where some know or believe they would receive more than an equal share in a testamentary disposition. We think a child's granting, selling, and conveying to trustees whatever he may acquire from his parent through a will or by the laws of descent, and providing that such interest shall become a part of an existing trust estate derived from the other parent, and shall be distributed agreeably with all instruments relating to such estate, where all such instruments provide for distributions share and share alike, and made along with other children's identical grants, is a conveyance to the trustees effectual to equalize the expectancies and may be enforced as such.

The judgment is affirmed.

MARSHALL v. MARSHALL

Texas Appeals—Texarkana 1990
786 S.W.2d 493
no writ

CORNELIUS, Chief Justice.

Thomas David Marshall, Jr. and Dana Jo Dunkerson appeal from a judgment which declared that a family trust was ineffective because the subject of the trust had not been transferred to the trustees. We will affirm the judgment.

On August 23, 1985, Thomas Marshall, Sr., as grantor, and his sons and daughter, Thomas Marshall, Jr., Douglas Marshall, and Dana Jo Dunkerson, as trustees, executed a trust indenture to create the Marshall Family Trust. The trust was to be irrevocable and was to consist of 5,000 shares of stock in Marshall Health Care, Inc. On November 15, 1985, Thomas Marshall, Sr. sought to dissolve the trust, contending that it was ineffective and void. The trustees filed a petition for declaratory judgment that the trust was valid and subsisting. The trial court found that the stock was never transferred to the trustees, and thus concluded that no valid trust had been created.

The trustees contend that the trial court's finding is against the great weight and preponderance of the evidence. To determine the factual sufficiency of the evidence, this Court must consider and weigh all of the evidence, including both that supporting and that which is contrary to the trial court's judgment. Burnett v. Motyka, 610 S.W.2d 735 (Tex. 1980).

A trust may be created by a property owner's inter vivos transfer of property to another person as trustee for the transferor or for a third person. Tex. Prop. Code Ann. § 112.001(2) (Vernon 1984)[1]. To constitute a valid gift inter vivos, there must be a written conveyance, or possession of the property must be delivered to the donee. Wells v. Sansing, 151 Tex. 36, 245 S.W.2d 964 (1952). Delivery requires that the property be placed within the control of the donee with the intention that a transfer of the title becomes currently operative.

Shares of stock in a corporation may be transferred by an assignment in writing on the certificate or in a separate document, and a delivery of the certificate to the transferee, or a surrender of the certificate and procuring another in which the transferee is named as owner. Tex. Bus. & Com. Code Ann. §§ 8.308, 8.309 (Vernon Supp. 1990); * * *. The by-laws of Marshall Health Care, Inc. provide that shares may be transferred by delivery of the certificates together with a written assignment of the shares or a power of attorney to sell or assign the shares.

---

[1]The declaration of trust alone, without an assignment of the stock, was not sufficient to create a trust in the stock pursuant to Tex. Prop. Code Ann. § 112.001(1) (Vernon 1984), because Thomas Marshall, Sr., the owner of the stock, did not declare that he held the stock as trustee, but rather purported to assign it to others as trustees.

The trust indenture executed by Thomas Marshall, Sr. and the trustees contains the language "The Grantor does hereby transfer and assign unto the Trustees, the property listed in Schedule A,* * *" The 5,000 shares of stock in Marshall Health Care, Inc. are described in Schedule A. Even if this instrument would suffice as a written assignment of the stock certificates, they must have been delivered to or placed in the control of the trustees in order for the assignment to be fully effective.

The evidence is conflicting as to whether the stock certificates were placed within the control of the trustees. The certificates were not endorsed or surrendered. There was testimony by Dana Jo Dunkerson that her father offered her the stock, but that she agreed that he could hold it for her. Thomas Marshall, Jr. testified that his father told him the certificates were in the bank in a safety deposit box to which he had a key. Thomas Marshall, Sr., however, denied that the certificates had ever been delivered to the trustees or to any safety deposit box.

Whether delivery has occurred is a question of fact. Ragland v. Kelner, 148 Tex. 132, 221 S.W.2d 357 (1949). The trial court, as the trier of fact, found that the certificates were not delivered to the safety deposit box and as such had not been placed within the control of the trustees. If there is sufficient evidence to support a finding of fact, the appellate court will not substitute its conclusions for that of the jury or the trier of fact. Pool v. Ford Motor Co., 715 S.W.2d 629 (Tex. 1986).

After reviewing all of the evidence, we find that there is some evidence to support the trial court's finding that the stock certificates were not transferred to the trustees, and that such finding is not against the great weight and preponderance of the evidence.

On cross-point, Thomas Marshall, Sr. contends that the trial court erred in not holding as a matter of law that the trust, if created, was unenforceable because he created the trust for the sole purpose of defrauding his creditors. It is not necessary for us to reach this point.

The judgment of the trial court is affirmed.

Notes and Questions

1. In *In re Estate of Kappus*, 242 S.W.3d 182 (Tex. App.—Tyler 2007, pet. denied), the trial court held that a testamentary trust was not created because no steps had been taken to fund the trust. The appellate court reversed. The court explained that the will left the residue of the testator's estate to a trust, the provisions of which were set forth in the will. Under Probate Code § 37, title to property devised in a will vests immediately in the beneficiaries upon the testator's death. The will

contained nothing which would delay this vesting. Thus, the property vested immediately in the trustee.

2.   The trust property must be adequately described. *In re Estate of Walker*, 250 S.W.3d 212 (Tex. App.—Dallas 2008, pet. denied), an inter vivos trust described trust property as:

All properties whether real or personal or mixed we [the two settlors] now own or will own in our names individually or in the name of B & W investments. * * *

We include all real or personal or mixed properties such as land, buildings, houses, stock, other securities, insurance policies, art, coin collections, automobiles, our companies other personal property with or without titles except that which we each maintain separately on our books and records * * *.

Both the probate and appellate courts held that this was an adequate description of trust property. The appellate court explained that there was sufficient testimony by a CPA and attorney that the precise property referenced by this description was ascertainable by consulting property and tax records.

3.   Generally, property may be added to an existing trust. However, additions are not permitted if either (1) the terms of the trust prohibit the addition or (2) the property is unacceptable to the trustee (the trustee's duties may not be enlarged without the trustee's consent). *Read* Trust Code § 112.006.

4.   If a settlor transfers property to a "qualifying trust" (basically a revocable inter vivos trust) which otherwise would qualify as the homestead of the settlor or the beneficiary had it not been transferred into the trust, this property may still qualify as the settlor's or beneficiary's homestead if the person occupies and uses it as his or her homestead. Prop. Code § 41.0021. Accordingly, the homestead does not lose the creditor protection it would normally have merely because the homestead property is being held in trust form.

5.   *See* Examples & Explanations § 19.6.

H. THE TRUSTEE

Read Trust Code § 111.004(18).

1. Capacity

Read Trust Code § 112.008.

The trustee must have the ability to take, hold, and transfer title to the trust property, that is, (a) an individual trustee must be of legal age (or have had the disabilities of minority removed) and competent and (b) a corporate trustee must have the power to act as a trustee in Texas. *See* Finance Code §§ 32.001(b)(3) & 182.001(b)(3) and Est. Code § 505.001-505.006 (foreign corporate trustees). Although the trustee may be a person unconnected with the rest of the trust arrangement, such detachment is not necessary. A trustee may also be the settlor or a beneficiary of the same trust as long as the sole trustee is not also the sole beneficiary. *See* Trust Code § 112.034 (merger).

See Examples and Explanations § 19.7.1.

2. Acceptance

Read Trust Code § 112.009.

A person does not become a trustee merely because the settlor names that person as the trustee of a trust. The settlor cannot force legal title and the accompanying fiduciary duties on an unwilling person. Thus, a person must take some affirmative step to accept the position. Once acceptance occurs, the person is responsible for complying with the terms of the trust as well as applicable law.

The trustee's acceptance of the trust may be established in two main ways. First, the trustee may sign the trust instrument or a separate acceptance document. When creating an inter vivos trust, it is common practice for attorneys to have the trustee sign the trust instrument at the same time as the settlor. The signature of the trustee is conclusive evidence of acceptance.

Second, the trustee's acceptance may be implied from the fact that the trustee has started to act like a trustee by exercising trust powers or performing trust duties. Note that certain acts of the trustee will not be considered acceptance such as acting to preserve trust property under limited circumstances and inspecting the property.

In *In re Estate of Kappus*, 242 S.W.3d 182 (Tex. App.—Tyler 2007, pet. denied), the appellate court explained that "[w]hen the same person is named as independent executor and as trustee of a testamentary trust, acceptance of the position of trustee will be presumed from his or her having acted as executor." *Id.* at 191. It appears that the court is engrafting this as either an additional method of acceptance or as coming within the two primary acceptance methods.

If the named trustee does not accept, the trust instrument is consulted to see if the settlor named an alternate or specified a method for selecting a replacement. If this does not result in a trustee who accepts the trust, the court will appoint a trustee upon petition of an interested person. *See* Trust Code § 111.004(7) (defining "interested person").

See Examples & Explanations § 19.7.2.

BLIEDEN v. GREENSPAN

Texas Supreme Court, 1988
751 S.W.2d 858

PER CURIAM.

This case arises out of a dispute over the administration of a trust. The trial court found that there were no genuine issues of material fact regarding the beneficiaries' claims against Greenspan in his capacity as trustee, and granted summary judgment in his favor. The court of appeals affirmed the trial court's judgment, holding that the beneficiaries had judicially admitted that Greenspan had never accepted the trust, and therefore, Greenspan could not be liable as trustee as a matter of law. 742 S.W.2d 93 (1987). We reverse the judgment of the court of appeals and remand the cause to the trial court.

On June 4, 1969, Hyman Blieden died testate, and the provisions of his will, which was admitted to probate, created two trusts. By the terms of the trust at issue in this case, the Blieden, Wolff, Tennenbaum Trust (hereinafter referred to as the "Trust"), Greenspan was designated as a co-trustee along with William Blieden, the testator's brother, and Doris Blieden, the testator's wife. The testator made his wife and the petitioners in this case the beneficiaries of the Trust. The testator's brother died on November 24, 1970, and his wife died on May 24, 1983, leaving Greenspan as the sole surviving trustee. After the wife's death, the beneficiaries demanded an accounting of the trust property from Greenspan, and when such was not done, they brought this action seeking an accounting. The trial court ordered Greenspan to furnish an accounting. He failed to do so; thus, the trial court set a show cause hearing on the matter. Before the hearing, Greenspan filed and signed an instrument entitled "Account of Arthur Greenspan * * *," wherein he asserted a claim for trustee's fees and attorney's fees. The beneficiaries filed objections to the accounting and requested the removal of Greenspan as trustee. The trial court entered an order finding that Greenspan did not comply with its order for an accounting and that Greenspan resign as trustee. Thereafter, Greenspan filed a motion for summary judgment wherein he contended that he never accepted the trust.

Greenspan, as the summary judgment movant, had the burden of showing that there was no genuine issue as to any material fact. *City of Houston v. Clear Creek Basin Authority*, 589 S.W.2d 671, 678 (Tex. 1979). Referring to "Plaintiff's List of Contested Issues of Fact and Contentions if Law," the court of appeals, in its majority opinion, held that by their "own solemn pleadings," the beneficiaries admitted that Greenspan never accepted the trust. The language in the document cited by the court of appeals is taken out of context. The quoted language, as shown in context, is set forth as follows:

> *Breach of duty to administer the trust.* The evidence will show that *Defendant never accepted the trust*, that he never undertook to administer the trust in accordance with his duties under the Texas Trust Code and at common law, and that he abandoned the administration of the trust to his co-trustees. Defendant's conduct constitutes a breach of his fiduciary duty to administer the trust * * * (emphasis added).

Taken in context, it is clear that the beneficiaries are referring to a failure by Greenspan to take possession of the trust assets because a breach of the duty to administer the trust can only occur if the trustee has accepted or acquiesced in his appointment as trustee. Similarly, a trustee could not have abandoned his duties as trustee if he had not accepted the trust. Consequently, although the phrase "Defendant never accepted the trust" may have been a poor choice of words, it does not constitute an admission by the beneficiaries that Greenspan did not accept his appointment as trustee.

Additionally, it is abundantly clear from the record in this case that there were fact issues regarding whether Greenspan accepted the trust. It was undisputed that Greenspan signed warranty deeds conveying property of the Testator in his capacity as trustee; that he filed a claim for trustee's fees in his Account as well as in his First Amended Answer and Cross-Action; and that he resigned as trustee on March 3, 1986. In light of these undisputed facts, summary judgment was improperly granted. The opinion and judgment of the court of appeals are thus in conflict with this court's holding in *City of Houston v. Clear Creek Basin Authority*, 589 S.W.2d 671 (Tex. 1979). Therefore, pursuant to Tex. R. App. P. 133(b), we grant the beneficiaries' application for writ of error, and without hearing oral argument, a majority of the court reverses the judgment of the court of appeals and remands the cause to the trial court.

3.   Bond

Read Trust Code § 113.058.

The trustee may need to post bond conditioned on the faithful performance of the trustee's duties. The court sets the amount of the bond based on the value of the trust property. The trustee may deliver that amount in cash to the court. However, the trustee typically obtains the bond from a surety company. In exchange for the payment of premiums, the surety company agrees to pay the amount of the bond to the beneficiaries if the trustee breaches the applicable fiduciary duties. Of course, if the surety is required to pay, the surety will seek reimbursement from the trustee.

The trustee is exempt from the bond requirement if either (1) the trustee is a corporation, or (2) the settlor waived bond in the trust instrument. However, the court may, for cause shown, require a noncorporate trustee to post bond even if the settlor waived bond in the trust. The court may order the bond to be payable to the trust estate or the registry of the court as well as the beneficiaries.

See Examples & Explanations § 19.7.3.2.

4. Multiple Trustees

Read Trust Code § 113.085.

The settlor may appoint more than one person to serve as co-trustees. The traditional rule requires all trustees to consent before taking any action with respect to the trust unless the settlor expressly provided otherwise in the trust. Texas rejects the unanimity rule in § 113.085 and permits a majority of the trustees to make decisions regarding the trust.

Under limited circumstances such as when one of the co-trustees is absent or ill, the other co-trustee (or the majority of the remaining cotrustees) may take action if it is necessary to achieve the purposes of the trust, to achieve the efficient administration of the trust, or to avoid injury to the trust property or a beneficiary.

Co-trustees also have a duty to prevent breaches of trust by another co-trustee and, if a breach is discovered, to compel a redress for that breach.

See Examples & Explanations § 19.7.4.

5. Resignation

Read Trust Code § 113.081.

A trustee is not stuck with serving as a trustee until the trust ends or the trustee dies. The trustee may resign either by (1) following the terms of the trust or (2) petitioning the court for permission to resign. The trustee cannot just "walk away" from the job.

See Examples & Explanations § 19.7.6.

6. Removal

See Trust Code § 113.082. Removal for cause is discussed later in Chapter 4(B)(2).

7. Successor Trustees

Read Trust Code § 113.083.

If no trustee remains (e.g., the sole or surviving trustee dies), a replacement trustee is selected by (1) the method specified in the trust instrument, (2) the court on its own motion, or (3) the court upon petition of an interested party.

A trust provision providing a method for the appointment of a successor trustee needs to be clearly stated and then clearly followed. For example, in *Alpert v. Riley*, 274 S.W.3d 277 (Tex. App.—Houston [1st Dist.] 2008, pet. denied), the court determined that the alleged successor trustee did not properly accept the position because the trustee did not execute "an acknowledged acceptance of the trusteeship" as required by the trust. Instead, the alleged successor trustee had only signed a letter which had not been notarized. Although this letter would be sufficient under Trust Code § 112.009(a), the trust itself prescribed a method and the settlor's instructions prevail over the Trust Code's default method under Trust Code § 111.0035(b) The court also rejected the alleged successor trustee's claim that equitable theories such as estoppel or deviation would allow him to assume the trusteeship without compliance with the express language of the trust.

If at least one trustee remains, however, the court will not fill a vacancy. However, the majority of the trustees of a charitable (not private) trust may by majority vote to fill the vacancy if they so desire.

Finance Code §§ 274.001-203 are often referred to as the "Substitute Fiduciary Act." This Act permits, under certain circumstances, one corporate fiduciary, such as a trustee or executor, to be substituted for another without obtaining court permission. The courts have held this Act to be constitutional. See *In re Estate of Touring*, 775 S.W.2d 39 (Tex. App.—Houston [14th Dist.] 1989, no writ).

The attorney who prepares a will or trust which names a corporate fiduciary should explain the potential operation of this Act to the client. If the client objects, the attorney should include a provision prohibiting a substitution as permitted by Finance Code § 274.201.

A successor trustee has the same rights, powers, authority, discretion, and title to trust property as conferred on the original unless the trust instrument or a court order provides to the contrary. *Read* Trust Code § 113.084.

See Examples & Explanations § 19.7.5.

8. Pro Se

According to *In re Guetersloh*, 326 S.W.3d 737 (Tex. App.—Amarillo 2010, no pet.), a trustee who is not an attorney may not appear in court pro se, that is, without an attorney, in the trustee's representative capacity. The trustee attempted to represent himself pro se, in both his capacity as a trustee and in his individual capacity. The appellate court held that the trustee had no right to proceed pro se in his representative (trustee) capacity but could proceed without an attorney with regard to claims in his individual capacity.

The court explained that allowing the trustee to proceed pro se in his representative capacity would be the unauthorized practice of law. The court stated that "if a non-attorney trustee appears in court on behalf of the trust, he or she necessarily represents the interests of others, which amounts to the unauthorized practice of law." The court relied on *Steele v. McDonald*, 202 S.W.3d 926 (Tex. App.—Waco 2006, no pet.) in which the court held that a non-lawyer may not appear pro se in the capacity as an estate's independent executor.

I. THE BENEFICIARY

Read Trust Code § 111.004(2).

1. Capacity

A person needs the capacity to take and hold title to property to be a trust beneficiary. A beneficiary does not need the ability to transfer or manage the property. Thus, any human who is alive can be a beneficiary. A legal entity, such as a corporation, limited liability company, partnership, association, or governmental unit, may also be a trust beneficiary provided the entity is otherwise empowered to take and hold title to property. *Read* Trust Code § 111.004(10).

The settlor may be a beneficiary of his or her own trust. A trustee may also be the beneficiary of a trust as long as the sole beneficiary is not the sole trustee. *See* Trust Code § 112.008.

The settlor may divide the equitable title among multiple beneficiaries. This division can occur along two lines. First, several beneficiaries may hold concurrent interests so that each is presently eligible for trust distributions. Second, the beneficiaries may hold successive interests. For example, one beneficiary may be entitled to the income from the trust until death with any remaining trust property passing to a remainder beneficiary.

See Examples & Explanations § 19.8.1.

2.   Adequacy of Beneficiary Designation

The settlor must designate the beneficiaries of a private trust so that their identity is definitively stated or clearly ascertainable. The trust will fail if the settlor fails to describe the beneficiaries with sufficient certainty. (Special rules for charitable trusts are discussed later in § J(2).)

Notes and Questions

1.   Settlor transferred $100,000 to Timothy, in trust, "to distribute to those individuals whom my trustee so desires." Is this a sufficient beneficiary designation?

2.   Settlor transferred $100,000 to Timothy, in trust, "to distribute to those of my children whom my trustee so desires." Is this a sufficient beneficiary designation?

3.   Settlor transferred $100,000 to Timothy, in trust, "to distribute to those of my friends whom my trustee so desires." Is this a sufficient beneficiary designation?

4.   In *Paschall v. Bank of America, N.A.*, 260 S.W.3d 707 (Tex. App.—Dallas 2008, no pet.), the settlor authorized the trustee to distribute trust principal and/or income to her grandchildren "or the descendants of a grandchild." Trustee distributed trust property to a grandchild's daughters under the belief that the great-grandchildren were current beneficiaries of the trust. The grandchild objected claiming that the trustee could make distributions to his daughters only after he dies. The trial court granted summary judgment that the great-grandchildren were eligible distributes even though their parent was still alive. The appellate court affirmed. Do you agree? Why or why not? How would you avoid this problem if you were the drafting attorney?

5.   *See* Examples & Explanations § 19.8.2.

3.   Honorary Trusts

An honorary trust is a gift which the donor intends to benefit a non-human, non-charitable purpose. Because equitable title is held neither by a human nor by a charity, no one can enforce the arrangement and thus the trustee is on the trustee's "honor" to carry out the settlor's instructions. Common examples of honorary trusts are to care for pet animals, maintain specified items of property in good condition (e.g., a car or a grandfather clock), and to erect monuments. In the past, providing donations for the saying of Masses to honor deceased individuals in a Catholic religious ceremony was also a common type of honorary trust. (Under modern law, such arrangements are deemed charitable in nature.)

Most American jurisdictions do not recognize honorary trusts. Instead, an attempted honorary trust fails and the property reverts to the "settlor," or, if the settlor has already died, to the settlor's successors in interest (heirs, if intestate; beneficiaries, if testate) under resulting trust principles. However, there is a growing trend to permit trustees to carry out these arrangements as long as the purpose is not unlawful or capricious and the duration does not exceed the Rule Against Perpetuities period.

See Examples & Explanations § 19.8.3.

4.   Trusts for Pet Animals

Traditionally, a trust in favor of specific animals failed for a variety of reasons such as for being in violation of the Rule Against Perpetuities because the measuring life was not human or for being an unenforceable honorary trust because it lacked a human or legal entity as a beneficiary who would have standing to enforce the trust. To get around this problem, pet owners who wanted to assure that their pets were properly cared for after they died created a traditional trust which indirectly provided pet care by instructing the trustee to help the person, the actual beneficiary of the trust, who is providing care to the pet by paying for the pet's expenses (and perhaps a fee) according to the pet owner's directions as long as the beneficiary takes proper care of the pet.

With the enactment of Trust Code § 112.037 in 2005, Texas joined the growing number of states which authorize statutory pet trusts. This type of trust is a basic plan and does not require the pet owner to make as many decisions regarding the terms of the trust. The statute "fills in the gaps" and thus a simple provision in a will such as, "I leave $1,000 in trust for the care of my dog, Rover" may be effective.

Read Trust Code § 112.037. For information on estate planning for pet owners, see http://www.professorbeyer.com/Articles/Animals.htm.

5. Incidental Beneficiaries

The term *incidental beneficiary* refers to someone who benefits from the trust but whom the settlor did not name as a beneficiary. Because incidental beneficiaries do not have equitable title to trust property, they usually do not have standing to enforce the trust. But, standing might be possible if the person qualifies as an *interested person* under Trust Code § 111.004(7).

See Examples & Explanations § 19.8.4.

6. Disclaimer

Read Prop. Code §§ 240.001-240.151.

Just as heirs may disclaim inheritances and beneficiaries may disclaim testamentary gifts, potential trust beneficiaries are not required to accept the proffered equitable title. In the normal course of events, the beneficiaries do not disclaim. Most people like the idea of getting something for free. However, there are many good reasons why a person may desire to forego the offered bounty. Three of the most common reasons are as follows: (1) the property may be undesirable or accompanied by an onerous burden (e.g., littered with leaky barrels of toxic chemical waste or subject to back taxes exceeding the value of the land); (2) a beneficiary who is in debt may disclaim the property to prevent the property from being taken by the person's creditors except for the federal tax lien under *Drye v. United States*, 528 U.S. 49 (1999); and (3) the beneficiary may disclaim to reduce the person's transfer tax burden (a "qualified disclaimer" under I.R.C. § 2518).

If the beneficiary properly disclaims, the disclaimed property passes under the terms of the trust as if the beneficiary had predeceased the settlor. *See* Prop. Code § 240.051.

Disclaimer law prior to September 1, 2015 imposed a nine month deadline to make a disclaimer. There is no longer a time-based deadline for Texas disclaimers although the nine-month rule still applies under Federal law to disclaimers that are made for tax purposes.

A person who is in arrears with his or her child support obligations may not disclaim property to avoid those obligations under the circumstances described in Property Code § 240.151(g).

Notes and Questions

1.   What are the prerequisites of a disclaimer? *See* Prop. Code § 240.151.

2.   May a beneficiary disclaim part, but not all, of the beneficiary's interest? *See* Prop. Code § 240.009(b).

3.   May a beneficiary undo a disclaimer if the beneficiary has second thoughts? *See* Prop. Code § 240.009(c).

4.   What are the formalities needed to make a disclaimer? Note the differences for a disclaimer of an interest in a testamentary trust under Prop. Code § 240.103 and an inter vivos trust under Prop. Code § 240.104.

5.   *See* Examples & Explanations § 19.8.5.

7. Characterization of Distributions

A very important issue is whether an interest in a trust held by a married beneficiary is the separate property of the beneficiary or the community property of the beneficiary and his/her spouse. The resolution of this issue is especially important if the spouses are in the midst of a divorce. Although a comprehensive treatment of this issue is left for courses in Marital or Community Property, below are some basic rules assuming the trust as not created by one or both of the spouses:

- Principal distributions are the beneficiary's separate property because the trust interest was acquired by gift, by intestate succession, under a will, or prior to marriage. See *Hardin v. Hardin*, 681 S.W.2d 241 (Tex. App.—San Antonio 1984, no writ).

- Undistributed income is neither community nor separate until a beneficiary has a right to demand income distribution. See *In re Marriage of Burns*, 573 S.W.2d 555 (Tex. App.—Texarkana 1978, writ dism'd).

- Discretionary income distributions are separate.

- The law is unclear with regard to mandatory income distributions. "If the trustee is required to distribute the trust's income to the married beneficiary, the income could be considered community once it is distributed since it arguably could be considered income from the beneficiary's equitable separate property. However, there is case authority that holds that trust income required by the trust document to be distributed to the beneficiary is the beneficiary's separate property. The commentators disagree on the proper result; case law is not definitive." Thomas M. Featherston, Jr., *Marital Property Characterization of Interests in Trusts, Including Distributed and Undistributed Income,* in STATE BAR OF TEXAS, ADVANCED ESTATE PLANNING AND

PROBATE COURSE ch. G, at G-11 (1999).

See Sharma v. Routh, 302 S.W.3d 355 (Tex. App.—Houston [14th Dist.] 2009, no pet.) ("in the context of income distributions under an irrevocable trust during marriage, these distributions are community property only if the recipient has a present possessory right to part of the corpus, even if the recipient has chosen not to exercise that right"); *Benavides v. Mathis*, No. 04-13-00270-CV, 2014 WL 1242512 (Tex. App.—San Antonio Mar. 26, 2014, pet. denied) (income distributions from an irrevocable trust are community property only if the beneficiary has a present possessory right to a portion of the corpus).

8. Effect of Divorce

Read Est. Code §§ 123.051-123.005.

The 2005 Texas Legislature added §§ 471-473 to the Probate Code (not the Trust Code) to address the situation of what happens if the settlor and beneficiary of a revocable trust are divorced and the settlor fails to amend the trust to address this change in circumstance. These sections were recodified into the Estates Code in 2009.

These provisions apply only if the divorce occurs on or after September 1, 2005. It does not matter when the settlor created the trust.

Only written revocable trusts are covered. The ex-spouse remains as the beneficiary of an irrevocable trust and of a revocable oral trust.

If the settlor of a written revocable trust divorces a beneficiary of that trust to whom the settlor was married before or at the time of trust creation, the following provisions of the trust in favor of the ex-spouse are automatically revoked:

- Beneficiary of a revocable disposition or appointment.
- Donee of a general or special power of appointment, and
- Designation as a fiduciary (e.g., trustee, personal representative, agent, or guardian).

Any property interest which is automatically revoked passes as if the ex-spouse executed a valid disclaimer of that interest under Texas law. If a fiduciary designation is automatically revoked, the trust instrument is read as if the ex-spouse died immediately before the dissolution of the marriage.

The automatic revocation of provisions in favor of the ex-spouse discussed above does *not* occur if one or more of the following instruments provides otherwise:

- A trust executed after the divorce,

- A court order,
- Express language in the trust, or
- Express language of a contract relating to the division of the marital estate entered into before, during, or after the marriage.

A bona fide purchaser from the ex-spouse of trust property or a person who receives a payment from the ex-spouse which is traceable to the trust, does not have to return the property or payment and is not liable for that property or payment.

If the ex-spouse receives property or a payment from a trust to which the ex-spouse is not entitled, the ex-spouse has a duty to return the property or payment and is personally liable to the person who is entitled to that property or payment.

9.   Transfers and Assignments of Beneficial Interests

The beneficiary of a trust has the power to transfer the beneficiary's interest to the same extent the beneficiary could transfer a non-trust interest. Thus, if the beneficiary has the capacity to transfer property generally, the beneficiary would also have the capacity to transfer the beneficial interest. While the beneficiary is alive, the beneficiary could give away the interest or could sell the interest. If the beneficiary's interest survives death, the beneficiary's interest would pass either to the beneficiary's heirs or to the takers under the beneficiary's will.

Despite the broad powers which a beneficiary may have to make inter vivos and at-death transfers of the beneficial interest, settlors rarely permit beneficiaries to exercise these powers. Instead, it is extremely common for settlors to limit the transferability of beneficial interests. First, settlors require beneficiaries to be alive to benefit from the trust. For example, beneficiaries who receive periodic payments only have life interests and remainder beneficiaries must be alive when the trust ends to receive the property. Second, settlors usually include spendthrift provisions which prohibit beneficiaries from transferring or assigning their interests.

Notes and Questions

1.   Settlor created a trust which provides that the trust terminates in the year 2020 and the trustee is then to distribute all remaining trust property to Randy. Randy's interest indefeasibly vested when Settlor created the trust because Settlor did not place any condition on Randy taking the property; he does not even need to be alive in 2020. Additionally, Settlor did not include a spendthrift provision. In 2015, Randy sold his remainder interest to Florence. In 2016, Randy sold the

same interest to Sam. To whom should the trustee distribute the remaining trust property when the trust ends in 2020? *See West Texas Lumber Co. v. Tom Green County*, 188 S.W. 283 (Tex. Civ. App.—Austin 1916, no writ).

2.   *See* Examples & Explanations § 19.8.6.

10. Duties of Beneficiaries to Each Other

Read Trust Code § 114.031.

11. Availability of Beneficiary's Interest to Creditors

The equitable interest of the beneficiary may be subject to attack from the beneficiary's creditors. Typical state law procedures that a creditor could use to reach this interest include a creditor's bill, a bill for equitable execution, levy, attachment, execution, and garnishment. Once the creditor obtains the interest, the creditor may elect to sell the interest or require the trustee to make distributions directly to the creditor as they come due.

The beneficiary's creditors, however, rarely have the ability to reach the beneficiary's interest in the trust. Almost all trusts contain spendthrift provisions which prevent the creditors from obtaining the equitable interest.

A spendthrift clause is a provision of a trust which does two things. First, it prohibits the beneficiary from selling, giving away, or otherwise transferring the beneficiary's interest. Second, a spendthrift clause prevents the beneficiary's creditors from reaching the beneficiary's interest in the trust. *Read* Trust Code § 112.035.

A spendthrift provision permits the settlor to carry out the settlor's intent of benefiting the designated beneficiary but not the beneficiary's assignees or creditors. Settlors include spendthrift restrictions in practically every trust because they protect beneficiaries from their own improvidence and their personal creditors. Note, however, that neither the settlor nor the beneficiary must show that a beneficiary is actually incapable of prudently managing property to obtain spendthrift protection.

Spendthrift restrictions are easy to create. The settlor does not need to use any particular language as long as the settlor's intent is clear. In fact, § 112.035(b) provides that it is adequate for the settlor to simply write, "This is a spendthrift trust."

A spendthrift provision has no effect once the trustee delivers a trust distribution to the beneficiary.

BOOTH v. CHADWICK

Texas Civil Appeals—Galveston 1941
154 S.W.2d 268
writ ref'd w.o.m.

CODY, Justice.

While William H. Langhorne was in prison serving a life sentence he, on December 21, 1933, executed to E.C. Chadwick, trustee, a kinsman, a general warranty deed in trust, by which he conveyed to his said trustee all of his property and estate, in trust, for a period of ten years therefrom, and for as much longer as he did not himself terminate the trust, upon certain terms and conditions which involved managing the property and estate, paying off the debts and incumbrances thereagainst, and preserving the property while Langhorne was in prison. The trust deed provided that any attempted alienation, or mortgaging any of the property thus conveyed in trust by Langhorne, if made during the term of the trust, should be invalid and of no effect. This deed was properly recorded.

Thereafter, on August 2, 1939, while still confined as a prisoner serving a life sentence, the said Langhorne executed a deed of conveyance to half of all his property and estate to C.C. Booth, which was promptly recorded.

* * *

It is doubtless true that ordinarily one may not create a spendthrift trust, wherein he is the sole beneficiary, which he may not revoke at any time. "It is against public policy to permit a man to tie up his property in such a way that he can still enjoy it but can prevent his creditors from reaching it." 1 Scott on Trusts, § 156, p. 782. There is every reason of morals, prudence and public policy why a wealthy man should not be allowed to tie up his wealth in such a fashion that he can enjoy the position of wealth, and yet not be answerable for debts which that position would enable him to incur, or for injuries which he might inflict on others. But circumstances alter cases. A wealthy man who is sentenced to prison for life does not come into contact with the public, and is by his situation separated from his friends. It takes no great foresight on his part and on the part of his friends to foresee that his wealth and his unfortunate situation will result in efforts being made by those who have access to him to obtain his wealth. It takes no great foresight on his part to foresee that imprisonment, which is punishment, will weaken his will, and that his desire for liberty will make him credulous. We see no reason, when there is no occasion to suppose that a trust in the nature of a spendthrift trust has been created by a man in prison to protect his estate, to hold such a trust to be against public policy. In such circumstances the tying up of a prisoner's property can work no injury to the public as the prisoner is in no position to defraud trusting creditors. Under such circumstances the man creating such a trust is protecting himself, not against his own folly, but against what other men may do while he is in a position where duress may very easily cause him to part with his property under circumstances where he might be afraid to claim duress. We will not rule on the point as it is not necessary to the disposition of the case. But the fact that it is against public policy for a man at large to tie up his property for himself, seems to present no valid reason for holding that a man in prison might not, consistent with sound public policy, create a spendthrift trust for himself during the period of his imprisonment.

Notes and Questions

1.   Under several circumstances, courts will not enforce spendthrift provisions for public policy reasons. The following is a nonexclusive list:

- A creditor may still reach trust property if the settlor is also the beneficiary under § 112.035(d). Note, however, that some states, such as Alaska, Colorado, Delaware, Hawaii, Mississippi, Missouri, Nevada, New Hampshire, Ohio, Oklahoma, Rhode Island, South Dakota, Tennessee, Utah, Virginia, West Virginia, and Wyoming, enforce spendthrift provisions under specified circumstances even if the trust is self-settled.

- The court may order the trustees of a spendthrift trust to make payments for the support of the beneficiary's child. *Read* Family Code § 154.005. Assuming the court first imposes a child-support obligation on the parent who is the beneficiary of a spendthrift trust, the court may order the trustee to make payments for the support of the child notwithstanding the spendthrift provision. *See Kolpack v. Torres*, 829 S.W.2d 913 (Tex. App.—Corpus Christi 1992, writ denied). If a trust payment is mandatory, then the full amount of that payment may be reached. However, if the trust is discretionary, the court is limited to ordering child support payments from trust income.

- Property in a spendthrift trust will not be protected from the beneficiary's federal tax obligations. *See United States v. Dallas Nat'l Bank*, 152 F.2d 582 (5th Cir. 1945).

2.   In the case of *In re Townley Bypass Unified Credit Trust*, 252 S.W.3d 715 (Tex. App.—Texarkana 2008, pet. denied), the settlor's will created a trust for his wife with the remainder to his two sons upon her death. Before the wife died, one of the son's died. When the wife died, the issue arose as to whether the predeceased son's share would pass to his

successors in interest or to the settlor's heirs via intestacy. The trust did not expressly require a son to survive to receive his interest and the trust contained a standard spendthrift provision.

Both the trial and appellate courts held that the deceased son's interest passed to his successors in interest. The court began its analysis by examining the remainder interest granted to each son by their father's will. Because the interest was in ascertainable persons and there was no condition precedent other than the termination of the prior estate (the wife's death ending her life estate), then the remainder was vested.

The court next determined as a matter of first impression in Texas that the spendthrift clause did not prevent the predeceased son's vested remainder interest from passing under his will despite the existence of a spendthrift provision restricting the transfer of the son's interest prior to his receiving the property. The court was impressed with the reasoning of RESTATEMENT (THIRD) OF TRUSTS § 58, reporter's notes, cmt. g (2003), which provides that "[a] continuing income or remainder interest in the trust, despite the spendthrift provision, is transferable by will or intestacy." *Townley*, at 720. The court stressed that a spendthrift provision is designed "to protect the beneficiary from his or her own folly, a purpose that cannot be promoted after the beneficiary's death." *Townley,* at 721.

3.   Section 112.035(e) prevents the beneficiary of a *Crummey* trust[6] from being deemed a settlor and thereby losing spendthrift protection if the beneficiary elects not to exercise the withdrawal right.

4.   Section 112.035(f) helps assure that a surviving spouse does not lose spendthrift protection under a bypass trust[7] under specified circumstances.

5.   A settlor will not be considered a beneficiary of a trust merely because the settlor's interest in the trust was created by the exercise of a power of appointment by a third party. Likewise, property contributed to a laundry list of trusts will not be considered to have been contributed by the settlor. These provisions help trusts retain spendthrift protection by

---

[6]A trust structured in a way that contributions to the trust qualify for the annual exclusion named for the case which first approved the technique, *Crummey v. Commissioner*, 397 F.2d 82 (9th Cir. 1968). *See* Examples & Explanations §§ 24.1.4.1.

[7]A trust funded by the settlor's will with property that qualifies for the federal exemption equivalent amount. Although this exemption amount could be given directly to an intended beneficiary without restriction, passage via a trust gives the settlor greater control over how the property is used. *See* Examples & Explanations § 24.3.2.

assuring that the settlor is not treated as a beneficiary. *See* Trust Code § 112.035(g) & (h) .

    6.   *See* Examples & Explanations §§ 19.8.7 & 19.8.8.

12. Discretionary Provisions

Settlors often create trusts for beneficiaries, such as children or grandchildren, whose future needs cannot be predicted with accuracy. For example, if the settlor's children are two and five years old when the settlor creates the trust, the settlor does not know whether one child will need extensive medical care because of a future accident or disease or whether one child will need additional funds to attend college (or, alternatively, will receive a scholarship and thus not need as much assistance). The settlor wants the trustee to make trust distributions in accordance with the beneficiary's needs just as the settlor would if the settlor were still in control of the property. In other words, the settlor is substituting the trustee's judgment for the settlor's judgment typically because the settlor will be deceased at the time the trust distributions are made. The settlor does not want to create a *mandatory trust* which requires the trustee to make predesignated distributions (e.g., "$1,000 per month for each beneficiary" or "50% of the trust's income in quarterly installments").

To accomplish this objective, settlors frequently give their trustees the discretion to determine which beneficiaries to pay and how much to pay each. A trust containing this type of provision is called a *discretionary trust.* You may also hear these types of trusts called *spray* or *sprinkle* trusts because of the trustee's power to spread the benefits among the beneficiaries.

The trustee's discretion may be very broad ("distribute to my children in your absolute discretion"), very narrow ("distribute to my children at your discretion for their dental expenses"), or anywhere in-between ("distribute to my children at your discretion for expenses relating to their health, education, maintenance, and support").

Trust Code § 113.029(a) codifies the common law rule that regardless of the extent of discretion the settlor grants to a trustee, the trustee must always act "in good faith and in accordance with the terms and purposes of the trust and the interests of the beneficiaries." Thus, even if the settlor provides that the trustee's discretion is "absolute" or "uncontrolled," the trustee's actions must still comport with fiduciary standards and are reviewable by the court. If a trustee actually could have uncontrolled discretion, no trust would exist because no one could enforce the trustee's duties. In addition, it would be against public policy to permit a trustee to have free reign over the property and to use it contrary to the settlor's intent but yet provide no remedy to the injured parties, the beneficiaries. Likewise, the trustee must exercise the discretion to pay or not to pay; the trustee cannot sit idly by doing nothing.

Federal gift and estate tax problems may result if a non-settlor beneficiary is also the trustee of a trust and is given the power to make self-distributions that are not limited by an ascertainable standard relating to health, education, support, or maintenance. A settlor may create this problem inadvertently by giving the trustee/beneficiary unrestricted discretion or may limit distributions to a standard that is not ascertainable such as for the trust/beneficiary's comfort, benefit, welfare, or well-being.

To remedy this problem, Trust Code § 113.029(b) provides that in such situations, the trustee/beneficiary's power to distribute is "cut back" to an ascertainable standard relating to health, education, support, or maintenance. Likewise, the trustee/beneficiary's power to distribute is restricted so that distributions cannot be made to satisfy a legal obligation of support that the trustee/beneficiary personally owes to another person.

If there are other trustees besides the beneficiary, a majority of the remaining trustees may exercise the power to make discretionary distributions to the "limited" trustee/beneficiary without regard to the cut-back. If there is no trustee who is not free of restrictions, the court may appoint a special fiduciary with authority to exercise the power. *See* Trust Code § 113.029(c).

The automatic cut-back will not apply if one of the following circumstances exists:

- The trust was created and became irrevocable before September 1, 2009. (If the trust was created before September 1, 2009 but did not become irrevocable until September 1, 2009 or thereafter, the cut-back will apply.)
- The settlor is the beneficiary/trustee.
- The settlor expressly indicated that the cut-back provisions of this section do not apply.
- The trustee/beneficiary is the settlor's spouse and a martial deduction was previously allowed for the trust.
- The settlor may amend or revoke the trust.
- Contributions to the trust qualify for the gift tax annual exclusion.

IN RE ESTATE OF DILLARD

Texas Appeals – Amarillo, 2003
98 S.W.3d 386
pet. denied.

BRIAN QUINN, Justice.

Ronald Glen Kirby (Kirby) and Glen David Dillard (Dillard) cross appeal from two orders involving the estate left and trust created by Iris Kirby Dillard upon her death. * * * Dillard challenges the trial court's * * * determination that Dillard "did not have the absolute right to withdraw all corpus and income from the trust." * * *

Background

The appeal involves the interpretation of a will left by Dillard's wife, Iris. The latter was also the mother of Kirby. Her will, which was subsequently offered for probate in the Yoakum County Court at Law, named Dillard as her independent executor, and Kirby as the alternate. Furthermore, she specifically bequeathed to her husband, "in fee simple," the following:

> ... all my personal property including jewelry, clothing, automobiles, furniture, silver, books, and pictures, but specifically excluding cash and certificates of deposit, or money in any financial institution, to my husband ... Dillard ... in fee simple absolute if he survive[d][her]....

The residue of her estate "whether community or separate, real or personal" was then "give[n]" to Dillard "as trustee, in trust for the benefit of ... Dillard." And, with regard to the disposition of the property held in trust, Iris directed that the trustee "shall pay to or apply for the benefit of ... Dillard during his lifetime all of the net income of the Trust...." Yet, according to the will,

> [i]f at any time in the discretion of the Trustee my husband should be in need of additional funds for maintenance and support, then the Trustee, in addition to the income payments provided, shall in his discretion pay to or apply for the benefit of ... Dillard such amounts from the principal of the Trust, up to the whole thereof, as Trustee deems necessary. In no event shall any trust income or principal be paid during the lifetime of ... Dillard to anyone other than my husband.

This provision was reiterated later in the will in virtually the same language. Regarding disposition of its assets upon termination of the trust, Iris directed that:

[u]nless the Trustee decides to use and does use all the principal of this trust, the trust shall continue in effect until the death of the beneficiary, at which time the trust shall be terminated and the principal and any accrued interest of the trust shall be distributed to the beneficiary in fee simple and in equal shares. * * *

After the order closing the estate was entered, Kirby sued Dillard, in the 121st District Court, for a declaratory judgment construing not only the will and trust but also the validity of Dillard's actions viz the trust. Allegedly, Dillard refused to fund the entity and instead converted the property for his own use. Kirby also sought a judgment declaring that * * * the trustee was entitled to invade the trust principal on behalf of Dillard only when necessary to maintain and support Dillard * * *.

Upon trial, the court entered its order (signed on September 18, 2000) * * * limit[ing] the trustee's ability to encroach upon the trust principal on behalf of Dillard to circumstances when additional funds were needed for his maintenance and support "when taking into account all other resources available to him." * * *

Issue Three-Absolute Right to Withdraw All Principal and Income

In his final issue, Dillard questioned whether the trial court erred in declaring that his ability (as trustee) to encroach on the principal for his benefit be limited to those events in which he "requires additional funds for his maintenance and support when taking into account all other resources available to him." This allegedly constituted error because he had the unfettered discretion or absolute right to distribute the principal. We overrule the issue.

Resolution of this dispute requires us to again read the will to determine Iris' intent per the rules of construction discussed in the preceding issue. Furthermore, the pertinent trust terms are found in § II(B) and (D) of the will. Through the former, Iris stated that:

... [i]f at any time in the discretion of the Trustee my husband should be in need of additional funds for maintenance and support, then the Trustee, in addition to the income payments provided, shall in his discretion pay to or apply for the benefit of ... Dillard such amounts from the principal of the Trust, up to the whole thereof, as Trustee deems necessary. In no event shall any trust income or principal be paid during the lifetime of ... Dillard to anyone other than my husband.

In paragraph (D), she wrote:

> ... If at any time in the discretion of the Trustee, my Husband should be in need of additional funds for his maintenance and support, then the Trustee shall in his discretion pay to or apply for the benefit of my Husband, in addition to the income payments, such amounts from the principal of the Trust, up to the whole thereof, as Trustee deems necessary. In no event shall any income or principal from the Glen David Dillard Trust be paid during my Husband's lifetime to anyone other than my Husband.

No one claims that any term in either provision is ambiguous or otherwise susceptible to different meanings. Nor do we view them as being so. Furthermore, as can be seen from the provisions themselves, Iris specified that the principal could be distributed to Dillard if he "should be in need of additional funds for his *maintenance and support*." (Emphasis added). Given this, we are obligated to determine the meaning of "maintenance and support."

Like words were used by the testatrix when creating a trust in State v. Rubion, 158 Tex. 43, 308 S.W.2d 4 (1958). There the Supreme Court had to decide what interest the beneficiary had when the trust instrument allowed the trustee to distribute assets for the beneficiary's support and maintenance. The court noted that those terms evinced the creation of support trust. Id. at 8. And, though a trustee's discretion viz distributions from such a trust may be considerable, it was not unbridled. Id. at 8-9. Quite the contrary, the trustee must nevertheless act reasonably and in a manner commensurate with the purpose of the trust. Id. at 9. This meant that his decision to distribute income or corpus for the beneficiary's support and maintenance could not be exercised at whim. Instead, the trustee was obligated to base his decision after considering indicia such as 1) the size of the trust estate, 2) the beneficiary's age, life expectancy, and condition in life, 3) his present and future needs, 4) the other resources available to him or his individual wealth, and 5) his present and future health, both mental and physical, to name a few. Id. at 10-11. With these words and directives in mind, we turn to the trust before us.

Admittedly, Iris used the word "discretion" when expressing the scope of the trustee's authority. Yet, she also incorporated therein the words "support and maintenance" and stated that the corpus could be expended when "necessary" to serve that purpose and when he was in "need of additional funds." "Support and maintenance," "additional funds," and "necessary" hardly connote utter discretion to do that which the trustee may care to at any given moment. Rather, they evince a restriction on the trustee's discretion and authority and denote an intent to permit expenditure when needed for Dillard's support and maintenance. So, like the testatrix in Rubion, Iris too created a support trust. Given that, distributions of principal therefrom could be made only in ways commensurate with that purpose. In other words, and contrary to the suggestion of Dillard, the discretion vested in the trustee under the instrument at bar was and is not unbridled or absolute. Instead, he, like the trustee in Rubion, must exercise it only after considering the beneficiary's needs, age, condition, separate resources, the size of the trust estate, health, and the like. And, if upon considering those factors, the trustee reasonably concludes that a distribution is warranted, only then can it be made. Finally, the wording used by the trial court at bar to describe the trustee's authority merely reflects the restrictions imposed by Iris and recognized by the Supreme Court long ago. * * *

Notes

1.   Under the terms of the trust in *Lesikar v. Moon*, 237 S.W.3d 361 (Tex. App.—Houston [14th Dist.] 2007, pet. denied), the trustee was instructed to use a designated portion of the property to fund a separate trust for the beneficiary. The trustee refused to do so and the beneficiary obtained a judgment from the trial court instructing the trustee to fund the trust. The trustee appealed alleging that the trial court interfered with his discretion as a trustee without a finding of fraud, misconduct, or abuse of discretion.

The appellate court recognized that a court "may not substitute its discretion for that of the trustee, and may interfere with the trustee's discretionary powers only in the case of fraud, misconduct, or clear abuse of discretion." *Id.* at 366. However, in this case, the trust directly instructed the trustee to fund the trust by using the mandatory term "shall." In other words, the Trustee had no discretion not to fund the trust and thus it was proper for the court to order the funding.

2.   *See* Examples & Explanations § 19.8.9.

13. Support Provisions

The settlor may restrict the use of trust income, principal, or both to the beneficiary's basic needs such as food, clothing, medical care, and educational expenses. A trust containing this type of provision is called a *support trust*. A support trust may either be mandatory or discretionary in nature. If mandatory, the trustee must make distributions to support the beneficiary. However, if the support trust is discretionary, the trustee may, but is not required, to pay for the beneficiary's support and may not, under any circumstances, make distributions for other reasons such as a vacation or second home.

Many courts treat support trusts as being spendthrift in nature even if they lack express spendthrift clauses. As a general rule, the beneficiary of a support trust may not convey the beneficiary's interest. If the beneficiary could alienate the beneficiary's interest, the settlor's purpose of providing for the beneficiary would be circumvented. For the same reason, the beneficiary's creditors may not reach the beneficiary's interest. This creditor protection is usually unavailable, however, in the same types of situations in which a spendthrift clause is ineffective such as where the settlor and the beneficiary are the same person.

Notes and Questions

1.   What does "support" mean – just enough to stay alive or something more?

2.   Does support include the support of the beneficiary's spouse and minor children?

3.   Should other assets and income of the beneficiary be considered in determining the amount needed for support?

4.   *See* Examples & Explanations § 19.8.10.

KEISLING v. LANDRUM

218 S.W.3d 737
Texas Appeals – Fort Worth 2007
pet. denied

TERRIE LIVINGSTON, Justice.

I. Introduction

Appellant Frankye Keisling, individually and as primary beneficiary under the Alfred Fate Keisling Trust, appeals from a declaratory judgment that prevents her from receiving trust distributions until her "other financial resources" are depleted save one home and one vehicle. In three issues, appellant argues that the trial court erred (1) in its construction of the terms of the trust, (2) by failing to find that appellant was entitled to distributions from the trust since Fate Keisling's death, and (3) by not awarding attorney's fees to appellant. We reverse and remand.

II. Background Facts

Fate and appellant married on April 26, 1997, in Ruidoso, New Mexico, and stayed married until Fate's death on July 25, 2000. Fate and appellant had both been in prior, long-term marriages. Before marrying Fate, appellant worked at Huff's Furniture Galleries for thirty-two years, starting out as a secretary and eventually becoming a licensed interior designer.

After marrying Fate, appellant quit working because Fate wanted her to travel with him. Appellant was earning a salary of approximately $70,000 a year when she stopped working.

Prior to marrying, Fate and appellant entered into an Agreement in Contemplation of Marriage ("pre-nup"). At the time of their marriage, Fate had significantly more assets than appellant; Fate's assets were in excess of $1.3 million while appellant's were approximately $300,000. Although Fate and appellant signed a pre-nup, Fate agreed to provide for the couple's standard of living and to pay appellant's mortgage, property taxes, and for repairs and maintenance for her home in Wichita Falls, Texas. Fate also granted appellant a life estate in his Ruidoso cabin.

During their three-year marriage, Fate and appellant enjoyed a high standard of living. They maintained a home in Wichita Falls, a home in Lubbock, and a cabin in Ruidoso. They had five vehicles, went on cruises to Alaska and Panama, and traveled throughout Texas and to Washington, D.C. Before he died, Fate also planned a trip for them to Carmel, California.

Fate died on July 25, 2000, leaving a testamentary trust for the benefit of appellant and his children from his earlier marriage. Except for personal effects and nontestamentary transfers, Fate's entire estate passed to the trust, including all of his interests in real property.

Lynn Landrum was good friends with Fate and his first wife, Jeanie Keisling, who died a year before Fate married appellant. Lynn served as the executor of Fate's estate and as the trustee of Fate's trust. After Fate died, Lynn made no trust distributions to appellant, reasoning that appellant was not entitled to distributions until she exhausted all of her "other financial resources," which included everything save one home and one vehicle.

Having received no trust income or principal distributions, appellant filed suit on May 31, 2002, under the Texas Declaratory Judgment Act and the Texas Trust Code for the court to declare the terms of the trust and the distributions to be made to her. Appellant also joined Fate's children ("appellees") as interested parties. After hearing evidence from both parties, the trial court determined that the trust language was ambiguous and that Fate had not intended for appellant to receive distributions from the trust until she had exhausted all of her "other financial resources," meaning income and assets, except for one home and one vehicle.

III. Appellant's Issues on Appeal

Appellant's first issue is dispositive, as this case's outcome depends on whether the trial court's interpretation of the phrase "other financial resources" in the trust is correct. Appellant contends that the trial court's interpretation is erroneous. The relevant portion of Fate's trust is as follows:

> 4. The primary purpose of "THE ALFRED FATE KEISLING TRUST" shall be to provide for the support, maintenance, and health of my wife *in the standard of living to which she is accustomed at my death. If my wife's own income and other financial resources from sources other than from this trust are not sufficient to so maintain her in such standard of living*, the Trustee *shall* distribute, from time to time, as much of the current trust net income, or accumulated trust net income, as shall be necessary to so maintain her. If my wife's own income and other financial resources, together with distributions of current and accumulated trust net income from this trust, are not sufficient to maintain her in such standard of living, then the Trustee *shall* distribute as much of the trust corpus as shall be necessary to so maintain her. After my wife has been provided for in the manner described above, and if in the Trustee's judgment, it will not endanger my wife's present or reasonably foreseeable future support, the Trustee may distribute to my descendants, from time to time, such amounts of the current or accumulated trust net income and as much of the trust corpus, as shall be necessary for their respective support, maintenance, health, and education.... [Emphasis added.]

At trial, no party disputed the fact that Fate and appellant were accustomed to a high standard of living. Additionally, no party disputed that Fate intended the trust to take his place supporting appellant's high standard of living after he died. The dispute arises in Fate's intended meaning of "other financial resources" in the trust instrument. Appellant asserts that Fate intended "other financial resources" to mean financial income and that Lynn should have distributed trust income payments to her as soon as her own income could not support her standard of living. Conversely, appellees argue that Fate intended "other financial resources" to mean assets and income and that appellant must first exhaust all of her assets except for one house and one vehicle before Lynn can distribute trust income payments. * * *

B. Applicable Law

The construction of a will or trust instrument is a question of law for the trial court. *Eckels v. Davis*, 111 S.W.3d 687, 694 (Tex.App.-Fort Worth 2003, pet. denied). Courts construe trusts to determine the intent of the maker. *Id.* The intent of the maker must be ascertained from the language used within the four corners of the instrument. *Id.* (citing *Shriner's Hosp. for Crippled Children of Tex. v. Stahl*, 610 S.W.2d 147,

151 (Tex.1980)). All terms must be harmonized to properly give effect to all parts, and if possible, the court should construe the instrument to give effect to all provisions so that no provision is rendered meaningless. *Id.* If the language used by the maker of a trust is unambiguous, it is unnecessary to construe the instrument because it speaks for itself. *Id.*; *Hurley v. Moody Nat'l Bank of Galveston*, 98 S.W.3d 307, 310 (Tex.App.-Houston [1st Dist.] 2003, no pet.); see *Moody v. Pitts*, 708 S.W.2d 930, 935 (Tex.App.-Corpus Christi 1986, no writ). The trial court's conclusion of law that the trust terms were unclear is reviewed de novo as a legal question. *Turner v. Mullins*, 162 S.W.3d 356, 364 (Tex.App.-Fort Worth 2005, no pet.).

C. Analysis

1. Ambiguity of the Trust

At trial, appellant introduced evidence that her regular monthly revenue was $1,137.75. Although the trial court did not determine appellant's standard of living at the time of Fate's death, neither party disputed that appellant's standard of living was high and included food, gas, gifts to church, gifts to children, utilities, a security system, maid service, yard maintenance, taxes, insurance, cruises to Panama and Alaska, dental and medical care, shopping, five vehicles, and costs to support multiple homes. Appellant argued that, based on these expenses, her standard of living at Fate's death was at least $5,600 per month. According to appellant, because Fate had paid for these expenses prior to his death, the trust should step in to cover any monthly costs that her income could not cover; these uncovered costs amounted to approximately $4,462.25 per month starting the first month after Fate died.

Appellant's expert witness, Charles King, an attorney specializing in wills and trusts, asserted at trial that the terms income and "other financial resources" were unambiguous, and that Fate never intended for appellant to exhaust all of her bank accounts, IRAs, and other assets save one house and one vehicle before receiving distributions. King further testified that the term "income" as used in the trust means compensation for personal services and work while "financial resources" means the cash flow from other assets such as Social Security, pension payments, annuity contracts, and similar items. As authority for his opinion, King cited section 50, comment e(2) of the Restatement of Trusts. Under this section, a beneficiary's "other resources" normally include "income and other periodic receipts, such as pension or other annuity payments and court-ordered support payments." Restatement (Third) of Trusts § 50 cmt. e(2) (2003).

John League, a trust officer and expert witness for appellees, testified that according to the terms of the trust, appellant must first exhaust all of her assets, including the four extra vehicles, cash, bank accounts, stocks, bonds, and other assets excluding one house and one vehicle before she can receive distributions. John Freels, Fate's attorney who drafted the trust, agreed with League and deposed that "if [appellant] has four cars and only needs one car, then she could liquidate the other three excess cars and use that for her support, maintenance and needs." Freels and League both reasoned that one house and one car are exempt from appellant's "other financial resources" because they provide basic maintenance support. At trial, however, neither expert elaborated on exactly how the trust instrument directed the trustee to limit appellant's maintenance support in this manner.

Appellant argues that appellees' interpretation of the will leaves her with two illogical choices: either stretch every dollar as far as possible or sell off all of her assets. However, according to appellant, there is no evidence in the trust instrument that Fate intended for her to exhaust all of her assets in this manner. We agree.

Both parties' experts testified that the primary purpose of the trust was to provide for appellant-the trust's primary beneficiary-as Fate had done during their marriage. Further, the trust language unambiguously states Fate's intent to sustain appellant's high standard of living and directs Lynn to use the trust income and even invade the trust corpus if appellant's income does not support her lifestyle.

The word "shall" means that the trustee must follow the maker's instructions. See *In re Orsagh*, 151 S.W.3d 263, 267 (Tex.App.-Eastland 2004, original proceeding); *Roberts v. Squyres*, 4 S.W.3d 485, 489 (Tex.App.-Beaumont 1999, pet. denied).

While Fate was alive, appellant enjoyed the benefits and luxuries of cruises and vacations, multiple homes, and multiple vehicles. There is no evidence in the wording of the instrument that Fate intended the trust to be a parachute to protect appellant from poverty after she had exhausted all of her own assets. On the contrary, the purpose of the trust was to step in and pay for appellant's high standard of living upon Fate's death. This high standard, which was established before Fate died, included use of and access to not just one vehicle, but to several. Appellant's standard of living also included use of both of the couple's homes plus use and access to her own home in Oklahoma. It would be nonsensical to require appellant to sell all of her vehicles and other assets save one home and one vehicle just so the trust could "step in" and provide her with funds to purchase new assets and vehicles to replace them. Further, if we construe "other financial resources" to mean all assets, nothing in the instrument shows an intent for appellant to keep one home and one vehicle; in that situation, appellant would have to sell everything she owns before receiving distributions, which is also nonsensical.

If the language of a trust instrument is unambiguous and expresses the intention of the maker, it is unnecessary to construe the instrument because it speaks for itself. *Corpus Christi Nat'l Bank v. Gerdes*, 551 S.W.2d 521, 523 (Tex.Civ.App.1977). In such a situation, a trustee's powers are conferred by the instrument and neither the trustee nor the courts can add to or take away from such powers, but must permit it to stand as written and give to it only such construction as the trustor intended. *Id.* Here, Fate's trust is unambiguous in its intent to maintain appellant in the standard of living to which she was accustomed at his death. By requiring appellant to use her own income and "other financial resources," Fate did not intend for appellant to become impoverished before the trust stepped in to again elevate her to a high standard of living. On the contrary, Fate designed the trust to provide appellant with a comfortable lifestyle, which included multiple vehicles, at least one vacation each year, and other reasonable luxuries.

During oral arguments and throughout their brief, appellees asserted that Fate and appellant enjoyed an inflated standard of living that was really just a "fantasy." Appellees base this argument on the fact that Fate was spending money from his deceased first wife's trust that he was not entitled to. Therefore, according to appellees, the trial court should establish a lower standard of living for appellant than she was accustomed to during marriage. We find this argument unpersuasive. First, when Fate died, Lynn used monies from Fate's estate to pay back these misused funds. More importantly, it is irrelevant that Fate and appellant enjoyed an inflated standard of living; what is relevant is the instrument language.

Because the trust language unambiguously shows Fate's intent to provide for appellant without her having to exhaust any assets, we hold that "other financial resources" as used in Fate's will means "income and other periodic receipts, such as pension or other annuity payments and court-ordered support payments." See Restatement (Third) of Trusts § 50 cmt. e(2). Accordingly, we hold that the trial court's conclusions of law numbers 5, 6, 9, and 10 are incorrect; thus, the findings of fact numbers 8-11 (which are more properly characterized as legal conclusions as they relate to the ambiguity of the trust language) and 14-16 (which deal with the parol evidence supporting Fate's intent) were unnecessary, and we "unfind" them.

2. Balancing Appellant's Current Support and Maintenance Needs with the Need to Preserve the Trust for Appellant's Future Support and Maintenance

Although Lynn, the trustee, has a responsibility to distribute the trust's income and principal to appellant to maintain her in the lifestyle to which she is accustomed, we recognize that he has a competing responsibility to manage the trust prudently and responsibly to preserve it for her future support and maintenance. See Tex. Prop. Code Ann. § 113.006 (Vernon Supp.2006) (stating that a trust may manage the trust property on the conditions and for the lengths of time as the trustee deems proper); *Brault v. Bigham*, 493 S.W.2d 576, 579 (Tex. Civ. App.-Waco 1973, writ ref'd n.r.e.) (holding that safety of the trust fund is the first care of the law, and on this depends every rule which has been made for the conduct of trustees). Here, the trust instrument does not state that Lynn must give into appellant's every support and maintenance whim; it simply notes that income and principal from the trust shall be distributed to appellant to support and maintain her if appellant's income does not suffice. Given this, we are obligated to determine the meaning of "maintenance and support." See *Estate of Dillard*, 98 S.W.3d 386, 395 (Tex.App.-Amarillo 2003, pet. denied).

Like words were used by the testatrix when creating a trust in *State v. Rubion*, 158 Tex. 43, 308 S.W.2d 4 (1957). See *Estate of Dillard*, 98 S.W.3d at 395 (analyzing *Rubion*). There, the court had to decide what interest the beneficiary had when the trust instrument allowed the trustee to distribute assets for the beneficiary's support and maintenance. *Rubion*, 308 S.W.2d at 8. The court noted that those terms evinced the creation of a support trust. *Id.* And, though a trustee's discretion regarding distributions from such a trust may be considerable, it was not unbridled. *Id.* at 8-9. Quite the contrary, the trustee must nevertheless act reasonably and in a manner commensurate with the purpose of the trust. *Id.* at 9. This meant that his decision to distribute income or corpus for the beneficiary's support and maintenance could not be exercised at a whim. Instead, the trustee was obligated to base his decision after considering indicia such as (1) the size of the trust estate, (2) the beneficiary's age, life expectancy, and condition of life, (3) his present and future needs, (4) the other resources available to him or his individual wealth, and (5) his present and future health, both mental and physical, to name a few. *Id.* at 10-11. With these words and directives, we turn to the trust before us.

Admittedly, Fate directed Lynn to distribute funds to beneficiaries other than appellant if, in Lynn's judgment, these distributions would not endanger appellant's future support and maintenance. This language exhibits Fate's desire for Lynn to manage the trust using reasonable judgment to preserve it for appellant's future support and maintenance. See *id.* at 8. At first glance, this wording seems to conflict with Fate's expressed intent for the trust to support appellant's high standard of living. However, Fate's two instructions can be reconciled. The trust instrument states that Lynn "shall distribute, from time to time, as much of the current trust net income, or accumulated trust net income, as shall be necessary to so maintain her." There is a similar provision allowing Lynn to use the trust corpus to maintain appellant if necessary. "Maintain," "time to time," and "necessary" hardly give Lynn utter discretion to fund appellant's every whim. See *Estate of Dillard*, 98 S.W.3d at 395. Rather, they evince a restriction on his discretion to distribute funds.

So, like the testatrix in *Rubion*, Fate created a support trust. Given that, distributions of principal therefrom could be made only in ways commensurate with that purpose. Because the trust's purpose is to provide for appellant's high standard of living both now and in the future, Lynn is required to use his discretion in distributing funds so that the trust is not depleted rapidly and wastefully. See *Rubion*, 308 S.W.2d at 8-9; *Brault*, 493 S.W.2d at 579. Lynn, like the trustee in *Rubion*, must exercise his discretion to distribute trust income and corpus to appellant after considering her lifestyle needs, age, health, income, and size of the trust estate. See *Rubion*, 308 S.W.2d at 10-11. And, if upon considering those factors, Lynn reasonably concludes that a distribution is warranted, only then can it be made. See *id.* * * *

Accordingly, we sustain appellant's first issue regarding the arguments (1) that the trust language is unambiguous and (2) that appellant must only exhaust her periodic receipts and income, and need not sell or exhaust other financial assets, before receiving trust distributions. We overrule appellant's first issue regarding her submission of receipts and expenses to Lynn and hold that the trial court did not err on that portion of this issue.

In her second issue, appellant argues that the trial court erred by failing to find that she was entitled to distributions from the trust since Fate's death. Having determined that the trust distributions are required to support appellant's standard of living at the time that Fate died, we hold that according to the trust language, the trial court must now determine what that standard of living was and then make trust distributions to compensate appellant from the date of Fate's death. Accordingly, we sustain appellant's second issue. * * *

IV. Conclusion

Having sustained appellant's three issues, we reverse the trial court's judgment and remand this case to the trial court for further proceedings consistent with this opinion.

J. CHARITABLE TRUSTS

A *charitable trust*, also called a *public trust*, is a trust established for the benefit of the community as a whole or for a relatively large segment of the community. Charitable trusts were originally enforced in England by chancery courts and were statutorily recognized by Parliament when they enacted the Statute of Charitable Uses, 43 Eliz. ch. 4, in 1601. This statute enumerated the purposes regarded as charitable which have remained relatively unchanged over the past 400 years. The five widely recognized categories of charitable purposes include (1) relief of poverty, (2) advancement of education, (3) advancement of religion, (4) promotion of health, and (5) governmental or municipal purposes (e.g., parks and museums). See *Boyd v. Frost National Bank*, 196 S.W.2d 497 (Tex. 1946). Courts retain considerable power to decide whether a particular purpose is or is not beneficial to the community.

For the most part, the law governing charitable trusts is substantially the same as the law for private trusts. There are, however, some very important differences and special concerns when the settlor creates a charitable trust.

1. Size of Charitable Class

Unlike private trusts, charitable trusts require a sufficiently large or indefinite class of beneficiaries so that the actual beneficiary of the trust is the public, not a particular person or small group of readily ascertainable people. If the trust fails as a charitable trust, it may nonetheless still be valid as a private trust. However, there are often advantages for the trust to be charitable such as not being constrained by the Rule Against Perpetuities and being eligible for significant tax breaks.

Notes and Questions

1. Settlor established a trust to pay the educational expenses of "some deserving student who wishes to pursue an acting career." Is this a charitable trust?

2. Settlor established a trust to provide a $1,000 scholarship to each student who receives an "A" in any law school course which spends at least six weeks on trust law. Is this trust charitable?

3. Settlor created a trust to pay for the medical care and housing expenses of victims of Hurricane Katrina. Is this trust charitable?

4. *See* Examples & Explanations § 19.10.1.

2. Description of Charitable Class

The settlor may specify the charitable class in extremely broad terms. Courts have held trusts charitable with language such as "for medical research," "to assist economically challenged families," and "for charity." The trustee and the court have the discretion to select the means for carrying out the settlor's charitable purposes. Broad designations are not, however, necessarily charitable. For example, a trust for "such objects of liberality that the trustee selects" would not be charitable because the recipients are not limited to those of a charitable nature.

3. Determination of Charitable Purpose

The court makes the determination of whether the settlor's purpose is charitable. The settlor's opinion that his or her purpose is charitable is irrelevant. As one judge stated, "If a [settlor] by stating or indicating [the settlor's] view that a trust is beneficial to the public can establish that fact beyond question, trusts might be established in perpetuity for the promotion of all kinds of fantastic (though not unlawful) objects, of which the training of poodles to dance might be a mild example." *In re Hummeltenberg*, 1 Ch. 237, 242 (1923).

How, then, do courts determine whether the settlor's purpose is charitable? Courts do not apply a bright-line rule. Instead, the resolution of any particular case depends on the exact facts and the philosophy of the judge. Courts frequently apply some version of a "generally accepted" standard. Thus, if the judge believes that the consensus of the community would be that the settlor's purpose is charitable, then the court will treat that purpose as being charitable. This test, however, is somewhat harsh because its application could prevent trusts from achieving charitable status if they are created for purposes not widely deemed charitable or if they involve new or controversial matters.

MARSH v. FROST NATIONAL BANK

Texas Appeals—Corpus Christi 2004
129 S.W.3d 174
pet. denied

Opinion by Justice RODRIGUEZ.

This is a declaratory judgment action. Appellants, Anna Spohn Welch Marsh, Noel Marsh, and Holly McKee, appeal from a probate order that modified a provision in the will of Charles Vartan Walker, deceased. Appellants raise four issues on appeal: (1) whether the trial court properly applied the cy pres doctrine to reform a will provision; (2) whether the trial court correctly ruled that tract 3 with its associated income, rather than the proceeds of the sale of that land, should be conveyed to the charitable beneficiary based on the cy pres reformation; (3) whether the abatement provisions of the order are appealable, and if so, whether those provisions were correct; and (4) whether the trial court properly awarded attorney's fees to the Attorney General. We reverse and remand.

I. Factual Background

Charles Walker died on March 13, 2000, leaving a holographic will. The will named appellee, Frost National Bank (Frost Bank), as independent executor. On July 11, 2000, Frost Bank filed an original petition for declaratory judgment for clarification of several probate matters including the construction of Article V of the Charles Walker will, the provision at issue in this appeal. Article V reads in relevant part:

I hereby direct my Executor to sell tract 3 of the V.M. Donigan 456.80 Partition for cash and to invest the proceeds in safe and secure tax-free U.S. government bonds or insured tax-free municipal bonds. This trust is to be called the James Madison Fund to honor our fourth President, the Father of the Constitution. The ultimate purpose of this fund is to provide a million dollar trust fund for every American 18 years or older. At 6% compound interest and a starting figure of $1,000,000.00, it would take approximately 346 years to provide enough money to do this. My executor will head the Board of Trustees.... When the Fund reaches $15,000,000 my Executor's function will cease, and the money will be turned over to the Sec. of the Treasury for management by the federal government. The President of the U.S., the Vice President of the U.S., and the Speaker of the U.S. House of Representatives shall be permanent Trustees of the Fund. The Congress of the United States shall make the final rules and regulations as to how the money will be distributed. No one shall be denied their share because of race, religion, marital status, sexual preference, or the amount of their wealth or lack thereof....

Appellants filed an answer to the petition for declaratory judgment alleging that Article V of the will is void under the rule against perpetuities. Appellee, John Cornyn, Texas Attorney General, intervened in this action pursuant to section 123.002 of the Texas Property Code, alleging that a general charitable intent could be found and that Article V of the will created a charitable trust. See Tex. Prop. Code Ann. § 123.002 (Vernon 1995). The Attorney General then moved for the application of the cy pres doctrine to Article V. After a hearing on this issue, the trial court found in relevant part that: (1) the will evidenced a general charitable intent; (2) Article V of the will established a valid charitable trust not subject to the rule against perpetuities; (3) the Attorney General's request to have the court exercise its cy pres powers should be granted; and (4) attorney's fees should be awarded to the Attorney General. The order was signed with the modification of the trust and charitable beneficiary to be determined after a second hearing. The second hearing was held before a different judge. After reconsidering the previous order, the second judge confirmed and ratified that order and signed a final judgment establishing the modifications of Article V. This appeal ensued.

II. Interpretation of Article V

In their first issue, appellants argue that Article V does not show a charitable intent and therefore is not subject to reformation under the cy pres doctrine. Furthermore, appellants argue that because Article V violates the rule against perpetuities and cannot be legally reformed, it is void, and the proceeds of the land that would fund the trust should pass through intestate succession.

In Texas, under the rule against perpetuities, an interest is not good unless it must vest, if at all, not later than twenty-one years after some life in being at the time of the creation of the interest, plus a period of gestation. Id. § 112.036; see Foshee v. Republic Nat'l Bank, 617 S.W.2d 675, 677 (Tex. 1981). Both perpetual trusts and trusts for an indefinite duration violate the rule against perpetuities and are void. Atkinson v. Kettler, 372 S.W.2d 704, 711 (Tex. Civ. App.-Dallas 1963), aff'd, 383 S.W.2d 557 (Tex. 1964). The rule against perpetuities does not, however, apply to charitable trusts. See Tex. Prop. Code Ann. § 112.036 (Vernon 1995); Foshee, 617 S.W.2d at 677. Therefore, we must first address whether Article V of the will establishes a trust for a charitable purpose.

Whether or not a given purpose is "charitable" is a question of law for the court to decide. Frost Nat'l Bank v. Boyd, 188 S.W.2d 199, 206 (Tex. Civ. App.-San Antonio 1945), aff'd, 145 Tex. 206, 196 S.W.2d 497 (1946). When an issue turns on a pure question of law, we apply a de novo standard of review, Tenet Health Ltd. v. Zamora, 13 S.W.3d 464, 468 (Tex. App.-Corpus Christi 2000, pet. dism'd w.o.j.) (citing State v. Heal, 917 S.W.2d 6, 9 (Tex. 1996)), and we are not obligated to give any deference to legal conclusions reached by the trial court. Id. at 468-69.

Where the question of whether a given purpose is or is not charitable arises, the words "charitable purpose" have a definite ascertainable meaning in law, and a judicial determination may be made with satisfactory certainty in every case. See Boyd v. Frost Nat'l Bank, 145 Tex. 206, 196 S.W.2d 497, 501-03 (1946). Legal concepts of what are "charitable purposes" are categorized in section 368 of the Restatement Second of Trusts. Id. at 502. Section 368 provides as follows:

Charitable purposes include

    (a) the relief of poverty;
    (b) the advancement of education;
    (c) the advancement of religion;
    (d) the promotion of health;

(e) governmental or municipal purposes;

(f) other purposes the accomplishment of which is beneficial to
     the community.

Restatement (Second) of Trusts § 368 (1959); see Boyd, 196 S.W.2d at
502.

Article V of the will clearly states that the purpose of the fund is to
provide a million dollar trust fund for every American eighteen years or
older with no one being denied his share due to race, religion, marital
status, sexual preference, or the amount of his wealth. Thus, it is clear
from the language of Article V that if the purpose is to be found charitable,
it must fall under the broad category (f) of section 368 of the Restatement;
other purposes the accomplishment of which is beneficial to the
community. Restatement (Second) of Trusts § 368 (1959). To be included
in category (f), the purpose set out in Article V must go beyond merely
providing financial enrichment to the individual members of the
community; the purpose must promote the social interest of the community
as a whole. See Restatement (Second) of Trusts § 374 cmt. a, f (1959). The
Restatement provides this Court with the following illustration applicable
to the facts of this case:

> [I]f a large sum of money is given in trust to apply the income each
> year in paying a certain sum to every inhabitant of a city, whether
> rich or poor, the trust is not charitable, since although each
> inhabitant may receive a benefit, the social interest of the
> community as such is not thereby promoted.

Id. § 374 cmt. f. Furthermore, trusts created to distribute money out of
liberality or generosity, without regard to the need of the donees and the
effect of the gifts, do not have the requisite public benefit necessary to a
charity. See G. Bogart, The Law of Trusts and Trustees § 379 (1991). With
these concepts in mind, we analyze Article V.

Charles Walker expressly states in Article V that "[t]he ultimate
purpose of this fund is to provide a million dollar trust fund for every
American 18 years or older." From this language, it is obvious Walker
intended nothing more than to financially enrich the American public.
While this act is generous and benevolent, it is not necessarily beneficial to
the community. There is no evidence referenced or argument made by
appellees to persuade us that the effect of the trust contemplated by Walker
would promote the social interest of the community. See Restatement
(Second) of Trusts § 374 cmt. a (1959). Article V does not place
restrictions or limitations on the beneficiaries of the trust, which would
allow them to use the funds for any purpose, whether it be one that benefits
the community or one that burdens it. The trust would provide a personal,

individual benefit to each beneficiary but would fail to promote the social interest of the community as a whole. See id. § 374 cmt. a, f. Furthermore, the trust is established without regard to the need of the beneficiaries or the effect of the trust and as a result lacks the requisite public benefit necessary to a charity. See G. Bogart, The Law of Trusts and Trustees § 379 (1991). The trust created by Walker is nothing more than a generous distribution of money with no contemplation or recognition of public benefit. We conclude the trust established by Walker is devoid of any charitable intent or purpose and is therefore not charitable as defined by law.

Appellees argue that Texas courts have a long history of favoring charitable bequests and use liberal rules of construction to fulfill the intent of the testator. They also urge that where a bequest is open to two constructions, the interpretation that gives the charity effect should be adopted, and that which will defeat the charity should be rejected. In support of their arguments, appellees cite Boyd; Blocker v. State, 718 S.W.2d 409 (Tex. App.-Houston [1st Dist.] 1986, writ ref'd n.r.e.); Taysum v. El Paso Nat'l Bank, 256 S.W.2d 172 (Tex. Civ. App.-El Paso 1952, writ ref'd); and Eldridge v. Marshall Nat'l Bank, 527 S.W.2d 222 (Tex. Civ. App.-Houston [14th Dist.] 1975, writ ref'd n.r.e.). We agree with appellees' contentions and the cases cited in support thereof. However, we find these cases distinguishable and the specific propositions stated inapplicable. In the cases cited, the courts, after finding an existing charitable intent as defined by law, used liberal rules of construction to sustain the charitable trust. In this case, however, we find no charitable intent or purpose. Therefore, these rules of law do not apply. Appellees would have us use these rules to create a charitable intent where none exists. We decline to do so.

Having concluded Article V of the will does not establish a charitable trust, the rule against perpetuities is applicable. In this case, the trust is of indefinite duration and therefore violates the rule against perpetuities. See Atkinson, 372 S.W.2d at 711. Accordingly, appellants' first issue is sustained.

III. Reformation of Noncharitable Trusts

When a noncharitable trust is in violation of the rule against perpetuities, a trial court is authorized to reform the trust pursuant to section 5.043 of the Texas Property Code. Tex. Prop. Code Ann § 5.043 (Vernon Supp. 2004). A court has the power to reform or construe the trust according to the doctrine of cy pres by giving effect to the general intent of the testator within the limits of the rule. Id. § 5.043(b). It is clear from the language in Article V that Walker's general intent in creating the trust was to financially enrich the American public. Therefore, application of section 5.043 requires the court to reform or construe Article V within the limits of the rule against perpetuities and consistent with this intent. If reformation is not possible however, the trust is void as being in violation of the rule.

Appellants contend in their second issue that the court erred in not selling tract 3 of the V.M. Donigan 456.80 partition for cash as stated in Article V. Because of the disposition of appellants' first issue, we need not address their second issue. However, as noted above, reformation under section 5.043, if possible, provides for the court to give effect to the general intent and specific directives of the creator. Tex. Prop. Code Ann. § 5.043(b) (Vernon Supp. 2004). The selling of the land provided for under Article V would constitute a specific directive and should be given effect in any reformation contemplated by the court.

Therefore, we remand this case to the trial court to consider the feasibility of reformation of Article V under section 5.043.

IV. Attorney's Fees

In their fourth issue, appellants complain that the court improperly awarded attorney's fees to the Attorney General. The trial court awarded reasonable and necessary attorney's fees totaling $24,500 to be paid out of the Estate of Charles Walker.

In proceedings under both the Texas Trust Code and the Uniform Declaratory Judgments Act, the trial court may award such costs and reasonable and necessary attorney's fees as are equitable and just. Tex. Prop. Code Ann. § 114.064 (Vernon 1995); Tex. Civ. Prac. & Rem. Code § 37.009 (Vernon 1997). In this case, the attorney's fees were awarded pursuant to both the trust code and the declaratory judgment act. Because we are reversing the trial court's judgment interpreting Article V as having a general charitable intent, the trial court may wish to reconsider the award of attorney's fees to the Attorney General. See Scottsdale Ins. Co. v. Travis, 68 S.W.3d 72, 77 (Tex. App.- Dallas 2001, pet. denied); see also JVA Operating Co. v. Kaiser Francis Oil Co., 11 S.W.3d 504, 508 (Tex. App Eastland 2000, pet. denied) (holding that because the trial court's judgment was reversed, the award of attorney's fees was no longer "equitable and just"); Fajkus v. First Nat'l Bank, 735 S.W.2d 882, 887 (Tex. App.-Austin 1987, writ denied). We therefore reverse the award of attorney's fees and remand for the trial court's reconsideration of this matter. See Barshop v. Medina County Underground Water Conservation Dist., 925 S.W.2d 618, 637-38 (Tex. 1996). Appellants' fourth issue is sustained.

V. Conclusion

Accordingly, we reverse the trial court's judgment to the extent it established a charitable trust and remand this case for further proceedings consistent with this opinion. We also reverse the trial court's award of attorney's fees and remand this issue to the trial court for further consideration.

Notes and Questions

1.   Settlor established a trust for the education and medical expenses of Settlor's children. Is this trust charitable?

2.   Settlor created two trusts, each with a different purpose. Settlor directed the trustee of the first trust to expend trust income and principal to advance the idea that the United States should become a communistic country run by one person who is not answerable to any court or legislative body. The trustee of the second trust was to use trust assets to fund the dissemination of Settlor's essays regarding Settlor's belief that operatives from a foreign government are conspiring with extra-terrestrial forces to take over the earth. Are either or both of these trusts charitable?

3.   Settlor's testamentary trust required the trustee to use trust property to build a small office at the entrance to the cemetery in which Settlor was buried. The trustee was then to pay a person to be stationed in this office for ten hours per day, 365 days per year, to greet individuals visiting Settlor's grave and guide them to the appropriate plot while relating stories about Settlor's life experiences. Is this trust charitable?

4.   Settlor established a trust for the promotion of Santeria, a religion which includes animal sacrifice in its ceremonies. Is this trust charitable?

5.   *See* Examples & Explanations § 19.10.3.

4.   Relocation

The 2009 Legislature enacted Trust Code § 113.029 to remedy the "orphan trust" problem which is described in the analysis of S.B. 666 as follows:

> The "orphan trust" or charitable foundations set up by donors who have no heirs or other family that they wish to carry out their wills, are often entrusted to lawyers or local banks who will keep the money invested in the local community. However, when an attorney retires or local banks are sold to multinational financial institutions, the foundations are no longer run by the people and banks familiar with the donors' specific wishes. The corporate trustees have wide latitude to change the way the trust operates, and to decide which charities will receive grants and thus the danger of distorting or altogether ignoring the donor's intent is increased with each transaction. Banks give fewer and smaller charitable gifts from the trusts they manage, all the while increasing the foundation's assets,

and increasing administrative fees that the banks charge to foundations for the services they provide. Additionally, banks as trustees will often provide grants which serve their own interests, but that do not honor the donor's favorite causes. * * * The consequences of charitable funds being moved and used as assets and revenue streams for large financial institutions is that communities that stood to benefit from the philanthropy of their citizens are denied the good works and good will of the original donors.

The statute provides that the location of a charitable trust's administration cannot be changed to an out-of-state location other than as (1) the settlor provided in the trust or (2) the court approves under the procedure set forth in the statute. *See* Trust Code § 113.029(b).

A trustee who wants to move the location out of Texas must first give proper notice. If the settlor is alive and competent, the trustee must consult with the settlor and submit the selection to the attorney general. Trust Code § 113.029(c)(1). If the settlor is dead or incapacitated, then the trustee must propose a new location and submit the proposal to the attorney general. *See* Trust Code § 113.029(c)(2).

The trustee must then file an action in the appropriate court to get permission to move the trust administration out of the Texas. Trust Code § 113.029(d). The court may not authorize a relocation unless it finds that the charitable purposes of the trust will not be impaired by the move. *See* Trust Code § 113.029(e).

The statute grants the attorney general the power to enforce this section. If a trustee does not comply with the statute, the court may remove the trustee and appoint a new trustee. The court may charge the costs of the removal, including reasonable attorney's fees, against the removed trustee. *See* Trust Code § 113.029(f).

K. POUR OVER WILLS

A pour-over provision is a clause of a will that leaves property to an inter vivos trust. *Read* Est. Code § 254.001.

BRINKER v. WOBACO TRUST LIMITED

Texas Civil Appeals — Texarkana 1980
610 S.W.2d 160
writ ref'd n.r.e

CORNELIUS, Chief Justice.

This suit was brought by Cynthia and Brenda Brinker, the daughters of Norman E. Brinker and Maureen Connally Brinker, deceased, to construe or reform three trust instruments so that children born to Norman Brinker's second marriage would be excluded as beneficiaries of the trusts, and to impose a constructive trust on certain assets removed from Maureen Brinker's estate and placed in a Bahamian trust which included children of the second marriage. In a bench trial the court refused to admit evidence seeking to establish Norman's and Maureen's intention in creating the trusts, or to show that in the drafting of the trust indentures a mistake had been made which would warrant reformation of the instruments to reflect the true intention.

Cynthia and Brenda are the only children born to Norman and Maureen Brinker. Maureen died on June 21, 1969. Norman married Magrit Fendt in 1971, and they had two children, Christina and Mark, before their marriage ended in divorce in 1977.

While Norman and Maureen were married they decided to establish a trust. The trust indenture named Norman as the "settlor" and Maureen and the First National Bank of Dallas were collectively named "trustee". The trust was designated the "Norman E. Brinker Family Trusts", and was to be funded principally by proceeds from insurance policies on Norman's life. As it developed, however, Maureen died first. In her will she bequeathed $65,000.00 to a testamentary trust for her children and left the rest of her estate to a residuary trust created in the will, the assets of which, after her mother and Norman died, would "pour over" into the Brinker Family Trust, "to be held or disposed of in accordance with the provisions of Article IV" of said trust. Article IV of the Brinker Family Trust provides that if the settlor's wife predeceases him, the trust principal and income shall be paid to the "issue of settlor". In 1970, after Maureen's death, Norman created two other, separate trusts for the benefit of Cynthia and Brenda, and presumably funded them with monies or properties from his share of the community estate. Those trust indentures name Norman Brinker as settlor, and provide that if the principal beneficiary dies without issue, the trust assets will be paid to "settlor's issue then living."

When Maureen died her net estate was valued at approximately $700,000.00. In 1973, when Norman was married to Magrit and they had one child, Maureen's estate as contained in the residuary trust, consisting principally of stock in Steak & Ale Restaurants, Inc., had grown much larger. At that time, Norman, who was trustee of the residuary trust, conferred with his attorney and decided on a plan to divide some of Maureen's estate with the children of the second marriage, and also take advantage of some tax saving opportunities. To effectuate the plan, Norman transferred assets from Maureen's residuary trust and placed them in the Wobaco Trust, a trust he created through the World Banking Corporation located in the Bahamas. Norman's attorney advised him at the time of this transfer that there was a risk of complaint by Cynthia and Brenda when they became adults, but he chose to proceed. After his second marriage ended in divorce, Norman had second thoughts about his transfer of the residuary trust assets to the Wobaco Trust, and he told Cynthia and Brenda what had been done. Although the residuary trust in Maureen's will has not yet poured over into the Brinker Family Trust, when Cynthia and Brenda became aware of the transfer of the residuary trust assets to a trust benefiting the children of the second marriage, they brought this suit seeking to establish that they and their descendants are the only beneficiaries of the Brinker Family Trust, as well as the other two trusts created for their benefit, and to impose a constructive trust upon the assets transferred to the Wobaco Trust on the grounds that those assets eventually will belong to them exclusively when the pour over provision becomes operative.

On a bill of exceptions, appellants produced evidence that Maureen and Norman Brinker intended for the trusts to benefit only the issue born of their marriage to each other, and that if the term "issue of settlor" as used in the trust indentures meant the issue of Norman Brinker by any other union, a mistake had been made in the drafting of the trust indentures which warranted reformation of the instruments. The evidence consisted of the testimony of Norman Brinker and Mr. Robert Taylor, a tax lawyer who prepared both the trust indentures and Maureen's will. The evidence may be generally summarized as follows: Mr. Brinker testified that he and Maureen primarily wanted to be certain that whatever assets went into the trust would go for the benefit of their two children at that time, i.e., Cynthia and Brenda. He said they knew Maureen could not have any other children and that they intended for the trust to be just for Cynthia and Brenda. He further testified that neither he nor Maureen was familiar with trusts or wills or legal terminology, and that they depended entirely on their lawyer to correctly put into the trust instruments what they wanted done; that neither he nor Maureen chose to use the word "settlor" or even knew what it meant; that the word was never mentioned or discussed with their lawyer or the bank; and that although they read the trust instruments before executing them they did not understand them, and in effect told their lawyer, "You are the lawyer; we don't understand this, did you do what we asked you to do?", and upon the lawyer's assurance that he had, they completed the transaction. Mr. Taylor testified in detail. He testified that the Brinkers instructed him to prepare the family trust; in the discussion it was mentioned that Maureen could not have any more children; he understood that they wanted only Cynthia and Brenda to share in that trust; and that was the way he intended to draw the instruments and thought he had done so. When asked if either Norman or Maureen said anything about wanting to include children who might be born of other marriages, he answered "No, just the opposite", although he admitted that they did not specifically tell him to cut out all afterborn children. He further testified that if the trust indentures were written so as to include other children as beneficiaries, he had made a mistake in drafting the trust instruments. Upon being questioned about Norman alone being named settlor, Mr. Taylor stated that he considered Maureen to be a co-settlor, and had intended to designate her as such in the same manner as he had designated her and the bank as co-trustees, and that was the reason he had her execute the trust indenture along with Norman. He also recalled that Maureen discussed with him the possible remarriage of her husband and that she shared "the normal concern of a wife that her husband, if something happened to her, might remarry and reiterated that she wanted her property to go to Cindy and Brenda." On cross-examination appellees brought out concessions from Mr. Taylor that the trusts did benefit Cynthia and Brenda, which literally complied with the directions he received from Norman and Maureen, and that the Brinker Family Trust indenture did not contain typographical errors, but contained the actual words he dictated. On the suggestion that many corrections would be necessary to change the trust indenture to designate Maureen as co-settlor, Mr. Taylor disagreed and said he intended to so designate her and then use the singular of the word "settlor" to refer to both Maureen and Norman as he had done with the singular word "trustee" to refer to Maureen and the bank. Other features of the drafting and signing of the trust indentures were pointed out which could be construed to impeach Mr. Taylor's testimony that a mistake in the drafting had been made.

The foregoing summary demonstrates that a fact issue was made on the question of mistake in the drafting of the trust indenture to correctly express the parties' intention. The evidence raising such issue should have been admitted on appellants' plea for reformation.

[reformation discussion omitted]

Appellees contend, however, that because the residuary trust in Mrs. Brinker's will eventually will pour over into the Brinker Family Trust, and Mrs. Brinker's will has now been probated, the Brinker Family Trust, so far as the pour over assets are concerned, has become testamentary and consequently it cannot be reformed. We disagree.

It is true that a testamentary disposition is not subject to reformation. *Jackson v. Templin*, 66 S.W.2d 666 (Tex. Com. App. 1933, judgmt. adopted); * * *. But we hold that the Brinker Family Trust did not become testamentary by reason of Mrs. Brinker's residuary trust pour over.

Prior to the drafting of the Uniform Testamentary Additions to Trusts Act, there were two legal doctrines concerning the validity and nature of testamentary additions to inter vivos trusts. One was the doctrine of incorporation by reference, which held that the terms of the inter vivos trust became incorporated into the will by reference and became a part of it, thus rendering the trust testamentary insofar as the gift was concerned. * * * The other was the doctrine of independent significance, which held that the trust did not become a part of the will, but that the testamentary bequest or devise simply was added to and augmented the trust corpus to be administered as a part of the trust according to its provisions. Under that doctrine the trust provisions concerning disposition of the gift did not become testamentary. * * * The Uniform Testamentary Additions to Trusts Act was designed to validate testamentary additions to trusts even though such trusts were amendable, and to prevent the trust provisions affecting such gift from becoming testamentary. The Act provides in part as follows:

> ". . . the property so devised or bequeathed (a) *shall not be deemed to be held under a testamentary trust of the testator but shall become a part of the trust to which it is given and (b) shall be administered and disposed of in accordance with the provisions of the instrument* * * * setting forth the terms of the trust, * * *". (Emphasis supplied.)

Texas adopted the Uniform Act in 1961. [court quotes § 58a] Although the Texas version does not specifically provide that such a gift will not be deemed to be held under a testamentary trust, in other respects it is essentially the same as the Uniform Act, and it specifically provides that the gift ". . . shall be added to the corpus of such trust to be administered as a part thereof and shall thereafter be governed by the terms and provisions of the instrument establishing such trust, * * *". We hold that the intention of the Texas Act was that the trust provisions would not become testamentary by reason of such a gift, but that the gift would simply augment the corpus of the trust and become a part of it.

Appellees assert that a reformation of the Family Trust would violate that portion of Section 58a which provides that a gift to a trust will be governed by the trust instrument *and any written amendments or modifications made before the death of the testator*. It is argued that to reform the Family Trust would be the equivalent of amending or modifying it after the death of Maureen Brinker. We cannot agree.

To amend or modify an agreement means to change it. * * * Reformation does not change the agreement; it enforces the agreement. It orders a change in the drafted instrument so that it will correctly express what has been the real agreement from its inception. * * *

The excluded evidence on the issue of reformation is before us in the bill of exceptions, but as indicated in our summary of that evidence it is not so conclusive that it determines the issue as a matter of law and allows us to render a judgment. There is positive evidence of mistake; yet there are circumstances which bear upon the credibility and accuracy of the testimony which might lead reasonable minds to reject it. A fact issue has been created which requires resolution by a trier of fact. The judgment will therefore be reversed and remanded for a new trial.

In view of our disposition of the point concerning the exclusion of evidence, it is not necessary for us to consider appellants' other points.

Notes and Questions

1.   Compare the requirements for a valid incorporation by reference and for something to be a fact of independent significance with the requirements for a valid pour-over provision under Estates Code § 254.001.

2.   On May 1, Testator created a valid inter vivos trust naming Floyd as the sole beneficiary. On June 1, Testator executed a valid will leaving $10,000 to the trust. On July 1, Testator validly amended the trust changing the beneficiary to Sharon. On August 1, the Testator died. Who will benefit from the pour-over provision assuming the jurisdiction uses:

   a. the incorporation by reference theory to uphold pour-over provisions?

   b. the facts of independent significance theory to uphold pour-over provisions?

   c. Estates Code § 254.001?

What are the pros and cons of each approach?

3.   Assume in Question 2 that Testator had not created the trust until June 10. Would your answers change?

4.   Assume in Question 2 that Testator's spouse was also a settlor of the trust who retained the power to change the beneficiary. On September 1, Testator's spouse changes the beneficiary to Albert. Who is entitled to benefit from the $10,000?

5.   Assume in Question 2 that on July 1 Testator had validly revoked the trust. Who will benefit from the pour-over provision under each of the three options?

6.   When would you suggest using a pour-over provision? Why might you suggest one rather than a testamentary trust?

7.   *See generally* Examples & Explanations § 9.6; Robert J. Lynn, *Problems With Pour-Over Wills*, 47 OHIO ST. L.J. 47 (1986); Alan N. Polasky, *"Pour-Over Wills": Use With Inter Vivos Trusts*, 17 SW. L.J. 410 (1963).

L. LIFE INSURANCE TRUSTS

The owner of a life insurance policy may name a trust as the beneficiary of the policy. In addition, the owner may transfer the policy itself to the trust. The trust property will then consist of the contract right to receive proceeds upon the insured's death or the life insurance contract itself. These contract rights are sufficient property to constitute trust corpus. *Read* Trust Code § 111.004(12).

For a variety of reasons, the owner of a life insurance policy may wish to name a trust as the beneficiary instead of the person the owner wishes to ultimately benefit from the proceeds. Ultimate Beneficiary (UB) may not have the legal capacity to handle the proceeds. For example, UB could be a minor or incompetent. If the proceeds were payable to UB directly, an expensive and inconvenient guardianship may be needed. Thus, anyone with life insurance and a desire to benefit their minor or incompetent children or grandchildren should seriously consider using a life insurance trust.

Even if legally competent, UB may be unable or unwilling to manage property in a prudent fashion. If UB were to receive the proceeds outright, they may disappear quickly. In addition, the insured may want to exercise control over how the proceeds are used after the insured's death, even if UB has both the legal and functional capacity to manage the property. Another benefit of life insurance trusts is their ability to help an individual create a unified plan for the insured's estate. The person may create one trust and have many different assets pour over into the trust, e.g., life insurance proceeds, pension and retirement plan death benefits, and the person's probate estate via a pour-over provision in the will.

Read Insurance Code §§ 1104.021-1104.025.

Notes and Questions

1.   Insured owns a life insurance policy with a face value of $500,000. Currently, Insured has named Spouse as the primary beneficiary and Children as the alternate beneficiaries. Insured realizes that it is not a good idea for the minor children to be named and has thus decided to create a life insurance trust. Should Insured create this trust immediately or would provisions in the Insured's will be sufficient?

2.   Insured created a valid inter vivos trust and has properly named the trust as the beneficiary of a life insurance policy. Should Insured add additional property to this trust, that is, should the trust be *funded*?

3.   Insured created a valid inter vivos trust and has properly named the trust as the beneficiary of a life insurance policy. Should this trust be revocable or irrevocable?

4.   *See* Examples & Explanations § 19.8.12.

Chapter Three

TRUST ADMINISTRATION[1]

The settlor's instructions with regard to the management of trust property and distribution to beneficiaries must be turned from mere words into action. The trustee is in charge of this process. This Chapter provides an overview of the administration process, analyzes the fiduciary duties, responsibilities, and powers of the trustee, and concludes with a discussion of the ability of a court and the parties to alter or terminate existing trusts.

A. OVERVIEW

A person who is considering the possibility of serving as a trustee must have a full appreciation of the burdens associated with the position to make an informed decision. This section provides an overview of the trust administration process.

1. Accept Trusteeship

A person must make a conscious decision to accept the office of trustee. No duties are imposed and no liability attaches until a trustee accepts the position. A person may be unwilling or unable to accept for many reasons. For example, the person may not want the responsibility or the potential liability of being a trustee. Lack of expertise, incompetence, or an insufficient trustee fee are other reasons a person may decline a trustee position. *Review* Trust Code § 112.009.

2. Post Bond

Unless the trustee is exempted from the bond requirement, the trustee must post bond. *Review* Trust Code § 113.058.

---

[1]Portions of this Chapter are adapted from GERRY W. BEYER, WILLS, TRUSTS, AND ESTATES: EXAMPLES & EXPLANATIONS ch. 20 (6th ed. 2015).

3. Register Trust

Under the law of a few states, the trustee has a duty to register the trust with the court. Texas does not have a registration requirement.

4. Possess and Safeguard Trust Property

As the holder of legal title, the trustee has the right to possess trust property. As soon as possible after accepting the position, the trustee needs to locate the trust property, assume control over it, and protect it. For example, the trustee should record deeds, buy insurance, keep the property repaired, place valuable personal property in a safe deposit box, and register corporate securities. *Read* Trust Code § 117.004.

a. Earmark Trust Property

The trustee must earmark the trust property, that is, label the property as belonging to the trust. Earmarking prevents trust property from being confused with the trustee's own property so that the trustee's personal creditors, heirs, beneficiaries, and other claimants do not take trust property under the mistaken belief that it belongs to the trustee.

Notes and Questions

1. Settlor placed two items of property into a valid trust — a collection of gold coins and 100 shares of Omnipotent Corporation stock. Trustee took possession of the coins and the stock but took no steps to label them as belonging to the trust. Trustee's finances suffered and one of Trustee's creditors successfully levied on the coins. When the United States Justice Department began an investigation of the top management of Omnipotent Corporation, the value of the stock dropped precipitously. Is Trustee liable for the lost coins and the decrease in value of the stock?

2. Settlor transferred an extensive stock portfolio to a valid trust. Trustee needs to buy and sell securities on a daily basis. Accordingly, it is not practical for Trustee to obtain stock certificates registered in the name of the trust. Instead, Trustee wants the stock to be held in nominee or *street name* form by a reputable and fully licensed stockbroker. May Trustee do so? *Read* Trust Code § 113.017.

3. *See* Examples & Explanations § 20.1.4.1.

b. Avoid Commingling

In addition to labeling property as belonging to the trust, the trustee must also keep trust property separate from the trustee's own assets and the property of others.

Notes and Questions

1. Settlor transferred a coin collection to Trustee. Trustee, also a collector, carefully placed the coins in Trustee's personal coin books. Trustee conspicuously noted the trust's ownership underneath each coin Trustee received from Settlor. A tornado struck Trustee's home and destroyed the collection. Is Trustee personally liable for the value of the coins?

2. *Read* Trust Code §§ 113.171 & 113.172 which permits corporate trustees to commingle the property from several trusts into a *common trust fund*. These funds permit trustees to diversify, lower transaction costs, and better leverage the trust property. Individual trustees do not typically have the option of commingling the property of different trusts. However, they can secure the same benefits by investing in regular commercial mutual funds.

3. *See* Examples & Explanations § 20.1.4.2.

5. Identify and Locate Beneficiaries

The trustee must ascertain the identity and location of the beneficiaries of the trust. The beneficiaries' names and addresses are needed so the trustee knows who receives the trust benefits and where to send them. The trustee may have some difficulty doing this if the trust instrument does not contain sufficient identifying information such as the beneficiaries' complete names, addresses, and relationships to the settlor. In such cases, the trustee may need to hire a professional search service.

6. Follow Settlor's Instructions

Unless prohibited by state law or public policy, the trustee must follow the settlor's wishes with regard to the trust property as stated in the trust instrument. The settlor inevitably provides instructions regarding the distribution of trust property. In addition, many settlors include directions regarding the investment and management of the trust property.

7. Act as Fiduciary

Read Trust Code § 113.051 (requiring the trustee to administer the trust "in good faith").

The trustee is subject to a broad range of fiduciary duties. For example, the trustee must exercise a high standard of care when investing trust property and otherwise managing the trust. The trustee is also bound by a duty of loyalty and thus must avoid self-dealing and being in any position in which the trustee has interests to serve other than those of the trust. If a trustee fails to comply with the requirements and duties of trust administration, the trustee can be held personally liable. A breach of duty may result in both civil and criminal penalties.

8. Support and Defend Trust

The trustee is responsible for defending attacks on the validity of the trust and its administration unless the advice of a competent attorney indicates that there is no reasonable defense. Likewise, the trustee has a duty to appeal an unfavorable verdict unless there is no reasonable ground for seeking a reversal.

See Examples & Explanations § 20.1.8.

9. Certification of Trust

If the trustee determines that a non-beneficiary's request for a copy of the trust is appropriate, the trustee has the option of providing a *certification of trust* rather than the a copy of the trust instrument itself. *See* Trust Code § 114.086.

B. STANDARD OF CARE & INVESTMENTS

1. Background

Until January 1, 2004, the propriety of the trustee's investments were judged according to the prudent person standard. A trustee was required to exercise the degree of care and level of skill that a person of ordinary prudence would exercise in dealing with that person's own property. The trustee was required to consider three main factors in selecting an investment. First, the trustee examined the safety of the investment. Risky or speculative investments were not allowed. Second, the trustee determined the investment's potential to appreciate in value. Third, the trustee evaluated the income which the investment was expected to generate. Prior law also contained a portfolio-type provision in that the determination of whether a trustee acted prudently was based on a consideration of how all the assets of the trust were invested collectively rather than by examining each investment individually.

The Texas version of the Uniform Prudent Investor Act took effect on January 1, 2004. *Read* Trust Code Ch. 117. Under this "total asset management" approach, the appropriateness of investments is based on the performance of the entire trust portfolio. A prudent investor could decide that the best investment strategy is to select some assets that appreciate and others that earn income, as well as some investments that are rock-solid balanced with some that have a reasonable degree of risk. In selecting investments, the trustee should incorporate risk and return objectives that are reasonably suited to the trust. Different trusts may call for different investment approaches depending on the trustee's abilities, the trust's purposes, the beneficiary's needs, and other circumstances. *Read* Trust Code § 117.004.

See Examples & Explanations § 20.2.

2. Settlor's Ability to Alter Standard

The prudent investor rule is the default standard of care for trustees under Trust Code § 117.003(a). However, § 117.003(b) authorizes the settlor to provide for a higher or lower standard of care. Why would a settlor raise or lower the standard?

The settlor is, for the most part, the master of the trust and thus may provide for things to be handled differently than the Trust Code indicates. The terms of the trust trump the Trust Code except as provided in § 111.0035.

The settlor may include an exculpatory clause to excuse breaches of the standard of care or to permit transactions that would otherwise be self-dealing or create a conflict of interest.

The 2003 and 2005 Texas Legislatures codified the rules regarding the enforceability of exculpatory clauses in trusts. *Read* Trust Code § 114.007. A settlor is prohibited from relieving a trustee of liability for a breach of trust committed (1) in bad faith, (2) intentionally, or (3) with reckless indifference to the interest of the beneficiary. In addition, the settlor may not permit the trustee to retain any profit derived from a breach of trust. An exculpatory clause is ineffective to the extent the provision was included in the trust because of an abuse by the trustee of a fiduciary duty to or confidential relationship with the settlor.

Note, however, that exculpatory provisions in management trusts under Property Code Chapter 142 (Property Code § 142.005(j)) and Estates Code Chapter 1301 (Estates Code § 1301.103) will be enforceable only if the following two requirements are satisfied.

- The exculpatory provision is limited to specific facts and circumstances unique to the property of that trust and is not applicable generally to the trust.

- The court creating or modifying the trust makes a specific finding that there is clear and convincing evidence that the exculpatory provision is in the best interests of the beneficiary of the trust.

This requirement for management trusts is a reaction to the Texas Supreme Court opinion in *Texas Commerce Bank, N.A. v. Grizzle*, 96 S.W.3d 240 (Tex. 2002), in which the court enforced a boilerplate exculpatory clause in a Chapter 142 trust.

Read Trust Code § 117.012. Pay careful attention to this section which indicates that certain phrases in trust instruments are deemed to trigger the prudent investor standard. Some of these phrases which invoke the prudent investor standard clearly appear to invoke a much different standard (e.g., "prudent person rule").

See Examples & Explanations § 20.2.3.

3. Trust Protectors

Read Trust Code §§ 114.003 & 114.0031.

Section 114.0031 was added in 2015 to provide more detailed governance for trust protectors in the private trust context.

The settlor may grant the protector any powers and authority which the settlor desires including, but not limited to, the power to remove and appoint trustees and advisors, the power to modify or amend the trust for tax purposes or to facilitate efficient trust administration, and the power to modify, expand, or restrict the terms of a power of appointment the settlor granted to a beneficiary.

By default, the trust protector is a fiduciary. However, the settlor may provide that a protector acts in a nonfiduciary capacity.

The trustee is liable for following the directions of a trust protector only if the trustee's conduct constitutes willful misconduct.

If the settlor requires the trustee to obtain the consent of a trust protector before acting, the trustee is not liable for any act taken or not taken as a result of the protector's failure to provide the required consent after being requested to do so unless the trustee's actions constitute willful misconduct or gross negligence.

Unless the settlor provided otherwise, the trustee has no duty to monitor the protector's conduct, to provide advice to or consult with the protector, or tell the beneficiaries that that the trustee would have acted differently from how the protector directed.

The trustee's actions in carrying out the protector's directions are deemed to be merely administrative actions and are not considered to be the trustee monitoring or participating in actions within the scope of the protector's authority unless there is clear and convincing evidence to the contrary.

Section 114.003 deals with trust protectors in charitable trusts providing more restrictive rules.

See Examples & Explanations § 20.2.4.

4. Trustees with Enhanced Skills

A trustee who has or represents as having more skill than a prudent investor has a duty to exercise those additional skills. *See* Trust Code § 117.004(f).

5. Compliance Review

Read Trust Code § 117.010.

A trustee's compliance with the prudent investor rule is measured by the facts and circumstances existing at the time of the trustee's action. In other words, a trustee's conduct is not judged with the benefit of hindsight (no "Monday morning quarterbacking").

6. Factors Trustee Must Consider

Trust Code § 117.004 is the key provision which explains how the prudent investor rule operates. Subsection (c) enumerates the factors a trustee must consider when making investment and management decisions. Note that no particular type of property is categorically improper and that some risk or speculation may be prudent. *See* Trust Code § 117.004(e).

See Examples & Explanations § 20.2.1.3.

7. Diversification

Read Trust Code § 117.005.

This section codifies the trustee's duty to diversify to spread the risk so that if one investment goes bad, the entire trust does not suffer. However, the trustee is not required to diversify if the circumstances demonstrate that the purposes of the trust would be better served without diversifying.

For example, assume that Settlor created a trust containing Settlor's heirloom jewelry and a 20,000 acre farm that has been in Settlor's family for almost 200 years. At the termination of the trust, all remaining trust property passes to Settlor's children. Should Trustee sell some of this property to create a balanced portfolio of investments? Retaining all trust property in two assets of this type is certainly not a proper diversification. On the other hand, it is reasonable to conclude that Settlor wanted the heirloom jewelry and the farm to remain in the trust so they would pass to Settlor's children and thus Trustee may retain the assets without diversification.

See Examples & Explanations § 20.2.2.

8.   Review of Trust Assets

Read Trust Code § 117.006.

The trustee must review trust assets within a reasonable time after accepting the trust or receiving trust property. The trustee must then bring the trust property into compliance with the prudent investor rule. This is a significant change from prior Texas law which permitted the trustee to retain the initial trust property without diversification and without liability for loss or depreciation.

See Examples & Explanations § 20.2.5.

9.   Loyalty to Beneficiaries

Read Trust Code § 117.007.

The trustee's loyalty is to the beneficiaries. Accordingly, social investing may be problematic, especially if the returns from a "politically correct" investment are lower than from other investments. Social investment refers to the consideration of factors other than the monetary safety of the investments and their potential to earn income and appreciate. Examples of these types of factors include a company's handling of environmental matters, whether a company does business with countries with policies that do not protect human rights, whether a company employs and pays substandard wages to workers in foreign countries, and the political party affiliation of the company's leadership.

10. Impartiality

Read Trust Code § 117.008.

The trustee must act impartially and not favor one beneficiary over another. This is especially important in the context of income and principal allocations under Chapter 116.

C. TRUSTEE POWERS

To carry out the trustee's duties relating to the management of trust property, the trustee needs a wide array of powers such as to buy, sell, rent, lease, lend, borrow, mortgage, settle claims, and manage corporate securities.

1. Sources of Powers

a. Trust Instrument

Read Trust Code § 113.001.

The first place a trustee looks for authority to act is the trust instrument. Section 113.001 provides that terms of a trust instrument granting additional powers or limiting powers will trump the statutorily provided powers discussed below.

See Examples & Explanations § 20.3.1.1.

b. Texas Trust Code

Read Trust Code §§ 113.002-113.028.

These provisions enumerate an extensive list of powers which trustees automatically receive. These provisions permit settlors to draft relatively short trust instruments because they do not need to enumerate all of the powers they wish the trustees to have.

See Examples & Explanations § 20.3.1.2.

c. Implied by Circumstances

Read Trust Code §§ 113.002 & 113.024.

Section 113.002 along with § 113.024 codify the principle of implied powers, that is, a trustee is deemed to have whatever powers which the settlor must have intended the trustee to have to achieve the objectives set out in the trust instrument. Implied trustee powers are analogous to the necessary and proper powers provided to Congress by the Constitution. U.S. CONST. art. I, § 8, ¶18.

See Examples & Explanations § 20.3.1.3.

d. Court Order

Read Trust Code §§ 113.001 & 115.001.

A court with proper jurisdiction may render a judgment affecting the trustee's powers. The court may grant additional powers beyond those the settlor or state statute provides. Likewise, the court may limit powers which were granted by the settlor or state statute.

See Examples & Explanations § 20.3.1.4.

2.   Delegation of Duties

The traditional rule regarding delegation of powers is that the trustee may delegate mere ministerial duties but may not delegate discretionary acts. Investment of trust property was deemed a discretionary act and thus was not subject to delegation.

In 1999, Texas altered this rule and allowed the trustee to delegate investment decisions to an investment agent. The statute required the trustee to send written notice to the beneficiaries at least 30 days before entering into an agreement to delegate investment decisions to an investment agent. Generally, the trustee remained responsible for the agent's investment decisions. However, the trustee could have avoided liability for the investment agent's decisions if all of the relatively strenuous criteria specified in the statute were satisfied.

Read Trust Code § 117.011.

Section 117.011, effective January 1, 2004, takes a very different approach. The trustee may delegate any investment or management decision provided a prudent trustee of similar skills could properly delegate under the same circumstances. Of course, the trustee must exercise reasonable care, skill, and caution in selecting and reviewing the agent's actions. In the usual case, the trustee is not liable to the beneficiaries or the trust for the decisions or actions of the agent. *See* Trust Code § 117.011(c).

See Examples & Explanations § 20.3.2.

3.   Multiple Trustees

The settlor may appoint two or more persons to serve as co-trustees. The traditional rule required all trustees to consent before taking any action with respect to the trust unless the settlor expressly provided otherwise in the trust.

Read Trust Code § 113.085.

Texas rejects the unanimity rule in § 113.085 and permits a majority of the trustees to make decisions regarding the trust. Under limited circumstances such as when one of two co-trustees is absent or ill, the other co-trustee may take action if it necessary to achieve the purposes of the trust or to avoid injury to the trust property. Co-trustees also have a duty to prevent breaches of trust by another co-trustee and, if a breach is discovered, to compel a redress for that breach.

Read Trust Code § 114.006

Generally, co-trustees are jointly and severally liable to the beneficiaries. Section 114.006 explains how a dissenting trustee may attempt to be protected from liability for the acts of the majority.

See Examples & Explanations § 19.7.4.

4. Decanting

Read Trust Code §§ 112.071-112.087.

In 2013, Texas joined the growing number of states which have statutes granting the trustee the power to decant, that is, to distribute trust principal to another trust for the benefit of one or more of the beneficiaries of the original trust under specified circumstances.

The summary of these provisions below is adapted from William D. Pargaman, *Out With the Old [Probate Code] and In With the New [Estates Code]: 2013 Texas Estate and Trust Legislative Update* (Sept. 20, 2013), at 9-10.

This new subchapter adds statutory decanting provisions that supplement any similar provisions in a trust, unless the settlor expressly prohibits decanting. (A standard spendthrift clause is not considered such a prohibition.)

If a trustee has "full discretion" (i.e., a power that is not limited in any manner), that trustee may distribute principal to another trust for the benefit of one or more of the current beneficiaries of the first trust. If there is more than one trustee and less than all have full discretion, those trustees may exercise this power without the participation of any "limited" trustee.

If the trustee could have made an outright distribution to the beneficiary, then the trustee may give the beneficiary a power of appointment in the second trust in favor of one or more of the current beneficiaries of the first trust. The permissible appointees may be broader than the beneficiaries of the first trust.

If a trustee has "limited discretion" (i.e., a power that is limited in some way), that trustee may distribute principal to another trust so long as the current beneficiaries of both trusts are the same, and the successor and remainder beneficiaries of both trusts are the same. The distribution language of the second trust must be the same as the first trust. If a beneficiary of the first trust has a power of appointment, the beneficiary must be given the same power over the second trust. In other words, this provision really is limited to changing administrative provisions.

In either case, the trustee must act "in good faith, in accordance with the terms and purpose of the trust, and in the interests of the beneficiaries."

Notice provisions include the attorney general if a charity is involved, and allow intervention by the attorney general.

A trustee may not exercise a decanting power if it would:

(1) reduce a beneficiary's current right to a mandatory distribution or to withdraw a portion of the trust;

(2) materially impair the rights of any beneficiary;

(3) materially lessen a trustee's fiduciary duty;

(4) decrease the trustee's liability or indemnify or exonerate a trustee for failure to exercise reasonable care, diligence, and prudence;

(5) eliminate another person's power to remove or replace the trustee; or

(6) modify the perpetuities period (unless the first trust expressly permits this modification).

The decanting power is reduced to the extent it would cause any intended tax benefits, such as the annual gift tax exclusion, the marital deduction, or the charitable deduction, to be lost.

A trustee may not exercise a decanting power without court approval solely to change the trustee compensation provisions. The trustee may, however, modify the compensation provisions in conjunction with other valid reasons for decanting if the change raises the trustee's compensation to reasonable limits in accord with Texas law.

In no case is a trustee deemed to have a duty to decant.

If there are one or more current beneficiaries and one or more presumptive remainder beneficiaries who are not incapacitated, neither consent of the settlor nor court approval is required to exercise the decanting power if the trustee has sent written, descriptive notice to those beneficiaries.

A trustee may elect to petition a court to order the distribution. If a beneficiary timely objects, either the trustee or the beneficiary may petition to court to approve, modify, or deny the power.

D. TRUST DISTRIBUTIONS

1. Standard of Care

Trustees are generally under an absolute and unqualified duty to make trust distributions to the correct persons. A trustee who makes an improper distribution is liable even though the trustee exercised reasonable care and made the mistake in good faith. This duty is stricter than the standard applicable to other aspects of trust management because the beneficiary is the owner of the equitable title and is thus entitled to the trust distributions according to the terms of the trust.

Read Trust Code § 114.004.

Section 114.004 provides protection for a trustee who makes a distribution without actual knowledge or written notice of a fact impacting distribution such as the beneficiary's marriage, divorce, attainment of a certain age, or the performance of educational requirements. The trustee still has a duty to seek recovery of the mistaken payment and the beneficiary who received the mistaken payment has a duty to repay it. *See* Trust Code § 114.031.

See Examples & Explanations § 20.4.1.

2. To Whom Made

The trustee should make trust distributions directly to the beneficiary if the beneficiary is a competent adult unless the settlor requires or authorizes the trustee in the trust instrument to make distributions in another manner. For example, the trust may permit the trustee to pay the beneficiary's college tuition by sending payments directly to the school.

Read Trust Code § 113.021.

If the beneficiary is a minor or is incapacitated and the trust does not provide distribution instructions, § 113.021(a) supplies the trustee with a variety of distribution options. Note that the trustee determines whether a beneficiary is incapacitated; neither a court nor medical determination of incapacity is necessary.

See Examples & Explanations §§ 20.4.2 & 20.4.3.

E. DUTY OF LOYALTY

A trustee owes the beneficiaries duties of undivided loyalty and utmost good faith with regard to all trust matters. In other words, the trustee must avoid self-dealing and all other conflict of interest situations. The trustee owes these duties to all beneficiaries and consequently the trustee cannot favor one beneficiary over another unless the settlor expressly permits favoritism in the trust instrument. In addition, the trustee cannot profit from being a trustee even if the trustee is not otherwise in breach of the trust. *Read* Trust Code § 114.001(a). There is, of course, an exception for the trustee's compensation. *Compare* Trust Code § 114.007(a)(2).

Loyalty duties are based on the common law. In some states such as Texas, these duties are extensively (but not completely) codified.

Although interrelated, loyalty duties and investment duties are different. Loyalty duties deal with self-dealing and conflicts of interest which could impact not just investments but any aspect of trust administration. An act could be self-dealing (for example, the trustee sells a personal asset to the trust) but not breach investment duties (for example, the asset is an extremely prudent one for the trust to own).

Loyalty duties are typically breached if the prohibited conduct occurs. There is no actual "standard" – if the conduct occurred, the trustee breached the duty. No evaluation needs to be done. On the other hand, investment and management duties are breached when the trustee's conduct falls beneath the applicable standard. Proving that the act occurred is not enough as it is for breach of a loyalty duty – you must also prove the act violated the standard.

1.   Buying and Selling Trust Property

Read Trust Code § 113.053.

A trustee may not purchase trust assets for the trustee's personal use. Likewise, a trustee cannot sell the trustee's personal assets to the trust. A trustee cannot be expected to act fairly in these situations because as a purchaser, the trustee wants to pay as little as possible and as a seller, the trustee wants to receive a favorable price. The prohibition also applies to closely related or connected persons.

See Trust Code § 111.004(1) (defining "affiliate") and § 111.004(13) (defining "relative" in a narrow fashion which excludes many close relatives, such as uncles, aunts, nephews, and nieces). Trust Code § 113.053(b)-(g) provide limited exceptions to the prohibition.

See Examples & Explanations § 20.5.1.

2.   Borrowing Trust Property

Read Trust Code §§ 113.052 & 113.057.

A trustee may not self-deal by borrowing property from the trust either for the trustee's personal use or for the use of closely related or connected persons. However, the settlor may expressly authorize these loans in the trust instrument. For example, Grandparent may establish a trust for Grandchildren naming Child as the trustee and permit Child to make educational loans to Grandchildren from trust property.

See Trust Code § 111.004(1) (defining "affiliate") and § 111.004(13) (defining "relative" in a narrow fashion which excludes many close relatives, such as uncles, aunts, nephews, and nieces).

Corporate trustees are allowed to deposit trust funds with itself (that is, loan trust funds to itself) under the circumstances set forth in Trust Code § 113.057. The operation of § 113.057 is demonstrated by the following example. Assume that Octopus National Bank (ONB) is serving as the trustee of a trust. ONB keeps $80,000 in one of its certificates of deposit which is earning a competitive rate of interest. In addition, ONB maintains a checking account for the trust which it uses to pay expenses and make distributions to beneficiaries. Both accounts are fully insured by the federal government.

Technically, both of these accounts violate ONB's duty of loyalty. In ONB's capacity as a trustee, it is a lender, while in its capacity as a bank, it is a borrower. Thus, ONB has actually lent funds to itself. Because it would be inefficient to force ONB to use another financial institution for banking services, § 113.057 permits certain self-deposits. The certificate of deposit is a long-term investment and thus the transaction has a significant self-dealing aspect and it would not be a great burden on ONB to search elsewhere for this type of investment. However, if the settlor authorized this type of investment, ONB may properly open the CD. (If the trust was created before January 1, 1988, a beneficiary may provide the necessary consent.) With regard to the checking account, the benefit to the trust of having fast and convenient access to trust funds outweighs the self-dealing nature of the deposit. Accordingly, § 113.057 permits self-deposits pending investment, distribution, or payment of debts under the statutorily mandated conditions.

See Examples & Explanations § 20.5.2.

3.   Purchase of Common Investments

Read Trust Code § 113.055.

A conflict of interest arises if a trustee invests in the same securities as both a trustee and an individual. This would place the trustee in a position of making decisions for both the trustee as an individual and the trust. The best choice for the trustee may not be the best option for the beneficiaries of the trust. Accordingly, § 113.055 prohibits a trustee from being in this conflict of interest situation.

Note that although a trustee may not purchase for the trust stock in corporations in which the trustee individually holds shares, a trustee may retain stock in the trust which the trust already owns when the trustee becomes the trustee as long as it is prudent to do so.

See Examples & Explanations § 20.5.3.

4.   Transfers Between Trusts

Read Trust Code § 113.054.

A trustee may not sell property to another trust for which the trustee is also serving as the trustee. A conflict of interest arises because as the trustee of the selling trust, the trustee has a duty to get the highest price possible for the asset. However, as the trustee of the purchasing trust, the trustee has the duty to secure the most economical price. Section 113.054 provides an exception for the transfer of obligations issued or fully guaranteed by the federal government and which are sold at their current market price.

See Examples & Explanations § 20.5.4.

5.   Dealings With Beneficiaries

A trustee owes a duty of fairness when dealing with beneficiaries even with regard to non-trust related business. The beneficiary should not be placed in a position where at times the trustee owes high fiduciary duties while at other times they deal at arms length or are in an adversarial context. If a trustee wishes to deal with a beneficiary about non-trust matters, the trustee should make a full disclosure of all applicable law and facts to prevent the beneficiary from claiming that the beneficiary either relied on the trustee being a fiduciary or was subject to overreaching.

See Examples & Explanations § 20.5.5.

6.   Self-Employment

A trustee with special skills may be tempted to employ him- or herself to provide those services to the trust. For example, the trustee may be an attorney, accountant, stockbroker, or real estate agent. If the trustee succumbs to the temptation, the trustee will create a conflict of interest situation. As a fiduciary, the trustee should seek the best specialist possible within the trust's budget. However, as a specialist, the trustee wants to get the job and secure favorable compensation. Dual roles permit the trustee to engage in schizophrenic conversations such as, "This is too complicated for my trustee mind so I need to consult myself using my attorney brain." Courts typically presume that self-employment is a conflict of interest and thus do not permit trustees to recover extra compensation for the special services. However, the court may permit the trustee to receive compensation in dual capacities if the trustee can prove that the trustee acted in good faith for the benefit of the trust and charged a reasonable fee for the special services.

See Examples & Explanations § 20.5.6.

7. Permitted Self-Dealing

Self-dealing is not necessarily a bad thing. Assume that Settlor places all of Settlor's property in a testamentary trust for Charity and names Settlor's child as the trustee. Child and Child's siblings may be the only individuals who would pay a fair price for some of Settlor's assets such as photograph albums, videotapes of family gatherings, jewelry, home furnishings, clothes, and interests in family businesses. A settlor who wants to permit self-dealing should include a trust provision giving the trustee permission to self-deal. Because courts construe waivers of fiduciary duties strictly, the clause must be clearly drafted and the permitted self-dealing should be expressly stated.

See Examples & Explanations §§ 20.5.7.1 & 20.5.8.

Review Trust Code § 114.007.

PRICE v. JOHNSTON

Texas Appeals—Corpus Christi 1982
638 S.W.2d 1
no writ

NYE, Chief Justice.

This is an appeal from a summary judgment in favor of defendants in a suit brought by the beneficiary of a testamentary trust. The suit sought removal of the trustee and cancellation of a deed which conveyed trust property from the trustee to a relative of the trustee.

The trust instrument was the will of Rose Morris. It created two trusts, one (which we will refer to as the "Price" trust) for the benefit of Cecile Morris Price, her daughter, and one (which we will refer to as the "Johnston" trust) for the equal benefit of her three grandsons, Robert Morris Johnston, Harold M. Johnston, Jr., and Thomas M. Johnston. The trust property for each trust was an undivided one-half interest in a house and the land on which it was located. Trustee for the Price trust was defendant Robert M. Johnston. We learn from the briefs that the Johnston trust was terminated and that, by means of various transfers, Harold M. Johnston became the sole owner of the one-half interest in the house originally owned by the Johnston trust. After giving notice to Cecile Morris Price, Robert M. Johnston, as trustee, sold the remaining one-half interest in the house owned by the Price trust to his brother Harold, thereby making him the owner in fee of the entire property. Cecile Price, joined by her husband, Orville Price, brought suit against Robert M. Johnston and Harold Johnston, defendants, to cancel the sale and against Robert M. Johnston to remove him as trustee of the Price trust.

As grounds for cancellation of the deed, the petition alleges that the trustee was without power under the trust instrument or by virtue of the Texas Trust Act to sell the trust property to a relative (his brother) and that the consideration for the interest sold was inadequate. As ground for removal, the petition alleges that Robert Johnston violated his fiduciary duties by selling the trust property for an inadequate consideration and by selling the property to his brother in violation of the trust instrument and the Texas Trust Act.

The trial court granted the defendants' motion for summary judgment in which defendants allege that, as a matter of law, "under the terms of the Will in question * * * that the Trustee was specifically vested with the power and authority to sell Trust property, to any person, whether a beneficiary of the Trust, a Co-trustee, or a member of his family." In this we find that the trial court erred.

The will provides that "The Texas Trust Act * * * shall govern and apply to the trustee, and trust under this Will, except where this Will may contain provisions contrary to or different from the provisions of said Act."

The Act, Tex. Rev. Civ. Stat. Ann. art. 7425b12 (Vernon Supp. 1981), provides in part:

> "A trustee *shall not . . . sell, either directly or indirectly*, any property owned by . . . the trust estate . . . *to a relative . . . .*" (emphasis supplied)

The defendant, in his motion for summary judgment, contends this restriction on the power of a trustee to sell trust property was removed by provisions of the will.[2]

---

[2][Relevant portions of the will contain these provisions:

III. "6. *Powers of Trustee*

The trustee hereunder, acting alone and in his sole discretion, *without the joinder or concurrence of any beneficiary or any other person, shall have and is hereby given and granted the full power and authority,* from time to time, and at any time the trustee may deem proper, and successively, without the necessity of any court proceeding, order, decree or confirmation, to do, execute and perform each and all of the following:

(a) *To sell and convey any or all of said trust estates, either real or personal property, on such terms, time and conditions,* either for cash or partly for cash and with deferred payments secured by liens on the property sold, as the trustee may see fit, and to receive the cash payment on any such sale or sales, and to execute, acknowledge and deliver good and sufficient transfers, assignments and bills of sale, all with covenants of general warranty;

* * *

(i) *To enter into any agreement deemed advisable by the trustee* for the partition and division of any real or personal property which may be owned in common by said trust estates or any of them, and any other person or persons, and to execute, acknowledge and deliver good and sufficient deeds of partition and deeds of conveyance carrying out any partition or division between said trust estates or any of them, and any other person or persons, of any property which may be so owned in common; and to partition and divide as between said trust estates any property owned by said trusts in common;

(n) To sell or purchase from any other trust estate, whether created hereunder or not, whether or not the same or a different beneficiary be involved, and whether or not the same trustee may be involved, any assets or property of any nature, and to exchange assets or properties with any such other trust estate, *all as the trustee may deem fit.*

* * *

The Texas Trust Act, and all future and subsequent amendments thereto, when and after same become effective, shall govern and apply to the trustee and trusts under this will, except where this will may contain provisions contrary to or different from the provisions of said Act.

7. *Individual Interest of Trustee*

If any trustee should be individually interested as a co-tenant or partner in any real or personal property in which said trust estates or any of them may also have or hereafter at any time possess any interest, *such individual interest of the trustee shall in no way limit the powers herein given and granted* to such trustee, and shall in no way disqualify such trustee from exercising any of such powers and authorities as trustee, including without limitation the power to enter into partnership agreements in which he may be involved individually, as well as other businesses and undertakings in which the trustee may have individual interest, and also including the power to carry into effect partitions and exchanges in which said trustee may be individually involved or interested, and including any and all other powers and authority which may have been granted hereinabove under this will . . . . The trustee shall not be liable for mistakes in business judgment honestly committed in regard to said trust estates, and shall not be liable for any depreciation in value of any property or securities belonging to the trust estates, regardless of whether or not such property and securities be purchased by said trustee under the powers of investment given above, *but all acts of the trustee under the terms hereof shall be valid and*

Article 7425b-22 permits the trustor to negate the prohibition on sales to relatives if the trust instrument makes specific provisions for the same in the trust instrument:

"The trustor . . . may, by provisions in the instrument creating the trust . . . relieve his trustee from any and all of the duties, restrictions and liabilities which would otherwise be imposed on him by this act . . . ."

In his brief, defendant points to certain phrases contained in the will (trust) which he argues gives him the power to sell trust property to a relative. Those phrases are the one in paragraph III, Sec. 6, which reads: ". . . without the joinder or concurrence of any beneficiary or any other person . . ."; the one in paragraph III, Sec. 6(a), which reads,". . . on such terms, time, and condition, . . . as the trustee may see fit . . ."; the one in paragraph III, Sec. 6(i), which reads, "To enter into any agreement deemed advisable by the trustee . . ."; the one in paragraph III, Sec. 6(n), which reads, ". . . all as the trustee may deem fit"; the one in paragraph III, Sec. 7, which reads ". . . such individual interest of the trustee shall in no way limit the powers herein given and granted . . ."; and the one in paragraph III, Sec. 7, which reads, ". . . but all acts of the trustee under the terms hereof shall be valid and binding upon the trust estates and the beneficiaries thereof, whether such acts prove of benefit to such trust estates or not." Defendant also points to the following sentence from paragraph IV: "I hereby authorize and empower my Executor to exercise and perform all of the powers of sale, leasing and disposition of the properties of my Estate as I have conferred upon my Trustee in the preceding Paragraph II of this Will, all free from the control of the Probate Court and without the joinder or concurrence of any beneficiary, to be exercised by my Executor in his sole discretion as he may deem fit."

Reading the entire trust instrument as a whole, we find that it does not specifically permit the trustee to sell the trust property to his brother. It would have been a very simple thing for the trustor, under paragraph III, Sec. 6(a), to have provided that the trustee could sell and convey any and all of the trust property to any person, firm, corporation, including relatives of the trustee—the Texas Trust Act, art. 7425b-12, prohibiting the same notwithstanding. The paragraphs referred to by the defendant in the trust instrument do not especially permit a sale to a relative; rather, these provisions define rather broadly the powers especially given to the trustee.

---

binding upon the trust estates and the beneficiaries thereof, whether such acts prove of benefit to such trust estates or not." (emphasis supplied)]

The Texas courts have never interpreted liberally the broad powers of management as a justification for lessening the high standards to which fiduciaries are held under the Texas Trust Act. See *Slay v. Burnett Trust*, 143 Tex. 621, 187 S.W.2d 377 (1945). When a derogation of the Act hangs in the balance, a trust instrument should be strictly construed in favor of the beneficiaries. Since the will does not specifically permit the sale to a "relative," the Texas Trust Act must apply, which prohibits the intended sale. Compare *Corpus Christi National Bank v. Gerdes*, 551 S.W.2d 521 (Tex. Civ. App.—Corpus Christi 1977, writ ref'd n.r.e.) with *Furr v. Hall*, 553 S.W.2d 666 (Tex. Civ. App.—Amarillo 1977, writ ref'd n.r.e.).

It is not necessary for us to consider appellants' point of error relative to inadequacy of consideration since the sale to the brother cannot take place.

The judgment of the trial court is reversed and the cause remanded for proceedings not inconsistent with this opinion.

Opinion on Motion For Rehearing

Both defendants below, Robert M. Johnston and Harold Johnston, Jr., have filed motions for rehearing. In point number two of Robert M. Johnston's motion for rehearing, he challenges the next to last sentence of our original opinion insofar as it may be read to prohibit a sale of the corpus of the Price Trust to Harold Johnston under *any and all circumstances*. This, we did not intend to do. A sale under the summary judgment evidence cannot take place.

The Texas Trust Act, Tex. Rev. Civ. Stat. Ann. art. 7425b-24 (Vernon 1960), provides in part, however, that:

> E. A court of competent jurisdiction may, for cause shown and upon notice to the beneficiaries, relieve a trustee from any or all of the duties, limitations, and restrictions which would otherwise be placed upon him by this Act, or wholly or partly release and excuse a trustee, who has acted honestly and reasonably, from liability for violations of the provisions of this Act.

Therefore, the trial court may, at the conclusion of a trial on the merits, for "cause shown," excuse the trustee for his acts and ratify a sale of the property.

Defendants also urge in their motions for rehearing that we sustain the trial court's summary judgment that the price given in the sale was adequate. This we cannot and should not do.

It appears that the only evidence bearing on the issue of adequacy of consideration consisted of the uncontroverted opinions of defendants' experts, offered through affidavits. These opinions are of questionable validity. One of the purportedly expert opinions was attached to the affidavit of a defendant who swore only that the attached document was relied upon in determining the consideration for the sale. There was no affidavit of the expert himself, proclaiming the required personal knowledge and competency to testify to the matter.

Rule 166-A, T.R.C.P., states that: "A summary judgment may be based on uncontroverted testimonial evidence of an interested witness, or of an expert witness as to subject matter concerning which the trier of fact must be guided solely by the opinion testimony of experts, if the evidence is clear, positive and direct, otherwise credible and free from contradictions and inconsistencies, and could have been readily controverted."

In this case, the summary judgment affidavits containing opinion evidence were insufficient to establish as a matter of law the adequacy of the price paid for the trust property. See *Mobil Oil Corp. v. Matagorda County Drainage Dist. No. 3*, 580 S.W.2d 634, 639 (Tex. Civ. App.— Corpus Christi 1979) *rev'd on other grounds*, 597 S.W.2d 910 (Tex. 1980).

As we have heretofore stated, upon a trial on the merits, should the proof offered be such that the sale should be authorized, then in the interest of justice, the adequacy of the consideration should also be fully developed before the sale should be approved.

The defendants' motions for rehearing are overruled.

F.   LIABILITY OF TRUSTEE TO THIRD PARTIES

1.   Contract Liability

Read Trust Code § 114.084.

A trustee frequently enters into contracts in the performance of the trustee's investment and managerial duties. For example, the trustee may contract with an attorney to provide legal services or with a janitorial service to maintain an office building that is part of the trust corpus. Unless the trustee takes special steps to avoid liability, the trustee is personally liable for any breach of contract. *See* Trust Code § 114.084(a). To recoup damages paid to a contract claimant, the trustee must prove that the trustee properly entered into the contract for the benefit of the trust and then seek reimbursement from the trust property. *See* Trust Code § 114.063. The trustee would be stuck with any loss that results if the trust does not have adequate property to make a complete reimbursement.

At common law, a contract plaintiff could not sue the trustee in the trustee's representative capacity and could not recover directly against trust property. The common law courts did not take notice of the trust relationship and thus did not recognize the trustee as an individual as being a separate entity from the trustee in a representative capacity. Section 114.063, however, permits contract plaintiffs to reach the trust property directly by proceeding against the trustee in the trustee's fiduciary capacity.

A trustee will usually want to take steps to prevent the trustee's exposure to personal liability on contracts entered into for the benefit of the trust. The trustee should include a provision in the contract which expressly excludes the trustee's personal liability. *See* Trust Code § 114.084(a). Instead, if the trustee only signs in a representative capacity (e.g., "as trustee"), the trustee may still be personally liable but the signature acts as prima facie evidence of an intent to exclude the trustee from personal liability. *See* Trust Code § 114.084(b).

See Examples & Explanations § 20.6.1.

2.   Tort Liability

Read Trust Code §§ 114.083 & 114.062.

A trustee may commit a tort during the administration of the trust. For example, the trustee may negligently injure someone or may convert the property of another believing it belongs to the trust. The trustee also may be liable for the tortious acts of the trustee's employees and agents which are committed in the scope of their work for the trust under normal respondeat superior rules. At common law, a tort plaintiff was required to sue the trustee personally and could not reach the trust property directly by suing the trustee in the trustee's representative capacity. The trustee could seek indemnification or reimbursement from the trust only if the trustee had not engaged in willful misconduct. If the trust property was inadequate, the trustee was stuck with the loss. Courts justified this strict rule on the grounds that it encouraged trustees to exercise a high level of care for fear of being personally liable and protected trust property from tort claimants.

The trustee is still personally liable for torts committed by the trustee or the trustee's agents/employees. *See* Trust Code § 114.083(c). However, Trust Code § 114.083(a) permits plaintiffs to sue the trustee in the trustee's representative capacity and to recover directly against trust property in three situations:

(1) the tort is a common incident of the business activity in which the trust was properly engaged (e.g., the trust owns a grocery store in which a customer slips, falls, and is injured because an employee negligently failed to clean up a spill);

(2) the trustee is not personally at fault because the tort is based on strict liability; and

(3) the tort actually increased the value of trust property, such as conversion. In these same three situations, the trustee is entitled to exoneration or reimbursement from trust property under § 114.062.

Because the trustee remains personally liable for amounts the trust cannot reimburse or exonerate, the trustee should purchase insurance. See Trust Code § 113.013.

See Examples & Explanations § 20.6.2.

3.   Notice to Beneficiaries

Read Trust Code § 115.015.

Contract and tort plaintiffs have an obligation to notify the beneficiary before being entitled to a judgment against the trustee. Section 115.015 explains the timing of the notice and how the plaintiff may obtain a list of beneficiaries and their addresses from the trustee. The purpose of the notice is to alert the beneficiary that something may be "wrong" with the trust administration. Once notified, the beneficiary may decide to exercise the right to intervene under § 115.011(d).

Note that § 115.015(a)(2) requires that the attorney general be given notice only in contract cases, not tort cases. This anomaly is traceable to Texas Trust Act § 21 which was written before Texas abolished charitable immunity. *See Howle v. Camp Amon Carter*, 470 S.W.2d 629 (Tex. 1971) (abolishing charitable immunity as of March 9, 1966); but see Charitable Immunity and Liability Act, Civil Practice & Remedies Code, ch. 84. The attorney general may nonetheless be entitled to notice under Property Code ch. 123.

G.   ALLOCATION OF RECEIPTS AND EXPENSES

The settlor may grant certain beneficiaries the right to trust income (income beneficiaries) and other beneficiaries the right to the principal when the trust terminates (remainder beneficiaries). This arrangement places these two types of beneficiaries in conflict. The income beneficiaries want the trust corpus invested in property which generates high rates of return such as corporate bonds and mutual funds. On the other hand, remainder beneficiaries want the trustee to invest in property which appreciates in value such as real property and growth stocks. Many investments that are good for one type of beneficiary will not benefit another. For example, assume that the trustee invested in a government insured certificate of deposit earning 7 percent interest. The income beneficiaries will be elated because the rate of return is relatively high and the investment is extremely safe. However, the remainder beneficiaries will be furious. The CD will not grow in value because the trustee will get back the same amount the trustee invested when the CD matures. In addition, because of inflation, the buying power of the proceeds will shrink to less than the amount invested so the remainder beneficiaries will actually incur a loss. To resolve this problem, a trustee either selects investments that earn both income and appreciate in value, such as rental real property and certain types of stock, or diversifies trust investments to balance investments that earn income and investments which increase in value.

A trustee also needs to know how to categorize property received from the trust assets to carry out the trustee's duty to be fair and impartial to both the income and remainder beneficiaries. *See* Trust Code § 117.008. Likewise, the trustee must determine whether to reduce income or principal when the trustee pays trust expenses. The trustee has three ways to determine how to allocate receipts and expenses between income and principal. First, the settlor may have provided instructions in the trust instrument. These instructions may state specific allocation rules or may merely give the trustee discretion to make the allocation. *See* Trust Code § 116.004(a)(1)-(2). Second, if the instrument is silent, the trustee must follow the rules in Chapter 116 which is the Texas adoption of the 1997 version of the Uniform Principal and Income Act. *See* Trust Code § 116.004(a)(3). Third, if neither the instrument nor the statute specifies the proper method of allocation, the trustee must allocate to principal. *See* Trust Code § 116.004(a)(4).

The Texas adoption of the 1997 UPIA took effect on January 1, 2004. Prior to this time, Texas followed the 1962 version. Many of the provisions of the 1997 version are significantly different from prior law. Perhaps the most controversial change is the trustee's ability to adjust between principal and income under § 116.005 discussed in more detail later in this section.

1.   Basic Allocation Rules

See Examples & Explanations § 20.7.1.

a. Capital Gains

Read Trust Code § 116.161.

When the trustee sells an asset, both the return of the investment and the profit (capital gain) are allocated to principal.

b. Interest

Read Trust Code § 116.163.

The trustee should allocate interest received on money lent (e.g., a certificate of deposit) to income. In a change from prior law, a trustee no longer may allot to income the increase in value of a bond which pays no interest but appreciates in value (e.g., U.S. Series E savings bonds and other zero-coupon bonds) unless its maturity date is within one year after acquisition.

c. Rent

Read Trust Code § 116.162.

Generally, receipts from rental real or personal property are income. However, certain receipts are principal, such as refundable security deposits.

d. Eminent Domain Award

Read Trust Code § 116.161.

Generally, eminent domain awards are principal.

e. Insurance Proceeds

Read Trust Code § 116.164.

Casualty insurance payments as well as life insurance proceeds are generally allocated to principal.

f. Corporate Distributions

Read Trust Code § 116.151.

Generally, cash dividends belong to income while stock dividends go to principal. The logic behind the latter rule is that the trust owns the same proportion of the corporation both before and after the stock dividend. The trust may own a greater number of shares but because all other stock holders also own proportionately the same number of additional shares, the stock dividend did not improve the trust's position. Consequently, it would be unfair to allocate stock dividends to income.

See Examples & Explanations § 20.7.2.

g. *Business and Farm Receipts*

Read Trust Code § 116.153.

A trustee may maintain separate accounting records to determine the income of trust property which is held as a business or farm. Instead of using the UPIA rules, the trustee computes income in accordance with generally accepted accounting principles (GAAP). The trustee may wish to hire an accountant or CPA to assist in this process. *See* Trust Code § 113.018.

See Examples & Explanations § 20.7.4.

h. *Liquidating Assets*

Read Trust Code § 116.173.

A liquidating or wasting asset is one which goes down in value as it is used to produce income beyond what would be considered mere depreciation from normal use and age. For example, the patent on the 8-track tape was very valuable in the 1970s but has little value today. Likewise, a royalty interest in today's blockbuster motion picture may have little value 50 years from now. The trustee needs to allocate a portion of the proceeds from liquidating assets to principal to compensate for the depletion of the principal which occurs as the proceeds are generated.

Trust Code § 116.173 governs assets such as leaseholds, patents, copyrights, and royalties. The trustee must allocate 10 percent of each receipt to income and the remaining 90 percent to principal. This allocation is significantly different from prior Texas law which provided that receipts up to 5 percent of the asset's value each year were income with any excess being principal.

See Examples & Explanations § 20.7.3.3.

i. *Oil and Gas Receipts*

Read Trust Code § 116.174.

Traditionally under Texas law, oil and gas royalties were allocated 72.5% to income and 27.5% to principal. These percentages were based on former federal income tax rules which used these percentages for depletion allowances.

The UPIA gives only 10 percent to income with the remaining 90 percent to principal. (Note how unfair this would be to a beneficiary who is receiving 72.5% and then discovers that the new law cuts the percentage way down to 10%.)

Texas deviates from the UPIA by requiring the trustee to allocate these receipts "equitably." In addition, the trustee may use the prior allocation percentages if the trust owned the natural resource on January 1, 2004.

It is irrelevant whether or not any natural resources were being taken from the land at the time the property was placed in trust. In other words, the open mine doctrine is not followed in a trust context. *See* Trust Code § 116.174(c).

See Examples & Explanations § 20.7.3.1.

j. Timber

Read Trust Code § 116.175.

Timber is unlike other natural resources because it is renewable; the trees will grow back. The time it will take the trees to regrow, however, depends on the type of trees. For example, some varieties of pine trees may be ready to harvest in 20 years while other trees such as redwoods may take over a century. Consequently, it is difficult to create a precise allocation rule. Section 116.175 explains that receipts are income if the timber removed does not exceed the rate of new growth but receipts become principal if they are from timber in excess of the regrowth rate. This provision provides more guidance than prior law which merely instructed the trustee to do what was reasonable and equitable.

See Examples & Explanations § 20.7.3.2.

k. Non-Income Earning Property

Read Trust Code § 116.176.

The trustee should not retain property that does not earn income absent express permission in the trust instrument unless it is prudent to retain it under Chapter 117. Although some nonproductive assets, such as collectible items and unleased land, may have the potential of significantly appreciating in value, the retention of nonproductive property usually would violate the trustee's duty of fairness to the income beneficiaries.

Under prior law, the trustee was required to promptly sell underproductive property which meant property that did not earn at least 1% of its value per year, assuming the trustee was under a duty to sell either according to the terms of the trust or because it was imprudent to retain the property. Once the trustee sold the underproductive property, the trustee was often required to allocate a portion of the sale proceeds to income as *delayed income* to make up for the income the trust should have earned had this portion of the trust been placed in income-producing investments.

See Examples & Explanations § 20.7.6.

2.　Trustee's Adjustment Power

Read Trust Code §§ 116.005 & 116.006.

Section 116.005 is the most innovative provision of the 1997 UPIA. Consider the following example: Settlor created a testamentary trust requiring trust income to be paid to Daughter for life with the remainder to Granddaughter. The trust corpus consists primarily of real estate which is appreciating in value at about 15 percent per year due to its proximity to the edge of a growing city. The land is still subject to a multiple-year lease which Settlor signed with Tenant many years ago. The rent Tenant pays is significantly below market value and is insufficient to support Daughter as Settlor intended. May Trustee sell part of the land and allocate a portion of the profits to income?

Under traditional trust rules, Trustee could not allocate any of the profits from the sale of the real estate to income. Granddaughter has a right to the principal and appreciation belongs to the principal. However, § 116.005 grants the trustee the power to adjust between principal and income under specified circumstances. The adjustment power section is quite lengthy and requires Trustee to consider a variety of factors such as the settlor's intent and the identity and circumstances of the beneficiaries. In this example, it appears that Settlor established the trust to provide for Daughter and Settlor's intent would be frustrated if Trustee did not allocate some of the profits to income to provide Daughter with an appropriate level of support.

The adjustment power has proven to be an extremely controversial aspect of the 1997 Act because of its tremendous departure from traditional law, the fear that trustees may abuse the power, and the potential of a beneficiary suing a trustee if the trustee does not exercise the adjustment power in the beneficiary's favor. Accordingly, many of the states enacting the 1997 version of the Act have omitted the adjustment provisions or have altered or restricted them in some way.

Notes and Questions

1.　What factors must a trustee consider before exercising the adjustment power?

2.　When is adjustment prohibited?

3.   Do the beneficiaries need to be given notice before the trustee exercises the adjustment power?

4.   Under what circumstances may the trustee seek court approval for an adjustment?

5.   What standard will the court use in evaluating whether the trustee properly exercised the adjustment power?

3.   Apportionment Upon Trust Creation, Termination, Change in Beneficiary

Read Trust Code §§ 116.051 – 116.103.

Section 116.051 provides guidance to the trustee for determining and distributing net income after (1) a decedent dies or (2) an income interest in a trust ends. In a significant departure from prior law, unpaid pecuniary gifts in a will (either outright or in trust) begin to earn interest one year after the decedent dies rather than one year after the court grants letters testamentary. In another change, the trustee may now allocate interest on estate taxes to either principal or income rather than only against principal.

Section 116.052 explains how a trustee is to determine the appropriate amount of trust income to distribute to the residuary and remainder beneficiaries once the income interest ends.

Sections 116.101 – 116.103 explain the amounts to which an income beneficiary is entitled both when the trust begins and when the trust terminates. Note that inter vivos and testamentary trusts have different rules. In addition, the applicable rule may depend on the precise type of asset involved (e.g., a periodic payment such as rent or interest, a corporate distribution, etc.).

See Examples & Explanations §§ 20.7.7 & 20.7.8.

4.   Allocation of Expenses

Read Trust Code §§ 116.201 – 116.205.

Notes and Questions

Against which interest (income or principal) are the following expenses allocated?

1.   Trustee compensation.

2.   Accounting expenses.

3.   Ordinary repairs.

4. Capital improvements and extraordinary repairs.

5. Interest on borrowed funds.

6. Debt repayment.

7. Insurance premiums on the principal.

8. Taxes.

9. Depreciation.

See Examples & Explanations § 20.7.9.

5. Unitrust

To avoid the accounting hassle of allocating receipts and expenses between the income and remainder interests, as well as to reduce the inherent conflict of interest between current and future beneficiaries, some settlors adopt a unitrust or total return approach. The current beneficiary of a unitrust is entitled to receive a fixed percentage of the value of the trust property annually. The current beneficiary may or may not also be entitled to additional distributions. For example, the trust could provide: "Trustee shall distribute 5% of the value of the trust property to Current Beneficiary on January 10 of every year. Trustee has the discretion to make additional distributions to Current Beneficiary for Current Beneficiary's health, education, and support. Upon Current Beneficiary's death, Trustee shall deliver all remaining trust property to Remainder Beneficiary."

Under a unitrust, both beneficiaries have the same goal — they want the value of the property in the trust to increase. It does not matter to them whether the increase in value is due to receipts traditionally nominated income (e.g., interest or rent) or principal (i.e., appreciation). All increases inure to the benefit of all beneficiaries. Likewise, all beneficiaries share in the expenses regardless of their usual characterization.

Because of the enhanced ability of trustees to make productive investments when they are concerned only about total return rather than balancing the interests of income and principal beneficiaries, the use of unitrusts is seen by courts and legislatures as desirable. Accordingly, a few states have recently enacted legislation permitting a trustee to convert a traditional income rule trust to a unitrust under statutorily-specified conditions.

H. TRUSTEE'S DUTY TO INFORM BENEFICIARIES

The 2007 Legislature made changes to the trustee's duty to keep the beneficiaries informed of the trust and its activities. To place the changes into perspective, it is important to appreciate how this duty has been treated in the past under Texas law.

Prior to January 1, 2006, trustees had a duty to disclose information to the beneficiaries either (1) upon request or (2) if the trustee was going to take some material and unusual action. *Read* Trust Code § 113.151 (beneficiary's right to an accounting) and *Montgomery v. Kennedy*, 669 S.W.2d 309, 313 (Tex. 1984) (trustee has "duty of full disclosure of all material facts * * * that might affect [beneficiary's] rights"). The existence of this duty was well accepted and did not cause significant problems for trustees.

The 2005 Legislature codified the duty to keep the beneficiary informed when it enacted Trust Code § 113.060. This section provided that the trustee had a duty to keep the beneficiaries reasonably informed regarding (1) trust administration, and (2) the material facts necessary for the beneficiaries to protect their interests.

At the same time, the Legislature enacted Trust Code § 111.0035(a)(5)(A) which authorized the settlor to limit this duty but only if either (1) the beneficiary was under age 25, or (2) the beneficiary was not eligible for current distribution or for a distribution if the trust were to terminate now.

The codification of the duty to inform raised significant concerns for trustees including the following:

- What does "reasonably" mean?
- Do the beneficiaries need to be told about all trustee actions, even day-to-day activities, because notice of virtually all actions may be necessary if the beneficiaries want to protect their interests?

These problems and others were triggered by the way the Legislature carved § 113.060, a very short and undetailed provision, out of Uniform Trust Code § 813 which includes an extensive explanation of the duty and how it may be satisfied.

The 2007 Legislature repealed the statutory duty (Trust Code § 113.060) and restored the common law duty. Acts 2007, 80th Leg., ch. 451, § 21 ("The common-law duty to keep a beneficiary informed that existed immediately before January 1, 2006, is continued in effect.").

However, under new Trust Code § 111.0035(c), the settlor may limit the duty to keep the beneficiary informed under the following conditions:

- The trust is revocable,
- The beneficiary is under age 25, or
- The beneficiary is not eligible for current distributions or a distribution if the trust were to terminate now.

I. ACCOUNTINGS

Read Trust Code §§ 113.151 & 113.152.

The trustee has a duty to keep accurate records of all transactions involving trust property and to provide accountings to the beneficiaries. This information helps the beneficiaries to determine whether the trustee is doing an acceptable job of administering the trust. Unlike some states, Texas does not require the trustee to render periodic accountings. Instead, § 113.151 provides that a trustee must account only if (1) a beneficiary makes a written demand, or (2) an interested party obtains a court order.

The trustee must provide the accounting on or before the 90th day after the trustee receives the demand unless a court order provides for a longer period.

If the beneficiary is successful in a suit to compel an accounting, the court has the discretion to award all or part of the court costs and all the beneficiary's reasonable and necessary attorney's fees against the trustee in either the trustee's individual or representative capacity. Note that the section does not seem to permit the court to award only a part of the attorney's fees; it appears to be an "all or nothing" situation unlike with regard to court costs where the court has the discretion to award "all or part."

Section 113.152 enumerates the items required in a trustee's accounting. A trustee may find it convenient to keep records in this format from the beginning to make it a relatively easy task to render an accounting.

Many good reasons exist for a trustee to render an annual accounting even though not required to do so by law or under the trust. The trustee will have an easier time preparing the accounting when the transactions are fresh in the trustee's mind. The trustee may have a difficult time recalling trust events years or decades later. Accountings also have a good psychological impact on the beneficiaries. Beneficiaries like to know what is going on and voluntarily submitted annual accountings may reflect highly on the trustee's conscientiousness and candor.

See Examples & Explanations § 20.8.

HOLLENBECK v. HANNA

Texas Appeals—San Antonio 1991
802 S.W.2d 412
no writ

PEEPLES, Justice.

Chrystella Hollenbeck, the remainder beneficiary under her deceased father's testamentary trust, brought suit in probate court to compel the trustee, Mark Hanna, to give her an accounting. Hollenbeck's mother, Chrystella Bacon, is the trust's income beneficiary for her lifetime. The trial court denied Hollenbeck's request, and she appeals that decision. She also appeals the trial court's denial of her motion to remove Hanna as trustee. We reverse and remand.

Hollenbeck's father, Joe H. Bacon, died on October 10, 1987, leaving a will and codicil dated October 7, 1983 and July 2, 1987 respectively. These instruments, which were admitted to probate on November 17, 1987, left the homestead and other items of property to his wife, Chrystella Bacon, and placed his remaining property, primarily a ranch, in trust. The trust provided that his surviving wife would enjoy the income for life and his daughter Hollenbeck would receive the remainder. Trustee Hanna was authorized to invade the corpus only for Chrystella Bacon's health, and Hollenbeck was given the right to oversee ranch operations.

Mother and daughter did not always agree on matters, and there was further litigation. On October 19, 1988 the court signed an agreed judgment that resolved various disputes between them and entitled Hollenbeck to visit the ranch and inspect operations twice a year. Eventually Hollenbeck started to question whether the day-to-day ranch operations were being overseen by a family member. Under § 2032A of the Internal Revenue Code, she says, farming and ranch property receives a tax break only if a family member oversees the daily operations. Failure to comply with § 2032A might endanger the estate's tax status and force Hanna to sell the ranch to pay taxes, leaving a much smaller remainder for her to take.

Unable to get an accounting from Hanna after several attempts, Hollenbeck brought this suit. Her petition sought an accounting, a written explanation of any action the trustee had taken to protect the § 2032A election, and removal of Hanna as trustee. At the hearing Hollenbeck also said she wanted to make sure that the corpus was not being improperly invaded. The court denied relief.

Hollenbeck contends that the court erred in ruling (1) that Joe Bacon intended to deny her an accounting and (2) that the will's provisions prevail over § 113.151 of the trust code. We agree with both of her contentions.

Section 113.151 of the Texas Trust Code authorizes beneficiaries to file suit to compel an accounting and says that upon such request the court may order one. Section 113.151, entitled "Demand for Accounting," provides in part as follows: A beneficiary by written demand may request the trustee to deliver to each beneficiary of the trust a written statement of accounts covering all transactions since the last accounting or since the creation of the trust, whichever is later. If the trustee fails or refuses to deliver the statement within a reasonable time after the demand is made, any beneficiary of the trust may file suit to compel the trustee to deliver the statement to all beneficiaries of the trust. The court may require the trustee to deliver a written statement of account to all beneficiaries on finding that the nature of the beneficiary's interest in the trust or the effect of the administration of the trust on the beneficiary's interest is sufficient to require an accounting by the trustee. TEX. TRUST CODE ANN. § 113.151 (Vernon 1984). Joe Bacon's will states that the trustee shall render an annual accounting and give a copy to Bacon's wife. Section IV(I) of the will provides, "The trustee shall render an annual accounting, a copy of which shall be delivered to my wife, CHRYSTELLA MAY BACON. Such accounting shall include the income and disbursements and the properties in the trust at the end of the accounting period."

The trial court ruled that under § IV(I) Hollenbeck was not entitled to an accounting and that this provision negated Hollenbeck's rights under § 113.151 of the trust code. The judgment states, [The court] finds that the Will of Joe H. Bacon establishing the Chrystella May Bacon Trust provides that an accounting shall be provided by the trustee to Chrystella May Bacon; that by exclusion of other directives to the trustee concerning delivery of an accounting, the testator's intent was that no other entity be provided an accounting; that the provisions of the Will prevail over the provisions of the Trust Code; and that therefore, Chrystella B. Hollenbeck is not entitled to an accounting. The judgment rests expressly on this interpretation of the will and the trust code. Hollenbeck asked for additional findings of fact and conclusions of law, which the court declined to make. Accordingly we cannot accept Hanna's invitation to uphold the judgment by presuming that the trial court exercised its discretion to deny an accounting under § 113.151, which clearly was not the court's reasoning. See Leonard v. Eskew, 731 S.W.2d 124, 132 (Tex. App.—Austin 1987, writ ref'd n.r.e.); Wilson v. O'Connor, 555 S.W.2d 776, 781 (Tex. Civ. App.—Dallas 1977, writ dism'd); Life & Casualty Ins. Co. v. Martinez, 299 S.W.2d 181, 182 (Tex. Civ. App.—San Antonio 1957, no writ). The court's ruling rests entirely on a legal interpretation of § IV(I) of the will and the trust code.

We believe that the trial court has incorrectly interpreted the will and also given too little weight to § 113.151. The will does not say that the trustee shall give an accounting only to Bacon. It does not say that Hollenbeck shall not receive one. It says simply that a copy shall be given to Bacon. We disagree that this language suggests that Joe Bacon meant to deprive his daughter of her statutory right to seek an accounting. This is especially true in view of his directive that Hollenbeck was to oversee the ranch operations.

We have found no Texas authority concerning the extent to which a settlor can excuse a trustee from accounting to beneficiaries. Certainly a settlor could not totally eliminate a trustee's duty to provide an accounting to the court. If the settlor attempts to eliminate any accounting duty of the trustee, by providing that it shall not be necessary for his trustee to account to anyone at any time, it would seem that the clause should be invalid and the duty of the trustee unaffected. The settlor ought not to be able to oust the court of its inherent equitable, constitutional or statutory jurisdiction, or to override the acts of the legislature concerning information to be furnished by trustees to their beneficiaries. Provisions of this sort in deeds and wills would seem against public policy and void.... There is a small amount of authority on the subject. The better reasoned decisions hold that the trustee still must account to the proper court. G. BOGERT & G. BOGERT, THE LAW OF TRUSTS AND TRUSTEES § 973, at 462-64 (2d ed. 1983). Similarly we question whether a settlor should be able to deprive any significant beneficiary of the statutory right to seek an accounting. A settlor who attempts to create a trust without any accountability in the trustee is contradicting himself. A trust necessarily grants rights to the beneficiary that are enforceable in equity. If the trustee cannot be called to account, the beneficiary cannot force the trustee to any particular line of conduct with regard to the trust property or sue for breach of trust. The trustee may do as he likes with the property, and the beneficiary is without remedy. If the court finds that the settlor really intended a trust, it would seem that accountability in chancery or other court must inevitably follow as an incident. Without an account the beneficiary must be in the dark as to whether there has been a breach of trust and so is prevented as a practical matter from holding the trustee liable for a breach. Id. § 973, at 467. The same considerations apply to a settlor's attempt to deprive some beneficiaries of an accounting while granting that right to others. We do not read Beaty v. Bales, 677 S.W.2d 750 (Tex. App.—San Antonio 1984, writ ref'd n.r.e.), to hold otherwise. The court there did say, "In Texas, unless there are provisions under the terms of an express trust, the Texas Trust Act generally grants to the district court original jurisdiction to require an accounting by the trustee." Id. at 754. See TEX. TRUST CODE ANN. § 115.001 (Vernon 1984). But Beaty did not purport to hold that a settlor could deprive a court of the power to require an accounting, an issue that was not before the court.

In any event the instruments before us do not suggest that the settlor meant to deny his sole remainder beneficiary her statutory right to ask for an accounting, particularly where she seeks primarily a copy of a document that already exists. The will and codicil simply grant that right to the lifetime beneficiary and are silent about the rights of the remainder beneficiary. We hold that the court erred in construing the instruments and the statute otherwise.

For the reasons stated we reverse the order denying an accounting. Section 113.151 requires the court to decide whether "the nature of the beneficiary's interest in the trust or the effect of the administration of the trust on the beneficiary's interest is sufficient to require an accounting by the trustee." The court has not decided that issue and therefore we remand the cause for further proceedings consistent with this opinion.

We overrule Hollenbeck's fourth point of error, which seeks the removal of Hanna as trustee. Nothing in this opinion is meant to prevent her from reurging on remand her motion to remove him.

J.   TRUSTEE COMPENSATION

Read Trust Code § 114.061.

At common law, a trustee was presumed to serve without compensation unless the trust instrument expressly provided otherwise. The policy behind this rule was that a trustee should not earn a profit by serving in a fiduciary capacity. Otherwise, the trustee might take certain actions which were not necessary or not in the best interest of the trust merely to increase the compensation.

Section 114.061 provides that a trustee is entitled to reasonable compensation unless the trust expressly provides that the trustee is not to be paid or provides a method for determining compensation. The following factors may be considered in determining the amount of compensation which is reasonable:

(1)   The amount of time the trustee spent working on trust matters;

(2)   the gross income of the trust;

(3)   the appreciation in value of trust property;

(4) the trustee's unusual or special skills or experience (e.g., being an attorney or accountant);

(5) the trustee's degree of fidelity or disloyalty to the trust;

(6) the amount of risk and responsibility the trustee assumed;

(7) the fees charged by other trustees in the local community for similar services;

(8) the character of the trustee's work, that is, did it involve skill and judgment or was it merely routine or ministerial; and

(9) the trustee's own estimate of the value of the services.

The trustee may then take this amount from the trust without court approval. If a beneficiary or co-trustee believes the fee is excessive, that person may seek judicial review. *See* Trust Code § 115.001(a)(9). The court may deny compensation to a trustee who commits a breach of trust. *See* Trust Code § 114.061(b).

See Examples & Explanations § 20.9.

K. TRUST MODIFICATIONS

1. By the Court

a. Deviation

Read Trust Code § 112.054.

A court may be willing to permit the trustee to deviate from the settlor's instructions as contained in the trust instrument if the court is convinced that the settlor would have consented to the change had the settlor anticipated the current situation. Deviation typically occurs if (1) the purposes of the trust have been fulfilled, (2) the purposes of the trust have become illegal, (3) the purposes of the trust are now impossible to fulfill, or (4) because of circumstances not known to or anticipated by the settlor, the deviation will further the purposes of the trust. The grounds for deviation were greatly expanded by the 2005 Texas Legislature when subsections (a)(3)-(5) were added and (a)(2) liberalized.

Using its deviation powers, the court may authorize a wide array of administrative revisions such as (1) changing the trustee, (2) permitting the trustee to perform acts that are not authorized or are forbidden by the trust instrument, (3) prohibiting the trustee from performing acts that the settlor mandated in the trust instrument, (4) modifying the terms of the trust, and (5) terminating the trust.

Although the trustee and the beneficiaries have standing to request deviation, the settlor lacks standing to do so.

Note

In the case of *In re Willa Peters Hubberd Testamentary Trust*, 432 S.W.3d 358 (Tex. App.—San Antonio 2014, no pet.), a father established a testamentary trust for his daughter. After a dispute arose regarding the depreciation allowance applicable to distributions from mineral income, all the parties and their attorneys signed a mediated settlement agreement modifying the terms of the trust. After the probate court issued orders in compliance with the settlement agreement, the daughter appealed.

Daughter claimed that the probate court erred in ordering the modifications under Trust Code § 112.054 because the order was inconsistent with the material purposes of the trust, she did not agree to them, they did not conform to the father's intentions, and one of the modifications was not contained in the agreement. The court carefully reviewed the trust and the modifications and decided that the probate court abused its discretion in ordering some, but not all, of the modifications. The court explained that the parties could not agree to modifications that are inconsistent with a material purpose of the trust because the statute does not authorize these deviations.

See Examples & Explanations § 20.10.1.1.

b. Cy Pres

BLOCKER v. STATE

Texas Appeals—Houston [1st Dist.] 1986
718 S.W.2d 409
writ ref'd n.r.e.

LEVY, Justice.

This is an appeal from an action brought by the Attorney General of Texas to prevent abuse of a charitable trust, pursuant to Tex. Rev. Civ. Stat. Ann. art. 4412a (Vernon 1986). The trial court entered judgment declaring a 1984 deed, purportedly conveying property of a charitable corporation to a private estate, void *ab initio* and awarded title and possession of the property and certain personalty to a newly constituted charitable organization, impressed with a public charitable trust in perpetuity under the *cy pres* doctrine.[3]

The appeal is before this Court on stipulated facts.

The Houston Conservatory of Music ("HCM") was granted a Texas charter on May 25, 1934. The corporation was created for the purpose of teaching music and its allied arts by C.A. Hammond, Ora B. Hammond, and their son, Mozart B. Hammond. On October 14, 1935, the charter of the corporation was amended to provide "that this corporation shall be non-profit-making in character and shall be maintained and operated strictly for the purpose of teaching the Youth of this land music and its allied arts." Its charitable identity was thus permanently and irrevocably established. [citations omitted]. The corporation had no members. On November 15, 1939, HCM was granted a federal tax exemption retroactive to 1934. Such exemption was effective "so long as there is no change in the form of the organization, your purposes or methods of operation." HCM was also exempt from state and local property taxes. The record indicates that the charitable nature of HCM was apparently relied on by third parties who made donations to HCM.

On August 12, 1941, Mozart B. Hammond ("Hammond") deeded property on Fannin Street in Houston to HCM. HCM agreed to assume payment of a vendor's lien note executed by Hammond. On March 29, 1950, HCM acquired property at 3614 Montrose in Houston, and shortly thereafter, HCM sold the Fannin Street location.

HCM conveyed the Montrose location on July 3, 1963, and following the sale, HCM acquired the current site on Milford Street, also in Houston. It was this site on Milford that HCM purportedly transferred to the estate of Mozart B. Hammond on May 4, 1984, by the deed which was declared void. No consideration for the transfer passed to HCM.

Sometime prior to March 12, 1984, Jean Blocker and Allison Frank became directors of HCM. On that date, a vacancy was declared on the board due to the earlier death of Mozart B. Hammond. The two remaining directors, Blocker and Frank, voted to expand the board to four members

---

[3]*Cy Pres* is equitable power authorizing a court to effectuate the *general* charitable purpose of a testator when his *particular* intention cannot be carried out, or becomes impractical or illegal, whereupon the court may direct the trust funds or property be expended or utilized in a charitable manner as near (*cy pres*) to the donor's intent as possible. *See Wooten v. Fitz-Gerald*, 440 S.W.2d 719 (Tex. Civ. App.--El Paso 1969, writ ref'd n.r.e.); *Coffee v. William Marsh Rice University*, 408 S.W.2d 269, 285 (Tex. Civ. App.--Houston [1st Dist.] 1966, writ ref'd n.r.e.).

and to elect Miriam Owen and Betsy Nalle as directors.[4] The board determined that the only substantial assets of HCM were the HCM Milford site and the musical instruments located therein. Upon determining that neither the articles of incorporation nor the bylaws specifically provided for the disposition of these assets, the directors unanimously voted to dissolve HCM, pay the liabilities of the corporation, and distribute any remaining assets to the Hammond estate.

Hammond had died in 1982 at the age of 70. The terms of his Will provided in part that "Miriam Blocker, Allison Blocker, and Betsy Blocker, share and share alike, all the property, real, personal and mixed, of which I may be seized and possessed at the time of my death after the payment of said debts and the expense of probating this Will, to be owned by them in fees simple and held or disposed of, as they may wish or deem practical." This will was offered for probate in Harris County on May 3, 1984, two months after the board action to dissolve HCM and one day before the effective date of the deed of the HCM site from the corporation to the Hammond estate.

By their sole point of error, appellants contend that the trial court erred in declaring void the deed conveying the Milford property to the Hammond estate. The contention involves interpretation of the dissolution and distribution section of the Texas Non-Profit Corporation Act, Tex. Rev. Civ. Stat. Ann. art. 1396-6.02 A (Vernon 1980) ["TNPCA"][5] It provides as follows:

Art. 1396-6.02.   Application and Distribution of Assets

A. The assets of a corporation in the process of dissolution shall be applied and distributed as follows:

(1) All liabilities and obligations of the corporation shall be paid, satisfied and discharged; in case its property and

---

[4]Appellant Lee Blocker was Mozart B. Hammond's first cousin and executor of his will. Jean L. Blocker is his wife. Appellants Allison Frank, Betsy Nalle, and Miriam Owen are their daughters and beneficiaries under Hammond's will.

[5]Paragraphs (3), (4), and (5) of this Act have been superseded by an amendment effective September 1, 1985, and applicable only to corporations formed thereafter. It provides generally that the remaining assets of a charitable corporation in process of dissolution, after debts are paid and conditionally held property is returned or transferred, shall be distributed only to tax exempt organizations pursuant to a plan of distribution adopted as provided in the Act, unless otherwise provided by the corporation's articles of incorporation. "Any distribution by the court shall be made in such manner as, in the judgment of the court, will best accomplish the general purposes for which the corporation was organized." See the newly effective art. 1396-6.02(3), TNPCA.

assets are not sufficient to satisfy or discharge all the corporation's liabilities and obligations, the corporation shall apply them so far as they will go to the just and equitable payment of the liabilities and obligations.

(2) Assets held by the corporation upon condition requiring return, transfer or conveyance, which condition occurs by reason of the dissolution, shall be returned, transferred or conveyed in accordance with such requirements.

(3) Assets received and held by the corporation subject to limitations permitting their use only for charitable, religious, eleemosynary, benevolent, educational or similar purposes, but not held upon a condition requiring return, transfer or conveyance by reason of the dissolution, together with any income earned thereon shall be transferred or conveyed to one or more domestic or foreign corporations, societies or organizations engaged in activities substantially similar to those of the dissolving corporation, pursuant to a plan of distribution adopted as provided in this Act.

(4) Other assets, if any, shall be distributed in accordance with the provisions of the articles of incorporation or the bylaws to the extent that the articles of incorporation or by-laws determine the distributive rights of members, or any class of classes of members, or provide for distribution to others.

(5) Any remaining assets may be distributed to such persons, societies, organizations or domestic or foreign corporations, whether for profit or not for profit, as may be specified in a plan of distribution adopted as provided in this Act.

Appellants contend that their actions were authorized under art. 1396-6.02(A)(1) and (5), and that "there was no trust of any sort attending the corporation's ownership of the Milford property," apparently on the theory that a charitable corporation owes no duty to donors to apply charitable donations upon dissolution to the charitable purposes of a corporation.

The State asserts that the actions of the directors were clearly governed by TNPCA art. 1396-6.02 A(3) and that HCM was a charitable trust. The failure of the directors to comply with art. 1396-6.02 A(3), and their actions in conveying the property to the Hammond estate, under which will three directors were individual beneficiaries, are described as breaches of fiduciary duty, properly remedied by the trial court imposing a constructive trust and by applying the doctrine of *cy pres* to form a new organization to continue the public trust.

A brief *amicus curiae*, filed by the reconstituted Houston Conservatory of Music, now entitled the "New Conservatory," essentially supports the State's position, emphasizing the alleged breaches of fiduciary duty and urging public policy considerations in enforcing non-distribution constraints to prevent abuse of charitable trusts.

The parties assert that this Court is bound by the stipulation of facts and is without authority to draw any inferences or find any facts not embraced in the agreement, unless as a matter of law such inferences are necessarily compelled by the facts agreed upon. *See Hutcherson v. Sovereign Camp, W.O.W.*, 112 Tex. 551, 251 S.W. 491 (1923).

Appellants contend that the directors' action was justified under TNPCA art. 1396-6.02 A(1), which provides for application and distribution of the assets of a dissolving nonprofit corporation.

There is no showing either in the stipulations or otherwise in the record that the corporation had any debts or other obligations to which the transfer of the Milford property was applied. Appellants do not contend that the property was applied to any obligation, but regard the transaction as "compensation" deserved in equity for the effort, economic support, and years Hammond dedicated to the HCM; that is, in the nature of a posthumous reward recognizing his service. This cannot properly be regarded as the type of "obligation" contemplated by art. 13966.02 A(1). Although the directors' action may have been in part so justified at some point, clearly their contention does not apply to their distributing assets remaining after obligations had been met, two years after the death of Hammond. A more logical posthumous recognition of his public service would surely be to continue the charitable trust he helped to establish and maintain, such socially beneficent purpose being more consistent with the declared educational objectives of the HCM than its dissolution for private gain.

Appellants also contend that the actions are justified under the following provision:

> Any remaining assets may be distributed so such persons, societies, organizations or domestic or foreign corporations, whether for profit or not for profit, as may be specified in a plan of distribution adopted as provided in this Act.

Id., art. 1396-6.02 A(5).

The structure of the Act reflects that this final paragraph applies only when the first four paragraphs have been satisfied.

It is undisputed that the property was initially conveyed to HCM without limitation requiring return, transfer, or conveyance in the event of dissolution. Therefore, art. 1396-6.02 A(2) is not applicable. Nor is it contended that the HCM had provisions determining distribution in the event of dissolution in the articles of incorporation or the by-laws.

Thus, article 1396-6.02 A(4) is inapplicable. Paragraph (5) effectively allows the directors, in their unrestricted discretion, to distribute assets remaining not subject to the preceding four application-and-distribution provisions. It follows that no breach of fiduciary duty could occur if the distribution is properly implemented under this paragraph. The core of the argument addresses the question whether the distribution plan adopted was subject to the provisions of article 1396-6.02 A(3), consequently authorizing the trial court's judgment and actions.

Appellants' primary contention is that, since the assets received and held over the years were not subject to limitations on their use, paragraph (3) does not apply. Texas courts have not yet directly addressed this point.

The California Supreme Court considered a similar factual situation. *In re Los Angeles County Pioneer Society*, 40 Cal. 2d 852, 257 P.2d 1, *cert. denied*, 346 U.S. 888, 74 S. Ct. 139, 98 L. Ed. 392 (1953). In that case, members of a non-profit corporation in voluntary dissolution sought distribution of the assets to themselves. The California Court held that the articles of incorporation provided that the society's purpose was the "[c]ommemoration of historical events and the collection and preservation of data of historical interest [which] are for the education and recreational benefit of the community as a whole and are recognized charitable purposes." *Id.*, 257 P.2d at 5. "[I]n cases where ... property is conveyed without restriction to a charitable corporation ... the charitable intent of the donor is ascertained by reference to the charitable purposes of the donee." *Id.* at 9. The Court further reasoned that an *inter vivos* gift made by a member "to a society organized for a charitable purpose *without a declaration of the use* to which the gift is to be put is given in trust to carry out the objects for which the organization was created." *Id.* at 6 (emphasis added). "[D]eviations from the purposes stated in [the] articles are thus subject to the same corrective measures that would be taken against a trustee of a charitable trust that similarly refused to carry out its duties." *Id.* at 6. The Court "should appoint a successor trustee to carry out the charitable intent of the donor whether the charitable purpose is found in the terms of the conveyance to the corporation or in the articles thereof, or whether the failure of the corporation is through dissolution or other disqualification." *Id.* at 9.

The Nebraska Supreme Court, *In re Harrington's Estate*, 151 Neb. 81, 36 N.W.2d 577 (1949), reached a similar conclusion. The Court stated that:

> [A] gift, donation, or bequest by name, without further restriction or limitation as to use, to a corporation organized and conducted solely for charitable purposes, will be deemed to have been made for the objects and purposes for which the corporation was organized. ...

[A] gift to a charitable corporation is equivalent to a bequest to a charitable trust, and will ordinarily be governed by the same rules.... In other words, the bequest at bar was in effect a gift to the objects and purposes of [the] corporation, and not to the corporation itself. It was in legal effect a charitable donation impressed with a public trust specifically imposed by [the] articles of incorporation.

Id. 36 N.W.2d at 582 [citations omitted].

Texas courts have apparently not yet adjudicated any cases addressing dissolution under the statute. However, in a Texas case decided prior to the California and Nebraska decisions, our Supreme Court made an extensive and scholarly analysis of Texas jurisprudence on charitable trusts vis-à-vis historical origins and applications by other jurisdictions. In *Boyd v. Frost National Bank*, 145 Tex. 206, 196 S.W.2d 497 (1946), the Supreme Court considered a testamentary trust established for general charitable purposes, where the appointed trustee was given unfettered discretion in determining beneficiaries of the trust. In reaching its holding that the trust was valid, the Court observed that Texas has a long history of preference for liberally upholding charitable trusts, often contravening the majority of jurisdictions, and broadly favoring charitable endeavors. The Court, quoting a New Jersey decision, stated:

A gift to a charitable institution or society will be presumed to be a charitable gift, though no purpose is named, and such institution or society will be presumed to hold such gifts in trust for those charitable purposes for which it exists.

Id., 145 Tex. at 220, 196 S.W.2d at 505 [citation omitted]. The single dissent did not argue against the policy statements, but rather with the difficulty in determining the beneficiaries of, and enforcing for the public, a general charitable purposes trust. Yet the facts of the case at bar would probably satisfy the dissent that an enforceable and specific public charitable trust exists. The dissent stated that:

[B]efore the Attorney General is authorized to sue to enforce a charity, it must be so public in nature or character as to be of interest to the entire public or the public in general. A charity for the orphan[ed] children of a state is a public charity, but a charity for the orphan[ed] children of deceased Masons, ... is not a public charity.

Id., at 511 (Slatton, J., dissenting) [citations omitted].

In the case at bar, the articles of incorporation specifically provided that the purpose of the corporation was the "teaching of the Youth of this land music and its allied arts." Education, both by the very terms of article

1396-6.02 A(3) and by general recognition as being for the advancement of society, is considered a charitable purpose. *See, e.g., Boyd*, 145 Tex. at 214, 196 S.W.2d at 502; *Coffee v. William Marsh Rice University*, 408 S.W.2d at 275.

We conclude that property transferred unconditionally to a non-profit corporation, whose purpose is established as or determined to be a public charity or an educational facility, is nevertheless subject to implicit charitable or educational limitations *defined by the donee's organizational purpose* and within the meaning of the statute, where no express limitation to the contrary is stated in the transfer, i.e., the transferred property is deemed a gift to the charitable purposes and objects of the corporation. No technical words or further manifestations of general charitable intent are necessary in order to create such a trust. *See Wooten v. Fitz-Gerald*, 440 S.W.2d at 723. Because a charitable corporation is organized for the benefit of the public, and not for private profit or its own benefit, the public has a beneficial interest in all the property of a public benefit, non-profit corporation. Such a corporation has legal title to the property but may use it only in furtherance of its charitable purposes.

The property deeded by Hammond to HCM, without any express or contrary limitation, was nevertheless subject to the implicit limitation of use for educational purposes within the meaning of paragraph (3) by reference to the stated corporate purposes. The property was used as collateral, before being sold, for the purchase of another piece of realty, in turn used to purchase the piece of property remaining at dissolution. This latter property was purchased for consideration furnished by the corporation and was, of necessity, subject to the limitations imposed on the corporation by the terms of its own articles of incorporation.

We hold that the real property and personalty were assets received and held by the corporation, whether from donation or purchase, subject to limitations permitting their use only for educational purposes, *by reference to the stated purposes set forth in the article of incorporation*. They were not purchased or donated subject to condition requiring their return or transfer elsewhere if the corporation should later dissolve. As such, they fall squarely within the provisions of article 1396-6.02 A(3). We further hold that the acceptance of such assets from donors established a charitable trust for the declared purposes as effectively as though the assets had been accepted subject to an express limitation providing that the gift was held in trust solely for such charitable purposes. *Pacific Home v. Los Angeles County*, 41 Cal. 2d 844, 264 P.2d 539, 542 (1953).

The directors were, accordingly, under a statutory duty to distribute the remaining assets to charitable organizations pursuing similar purposes. Instead, they attempted to distribute the corporate assets indirectly through the Hammond estate to three of the four directors, for their personal gain. This necessarily constitutes a breach of their fiduciary duty. *See Peterson v. Greenway Parks Home Owners Association*, 408 S.W.2d 261, 265-67 (Tex. Civ. App.—Dallas 1966, writ ref'd n.r.e.). Article 1396-6.02 A(3) of the TNPCA required the directors of HCM to transfer its assets upon dissolution to entities engaged in activities substantially similar to those of HCM. To permit the transfer of donated or acquired assets to non-charitable entities would defeat both the intent of donors and the purposes to which such assets were dedicated upon their acquisition, and permit the directors to profit from the dissolution of the charity. It seems fair to conclude that appellant's interpretation of 6.02 A(3) would encourage the dissolution of ongoing charities and the distribution of assets, directly or obliquely, to the directors serving at the time of dissolution.

The State contends that "[b]y their very incorporation for purely charitable and benevolent purposes [charitable corporations] have made a contract with the State and with the beneficiaries named in the charters effectually constituting those in charge of the enterprise *trustees of an express trust, and their charters in their last analysis and in their legal effect become declarations of trust.*" *Santa Rosa Infirmary v. City of San Antonio*, 259 S.W. 926, 935 (Tex. Comm'n App. 1924, judgment adopted) (emphasis added). We agree. This contention, and the case cited, confer additional authority for our deducing the same conclusions reached by the California and Nebraska courts: the articles of incorporation in the case at bar established an organization constituting a public charitable trust, in perpetuity, enforceable and subject to the same corrective measures available to protect any other charitable trust in the event of fiduciary breach by its directors. Because HCM was incorporated for purely educational, and therefore charitable, purposes, it functioned as a public charity whose directors managed the charity and its assets as trustees of an express trust. *Id.* at 935.

Thus, it would fall to the Attorney General as a representative of the State to take action to remedy the "use or appropriation of the trust estate ... for purposes of private gain or ... [for purposes] ... inconsistent with their charter provisions." *Id.* at 935. Imposition of a constructive public charitable trust upon breach of a fiduciary relationship is a well established remedy for the breach. *See Slay v. Bennett Trust*, 143 Tex. 621, 640, 187 S.W.2d 377, 388 (1945); [additional citations omitted].

Because our law favors the protection and preservation of charitable trusts, the trial court properly impressed the assets of the dissolved HCM with a public charitable trust in perpetuity and correctly applied the doctrine of *cy pres*, as embodied in art. 1396-6.02 A(3) of the TNPCA, to transfer the assets to the "New Conservatory," an organization dedicated to a similar, if not identical, purpose.

We overrule the point of error. The judgment of the trial court is affirmed.

Notes and Questions

1. Settlor created a trust to pay for the expenses of law students who attend your law school. Settlor stated that the trust income was to be divided equally among the law students to offset their tuition and living expenses. When the trust was originally created, the trust generated enough income to pay about one credit's worth of tuition per student per year. Due to Trustee's phenomenal investing abilities, the trust income is now enough to pay 100% of the tuition of all law students and give each a sizeable living allowance as well. The undergraduate students are jealous and petition the court for cy pres. They claim that the money would be better spent subsidizing undergraduate expenses because the trust would then benefit a greater number of students who are pursuing diverse occupations. Should the court grant cy pres? This example is loosely based on the 1986 California Superior Court of Marin County case of *In re Estate of Buck* as found in 21 U.S.F.L. Rev. 691 (1987).

2. How should a settlor take the potential application of cy pres into account when preparing the trust?

3. *See* Examples & Explanations § 20.10.1.2.

2.   By the Parties

a. *The Settlor*

Read Trust Code § 112.051.

Unlike under the common law, trusts are presumed revocable in Texas. A trust may, of course, be made irrevocable by its express terms.

The settlor may not enlarge the duties of the trustee without obtaining the trustee's express consent.

Subsection (c) augments § 112.004, the Statute of Frauds provision, by requiring a written trust to be revoked, modified, or amended in writing even if the trust originally would not have had to be in writing (e.g., an oral trust of personal property).

See Examples & Explanations § 20.10.2.1.

SANDERSON v. AUBREY

Texas Civil Appeals—Fort Worth 1971
472 S.W.2d 286
writ ref'd n.r.e.

MASSEY, Chief Justice.

The question posed by the instant appeal is whether the attempted revocation of a trust was effective. Holding that such was effective, judgment is affirmed.

In Texas "Every trust shall be revocable by the trustor during his lifetime, unless expressly made irrevocable by the terms of the instrument creating the same or by a supplement or amendment thereto." Vernon's, Ann. Civ. St., Title 125A, and "The Texas Trust Act", Art 7425b et seq., specifically Sec. 41, "Revocable unless expressly made irrevocable".

Restatement of the Law, Trusts, and under Chapter 10, "The Termination and Modification of the Trust", Sec. 330, "Revocation of Trust by Settlor", Subsection (i), "Where no method of revocation specified", contains language as follows:

"If the settlor reserves a power to revoke the trust but does not specify any mode of revocation, the power can be exercised in any manner which sufficiently manifests the intention of the settlor to revoke the trust.

"Any definitive manifestation by the settlor of his intention that the trust should be forthwith revoked is sufficient. * * * It is not necessary, however, that the communication should be received by the trustee. * * *

"A revocation may be effective even though the settlor does not attempt to communicate his decision to the trustee. * * *

"Even though the settlor has revoked the trust, the trustee incurs no liability for acts done by him in accordance with the terms of the trust before he receives notice of the revocation. *A beneficiary, however, who has received the trust property after the trust has been revoked will not be permitted to retain the property merely because neither he nor the trustee had notice of the revocation of the trust when he received the property.*"
(Emphasis supplied.)

See also 18 A.L.R.2d, p. 1010, Annotation: "Exercise by will of trustor's reserved power to revoke or modify inter vivos trust"; Restatement of the Law, Trusts, in the previously cited Chapter 10, Sec. 330, the discussion under Subsection (e), "Where creation of trust incomplete", and under Chapter 2, "Creation of a Trust", Section 57, "Disposition Inter Vivos Where Settlor Reserves Power to Revoke, Modify or Control". See also the discussion at Section 58 under the "Comment" on Subsection (1) thereof at (b) "Revocation of tentative trust". Though not directly upon the matter to be resolved on appeal language found in these authorities is informative and worthy of attention.

Factual background: A Mrs. Lucas was the settlor. She died, testate, in September, 1969. In May, 1954, she conveyed the real estate interest in question to a Mr. Eskridge, trustee, to hold the same in trust for her grandson during his minority—to be conveyed to him upon becoming 21 years of age. (This grandson is the appellant who received an adverse ruling in the trial court.) In July, 1965, Mrs. Lucas made her will. On the theory that the *inter vivos* trust instrument of May, 1954, was of testamentary character and might be revoked by her will she provided in the body of the will, by reference to it, that: "This instrument is specifically included in the revocation clause above (where she had revoked all prior wills, etc.), *and same is now formally revoked* because the beneficiary of said instrument * * * has been a bitter disappointment to me. * * *" (Emphasis supplied.)

There was no publication of the will. Only the settlor and her attorney knew of it. No notice of revocation by any means was conveyed to either the trustee or the *cestui que trust*, the latter individual being the appellant grandson of the settlor. In September, 1969, Mrs. Lucas died. Later in that same September the trustee executed an instrument conveying his interest in the subject realty to the appellant, he having reached the age of 21 years. Mrs. Lucas' will, having never been revoked, was admitted to probate in March, 1970. By it Annie Eva Aubrey, the appellee, was granted that same interest in realty which had been the subject of the trust. By this there was a first publication of the will and the revocation of trust recited therein. The trustee and the appellant (trust beneficiary) received their first notice that there had been a revocation of the trust in consequence of this publication.

We are not troubled with the fact that Mrs. Lucas, when she made her will, erroneously deemed the trust to have been of testamentary character, and, in consequence, one which by her 1965 will she could properly revoke. What we are concerned with is whether the trust revocation language in such will—which will could not have effect as such until the date of her death—operated and was immediately effective as a revocation of the trust. Concededly, if either the trustee or the settlor's grandson had received notice thereof by a copy of the will or by information otherwise there would have been an effective revocation.

The situation is not to be distinguished from one hypothesized, wherein among the effects of Mrs. Lucas found after her death in September, 1969, a written instrument was discovered wherein she had written to the effect that the *inter vivos* trust created for the benefit of the appellant in May, 1954, "is now formally revoked".

Our holding is that there would be an effective revocation. Here, in view of the express written language of Mrs. Lucas, as settlor, there was evidenced a "definitive manifestation" of like revocation as of the date she signed her instrument of will in July, 1965. The language of revocation appearing as part of her will was not testamentary in its operation or effect so as to become effective later on and as of the date of her death, but actually became effective on the date of the will (July, 1965). Since as of the time of her signatory action the trust had been extinguished the property "reverted" to her so that she could dispose of it by will. In view of her will it became the property of the appellee, Annie Eva Aubrey, upon her death in September, 1969.

Appellant's attorney concedes that there is no Texas authority decisive of the point. However, there is pertinent *dicta* in a case cited, Appling v. Jay, 390 S.W.2d 799 (Texarkana, Tex. Civ. App., 1965, writ ref., n.r.e.), in language under syllabus No. 3 (on page 802). The court observed that an instrument such as the will under consideration might have a dual character, i. e. be testamentary in part, but operative *in praesenti* in other parts. (Citing 94 C.J.S. Wills § 165, p. 963.)

Under the citation from Corpus Juris Secundum is to be found the case of First National Bank of Cincinnati v. Oppenheimer, 190 N.E.2d 70 (Ohio Probate Court, Hamilton County, 1963) which is in accord. Therein by the exact test applicable under the aforementioned provisions of the Restatement, altered in accord with necessity by reason of a method of revocation specified, was a test made of the efficacy of the revocation under consideration by the Ohio Court.

We have concluded that proper disposition of the appeal should be likewise determined. Thereby is demonstrated the appellee's right to prevail.

Supplying additional logic for our conclusion are principles of law applicable to wills. When an original will has been made and there is a subsequent will executed upon declaration therein contained that "all wills by me heretofore made are revoked", the revocation of the prior will takes effect *in praesenti* as of the time the new will is executed. Should said new will be revoked or annulled by a subsequently executed instrument or by the testator's intentional destruction of it the will which had been earlier revoked would not be reinstated in consequence. Indeed, if there should occur a death of such a person it would be correct to say that he had died intestate, because no former will which had been revoked could be said to have become revived. 61 Tex. Jur. 2d, p. 209, "Wills", Sec. 95, "Recession of revoking instrument as revival of prior will."

Judgment is affirmed.

Notes

1. In *Soeffe v. Jones*, 270 S.W.3d 617 (Tex. App.—San Antonio 2008, no pet.), Brother and Sister disputed the construction an amendment to Mother's trust. Brother argued that the amendment only added to the property to which Sister was entitled under the original trust instrument but left the property to which he was entitled intact. On the other hand, Daughter claimed that the amendment revoked the entire property distribution provided for in the original trust causing property originally given to Brother to pass under the trust's residuary clause permitting her to share in that property. The trial court agreed with Daughter and Brother appealed.

The appellate court reversed. The court began its analysis by recognizing that a trust amendment does not revoke a provision of the original trust "unless the words used in the amendment clearly show the [settlor's] intent to revoke the trust." *Id.* at 629. The court studied the trust and the amendment and held as a matter of law that the instruments are unambiguous. The amendment merely added to Sister's entitlement by giving her certain properties to which Brother was originally entitled under the original trust. The amendment did not act to revoke gifts of other property to Brother. The amendment expressly stated that the new terms "shall be added" to the trust; there was no language revoking other gifts not disposed of by the amendment.

Accordingly, trust amendments need to be extremely clear to avoid later disputes. Prudent practice may be to restate completely the dispositive provisions rather than change them "bit-by-bit."

2. In *Gordon v. Gordon*, No. 11-14-00086-CV, 2016 WL 1274076 (Tex. App.—Eastland Mar. 31, 2016, pet. denied), a husband and his wife created a revocable trust which required a revocation to be in a signed acknowledged writing delivered to the trustee. Thereafter, they executed a joint will which provided that the will overrides "any prior allocations described in trust documents." After the husband's death, a dispute arose as to whether the property they had transferred to the trust would be governed by the terms of the trust or the will. The wife claimed that the trust controlled and the executor of the husband's will contended that the will controlled. The trial court held that the will provision did not act to revoke the trust and thus the trust assets pass under the terms of the trust. The executor appealed.

The appellate court affirmed. The court explained that the language of the will addressing the disposition of property was testamentary in nature, that is, it would take effect after death even though the language of the will revoking previous wills was effective immediately. The will did not contain a provision revoking the trust which complied with the requirements for revocation set forth in the trust.

b. The Trustee

The trustee normally lacks the power to make unilateral changes to the terms of the trust. However, there are a few situations where the trustee may make significant changes to the trust.

Read Trust Code § 112.057.

Section 112.057 allows trustees to divide or merge trusts if the result does not impair the rights of any beneficiary or adversely affect the achievement of the purposes of the original trust. Prior to January 1, 2006, such an action was allowed only if it would achieve significant tax savings.

Read Trust Code § 113.026.

Section 113.026 permits the trustee, under specified circumstances, to exercise cy pres to replace a charitable beneficiary without the necessity of obtaining a court order if the charity (1) did not exist when the interest vested, (2) ceases to exist, or (3) ceases to be charitable in nature.

See Examples & Explanations § 20.10.2.2.

c. The Beneficiaries

The beneficiaries may consent to a trust modification. *See* Trust Code § 114.005. The trustee should not rely on a consent unless all beneficiaries agree. Some courts may permit a modification even if all the beneficiaries do not agree provided the interests of the non-consenting beneficiaries are adequately protected. Consent may be difficult to obtain because some beneficiaries may be unborn or unascertainable. *See* Trust Code § 115.013.

d. The Beneficiaries Plus the Settlor

MUSICK v. REYNOLDS

Texas Appeals—Eastland 1990
798 S.W.2d 626
writ denied

ARNOT, Justice.

This is a summary judgment case. Steven Patrick Musick and John Kenneth Musick, appellants, brought a declaratory judgment action each seeking to establish a one-fourth ownership in the "Revised Ted Musick Trust," an irrevocable spendthrift trust. Because their ownership in the trust had been previously litigated in a suit which had resulted in a settlement agreement, the trial court granted a summary judgment in favor of appellees: Joe Reynolds, present trustee of the trust; Rafael Gonzalez (R.G.) de Alba, former trustee of the trust; and Holly Lynne Musick and Susan Dee Warren Musick Walters, named beneficiaries under the trust. Because there is a material issue of fact as to whether appellants own an interest in a 100-acre tract of land, we reverse the judgment of the trial court and remand the cause for trial on the merits.

On March 10, 1972, Ted Musick executed a document entitled the "Revised Ted Musick Trust." The trust was made irrevocable for a period of ten years. The relevant portions of the trust are as follows:

I.

WHEREAS, the said property is the separate property of Ted Musick; and, whereas, it is necessary for him to receive the rents, profits, increase and income of all said property hereinafter described as a maintenance for the property; as a maintenance for the proper care and education of his children and any other children born to him or legally adopted by him, who are designated as beneficiaries of this Trust, SUSAN DEE WARREN MUSICK WALTERS, age 22 and HOLLY LYNN MUSICK, age 14 and the necessary care of his ex-wife, ALMITA H. MUSICK and the necessary care, education and maintenance of his nephews, STEVEN PATRICK MUSICK and JOHN KENNETH MUSICK, all beneficiaries of this trust.

XVI.

No interest or any part of the interest of any beneficiary of this Trust shall be subject in any event to sale, alienation, hypothecation, pledge, transfer, or subject to any debt of said beneficiary or any judgment against said beneficiary or process in aid of execution of said judgment. On the same day that the trust was created, Ted Musick funded the trust by conveying to the trustee two separate pieces of real property identified by the litigants as the "Woodlands 618 Property" and the "San Jacinto Street Property."

In 1979, litigation styled Hollingsworth v. Lucas, Cause No. 594,300, was pending in the 113th District Court in Harris County. The basis of that lawsuit was various claims of ownership in four tracts of land. One of the tracts of land, designated as "TRACT NO. 2," was the "San Jacinto Street Property." The parties involved in that lawsuit were: Mary Ann Musick (appellants' mother and widow of Levoy Musick [Ted Musick's brother]); TWI Development Corporation; Ted Musick (individually and as agent for and beneficiary of the "Revised Ted Musick Trust"); R.G. de Alba (trustee of the "Revised Ted Musick Trust"); Almita Musick (ex-wife of Ted Musick); Susan Dee Warren Musick Walters; Holly Lynne Musick; Steven Musick; and John Musick.

To settle the dispute as to the ownership of the four tracts of land, the parties entered into a settlement agreement in 1979. The parties agreed that title to the "San Jacinto Street Property" would be vested in the trust. The agreement expressed the intention of the parties that each appellant retain his undivided one-sixth beneficial interest in the "San Jacinto Street Property" under the terms of the trust. To assure appellants that the interest would be maintained, Ted Musick agreed to relinquish any power to terminate the trust as to appellants' interest. Also, the trustee agreed to execute a deed of one-sixth interest to each appellant that would come into effect in the event: (a) the trust was terminated by the settlor, Ted Musick; (b) the trust was terminated by the trustee under the terms of the trust; or (c) Ted Musick revised the trust in an attempt to change appellants' interest in this tract.

Pursuant to the settlement agreement, the parties executed various documents. On May 23, 1979, Mary Ann Musick, TWI Development Corporation, and the two appellants conveyed by quitclaim deed any right, title, or interest, legal or beneficial, that they had in the "San Jacinto Street Property" to R.G. de Alba, trustee for the "Ted Musick Trust." Ted Musick executed a "Limited Renunciation of Power to Terminate Trust" on May 24, 1979. On May 23, 1979, R.G. de Alba, as trustee, conveyed to each individual appellant an undivided one-sixth interest in the "San Jacinto Street Property," subject to the three conditions precedent.

With regard to the "Woodlands 618 Property," the parties in the litigation recognized that neither Mary Ann Musick nor TWI had any interest in this property. Appellants had a one-sixth interest each by the terms of the trust. The settlement agreement recites that appellants agreed to quitclaim this beneficial interest in this tract as an "inducement to Ted Musick and to the remaining beneficiaries of the Trust to approve and enter into this settlement agreement." On June 11, 1979, by quitclaim, appellants conveyed whatever right, title, or interest that they had in the "Woodlands 618 Property" to R.G. de Alba as trustee for the trust. The settlement agreement also provided that the quitclaim deed would not pass any title which appellants may subsequently acquire in the 618 acres.

Almita Musick, ex-wife of Ted Musick and named beneficiary in the trust, died on March 29, 1981. The "Woodlands 618 Property" was sold in April 1981. Ted Musick died on December 14, 1981, which was during the period of time that the trust was, by its terms, irrevocable. His will provided that all of his property was to go into the trust. Musick's property included 100 acres of land in Harris County conveyed to Musick in December 1980. The 100-acre tract was ultimately sold to Harris County in August 1985.

On May 8, 1985, appellants brought this suit seeking a determination that they were equal beneficiaries with Holly Lynne Musick and Susan Dee Warren Musick Walters of the entire trust estate. The substitute trustee, Joe Reynolds, pursuant to the settlement agreement and quitclaim deeds, refused to apportion any interest in the trust to appellants.

The trial court, after both sides moved for summary judgment, granted appellees' motion and denied appellants' motion. The trial court specifically stated in its judgment that: (1) [T]he [appellants] have no right or interest in the real property commonly referred to as the Woodlands 618 Property; (2) [T]he [appellants] have no interest in that certain 100 acres of land located in Harris County, Texas, conveyed ... by Ted Musick, et al; (3) [T]he [appellants] are entitled to none of the proceeds derived from the sale of said 100 acres to the County of Harris by Ted Musick, et al; (4) [T]he [appellants] have an undivided one-sixth (1/6) interest in the parcel of property commonly referred to as the San Jacinto Street Property.

In their first point of error, appellants argue that the trial court erred in not granting their motion for summary judgment. In their second point of error, appellants argue that the trial court erred in granting appellees' motion for summary judgment.

When reviewing a summary judgment, this Court will adhere to the following standards: (1) The movant for summary judgment has the burden of showing that there is no genuine issue of material fact and that it is entitled to a judgment as a matter of law; (2) In deciding whether there is a disputed material fact issue precluding summary judgment, evidence favorable to the non-movant will be taken as true; and (3) Every reasonable inference must be indulged in favor of the non-movant and any doubts resolved in its favor. Goswami v. Metropolitan Savings and Loan Association, 751 S.W.2d 487, 491 (Tex. 1988); Nixon v. Mr. Property Management Company, Inc., 690 S.W.2d 546, 548-49 (Tex. 1985).

When both appellants' and appellees' motions for summary judgment are properly before the trial court, all evidence accompanying both motions is considered in deciding them. DeBord v. Muller, 446 S.W.2d 299, 301 (Tex. 1969). In discharging their burden of demonstrating that the trial court's decision was erroneous because appellees failed to establish as a matter of law the absence of an issue of material fact, appellants must point out any fact question which allegedly existed on material issues. Kimble v. Aetna Casualty and Surety Company, 767 S.W.2d 846, 847 (Tex. App.—Amarillo 1989, writ den'd).

Appellants' points of error are predicated in part on the proposition that an irrevocable spendthrift trust cannot be modified. In Sayers v. Baker, 171 S.W.2d 547 (Tex. Civ. App.—Eastland 1943, no writ), this Court held that if a settlor of a trust is alive and all of the beneficiaries of an irrevocable spendthrift trust consent (and there being no incapacity to consent by any of the parties), the settlor and all of the beneficiaries may consent to a modification or termination of the trust. Because an irrevocable spendthrift trust can be modified, we reject appellants' contentions. See also Becknal v. Atwood, 518 S.W.2d 593 (Tex. Civ. App.—Amarillo 1975, no writ).

Having determined, as a matter of law, that an irrevocable spendthrift trust can be modified, we will now examine the summary judgment proof to determine if the trust was in fact modified. The summary judgment proof before the trial court was as follows: (1) the "Revised Ted Musick Trust"; (2) a 1972 deed executed by Ted Musick, individually and as settlor, conveying the "Woodlands 618 Property" to Janet Sue Weeren, trustee; (3) a 1972 deed executed by Ted Musick conveying the "San Jacinto Street Property" to Janet Sue Weeren, Trustee; (4) the 1979 settlement agreement in which all of the parties agreed to settle the litigation styled Hollingsworth v. Lucas; (5) an affidavit by Joe Reynolds (the present trustee of the trust) which stated the present status of the corpus of the trust; (6) appellants' 1979 quitclaim deed, executed individually and as beneficiaries of the trust, conveying whatever right, title, and interest they owned in the "Woodlands 618 Property" to R.G. de Alba, as trustee of the trust; (7) appellants' 1979 quitclaim deed conveying whatever right, title, and interest they owned in the "San Jacinto Street Property" to R.G. de Alba, as trustee for the trust; (8) R.G. de Alba's 1979 deed to appellants conveying an undivided one-sixth interest each in the "San Jacinto Street Property" subject to the conditions precedent; (9) a 1979 "Limited Renunciation of Power to Terminate Trust" executed by Ted Musick; (10) Ted Musick's will and probate proceedings; (11) a warranty deed conveying approximately 100 acres to "Ted Musick, Agent"; and (12) a special warranty deed conveying the 100 acres to Harris County, Texas.

There is no material issue of fact that appellants executed the 1979 settlement agreement. The settlement agreement recites that its purpose is to determine the ownership of certain tracts of land including the "San Jacinto Street Property." To settle the Hollingsworth v. Lucas litigation, appellants conveyed any and all beneficial interest they had in the trust as to the "Woodlands 618 Property." In exchange, they received assurances that their undivided one-sixth interest each in the "San Jacinto Street Property" would not be lost. As consideration for entering into the settlement agreement, Ted Musick executed the "Limited Renunciation of Power to Terminate Trust" which expressly prohibited Ted Musick from doing anything which might affect appellants' interest in the "San Jacinto Street Property." Appellants argue that the quitclaim deeds they executed were legal nullities because a beneficiary cannot alienate his interest in a spendthrift trust and because appellants' interest in the trust was only a future contingency or expectancy at the time of the execution of the quitclaim deeds. We do not agree with appellants' assertions. The settlement agreement and quitclaim deeds were executed to effectuate a modification of the trust in conformity with the settlement agreement.

Appellants argue that, even if an irrevocable spendthrift trust can be modified and if the trust was in fact modified, the trust was not properly modified because "all" of the parties did not consent to the modification. Paragraph No. I of the trust provided that "any other children born to [Ted Musick] or legally adopted by him, who are designated as beneficiaries of this Trust" would be additional beneficiaries under the trust. Because these unborn beneficiaries did not consent to the modification, appellants urge that "all" of the beneficiaries did not consent to the modification. It is undisputed that, at Ted Musick's death, no children other than his two named beneficiary daughters had been born to or adopted by him. Therefore, all of the beneficiaries consented to the modification. Moreover, a trust can be modified without the consent of unascertained beneficiaries if their interests are not prejudiced by the modification. RESTATEMENT (SECOND) OF TRUSTS § 338(2) (1959). It is apparent, through the modification, that an additional beneficiary's interest would not have been prejudiced because appellants reduced their present interest in the trust to a mere undivided one-sixth interest each in the "San Jacinto Street Property."

Having determined that an irrevocable trust can be modified and having determined that the trust was in fact modified, we will address appellants' contention that the trial court erred in finding that they have no interest in the 100-acre tract of land and that they are not entitled to the proceeds of the sale of the 100-acre tract of land. Appellants urge that there is an issue of fact as to whether they are entitled to an interest in the proceeds from the sale of the 100-acre tract of land. We agree.

The summary judgment proof includes a warranty deed dated December 1, 1980, from Frederick H. Weihrich and wife to "Ted Musick, Agent," conveying a 100-acre tract of land and securing a $427,185.78 purchase price obligation with a vendor's lien.

Ted Musick died on March 29, 1981. Ted Musick's will devised all of his property to the trust. Paragraph No. V of the "Revised Ted Musick Trust" provides: The Grantor reserves the right to himself or to any other person at any time by will or deed to add to the corpus of the Trust created herein, and any property so added shall be held, administered and distributed under the terms of this agreement. The inventory and appraisement of Musick's estate do not include the 100- acre tract, even though the summary judgment proof does not reveal any conveyance by "Ted Musick, Agent," prior to his death.

The "Woodlands 618 Property" was sold in 1981. This deed is not included in the summary judgment evidence. However, the summary judgment evidence does include a deed of trust dated May 15, 1981, from Stacy Crumley, trustee, to Ted Musick. This instrument conveyed a 627-acre tract of land which included the "Woodlands" 618 acres. This instrument was given to secure other indebtedness and recites that Stacy Crumley, trustee, assumed the $427,185.78 obligation owed to the Weihriches by "Ted Musick, Agent," for the purchase of the 100-acre tract. The lien is given in security for Ted Musick; R.G. de Alba, trustee of the "Ted Musick Trust"; Almita Musick; Susan Dee Warren Musick Walters; and Holly Lynne Musick.

On August 22, 1985, Joe Reynolds, acting as Independent Executor of the Estate of Ted Musick and acting as successor trustee of the "Revised Ted Musick Trust"; Susan D. Bristol (formerly Walters); and Holly Lynne Musick conveyed the 100-acre tract of land in dispute to Harris County.

In his affidavit to support appellees' motion for summary judgment, Joe Reynolds states that the "100 acres were sold to Harris County as a part of the consideration of the Woodlands 618 Property sale."

Appellees assert that the record conclusively establishes that the 100 acres was acquired in exchange for the "Woodlands 618 Property"; therefore, appellants are not entitled to any interest in this tract. We disagree. The Crumley deed of trust states that the purchaser of the 618 acres assumed the obligation owed on the 100 acres. Yet, the record shows that title to the 100 acres was in "Ted Musick, Agent," at his death. Ted Musick's estate passed to the trust. However, the affidavit of Joe Reynolds states that the primary assets of the trust are the "San Jacinto Street Property" and the remaining proceeds of the sale of the 618 acres.

There appears to be a material issue of fact as to how the 100-acre tract became part of the corpus of the trust: was it in fact in exchange for "Woodlands 618 Property" in which appellants owned no interest or was it in fact devised to the trust by Musick's will in which event appellants may own an interest. To the extent that proceeds from the sale of appellees'

"Woodlands 618 Property" was used to pay for the purchase of the 100-acre tract now in trust, appellees may be entitled to a reimbursement.

Reviewing all of the summary judgment evidence, we hold as a matter of law that the settlor and all of the beneficiaries modified the "Revised Ted Musick Trust." However, because there are material issues of fact as to whether appellants owned an interest in the proceeds of the sale of the 100- acre tract, the trial court erred in granting appellees' motion for summary judgment. Therefore, appellants' second point of error is sustained. We overrule appellants' first point of error in which they complain that the trial court erred in not granting their motion for summary judgment.

The judgment of the trial court is reversed, and the cause is remanded for trial.

e. Family Settlements

Because of potential or ongoing litigation, trust beneficiaries and trustees often try to reach an amicable resolution of their differences. As a result of these negotiations, the parties may agree to a settlement which includes various changes to the terms of the trust. Courts look favorably at these types of agreements because they seek to preserve property and reduce the amount of trust property wasted on litigation expenses. In addition, non-judicial settlements encourage harmony among the parties who are in many cases family members.

See Examples & Explanations § 20.10.2.4.

L. TRUST TERMINATION

Most trusts eventually terminate unless they are charitable or are permitted to continue indefinitely unfettered by the Rule Against Perpetuities because the state has abolished the Rule. Upon termination, all legal and equitable title to any remaining trust property becomes reunited in the hands of the remainder beneficiaries.

1.   Methods

a. Express Terms of the Trust

Read Trust Code § 112.052.

b. Revocation by the Settlor

Read Trust Code § 112.051.

If a settlor specifies a method of trust revocation, the settlor must comply exactly with that method for a revocation to be effective. For example, in *McClure v. JPMorgan Chase Bank*, 147 S.W.3d 648 (Tex. App.—Fort Worth 2004, pet. denied), Settlor created an inter vivos trust. Settlor retained the power to revoke the trust provided the revocation was in writing and the writing was delivered to Trustee. Later, Settlor executed a will leaving the majority of her estate to this trust. After Settlor' death, a dispute arose as to whether a subsequent holographic will operated to revoke the trust so that trust property would pass under the terms of this will rather than the trust. The trial court granted a summary judgment holding that the holographic will did not revoke the trust.

The appellate court agreed. The court began its analysis by recognizing that if a settlor specifies the method of revocation, that method must be followed for an attempted revocation to be effective. The court explained that the key to deciding the case was whether this holographic will was delivered to Trustee prior to Settlor's death. After examining the evidence, the court found nothing to raise a fact issue about Trustee's lack of receipt of a notice of revocation. Accordingly, the court affirmed the summary judgment that Settlor had not effectively revoked the trust.

c. *Exhaustion of Trust Property*

Read Trust Code § 112.005.

d. *Uneconomic*

The trustee may terminate an uneconomic trust if the conditions listed below are satisfied. *Read* Trust Code § 112.059.

- Notice is given to (1) current distributees of trust income or principal, (2) permissible distributees of trust income or principal, and (3) future distributees, or permissible distributees, if the trust were to terminate and no powers of appointment were exercised.
- The total value of trust property is less than $50,000.
- "[T]he trustee concludes after considering the purpose of the trust and the nature of the trust assets that the value of the trust property is insufficient to justify the continued cost of administration."
- The trustee's possession of the power would not cause trust assets to be included in the trustee's estate for federal estate tax purposes.
- The trust does not involve an easement for conservation or preservation.

When the trust terminates, the trustee must distribute the property "in a manner consistent with the purposes of the trust."

e. Court Order

Read Trust Code § 112.054.

f. Merger

Read Trust Code § 112.034.

2. Trustee's Duties Upon Trust Termination

Read Trust Code § 112.052.

The trustee's powers do not end immediately upon trust termination. Section 112.052 permits the trustee to continue to exercise trust powers for the reasonable period of time necessary to wind up the affairs of the trust and distribute to the remainder beneficiaries. The length of this period depends on the circumstances of each case and the type of property involved. More sophisticated investments and businesses may take longer to wrap up and transfer to the beneficiary than other assets which need a mere change in registration or physical delivery.

See Examples & Explanations § 20.11.8.

Chapter Four

TRUST ENFORCEMENT

If everything proceeds smoothly, the judicial system is not involved with the administration of a trust. The trustee invests property, makes distributions to beneficiaries, and does everything else necessary to carry out the settlor's wishes without court supervision. The trustee does not need to seek court permission or authorization. However, if a dispute arises which cannot be settled amicably, the aggrieved parties are forced to seek the assistance of the courts to enforce their rights.

Read Trust Code § 114.008 (providing a non-exclusive listing of possible remedies for a breach of trust).

A. PROCEDURAL MATTERS

1. Standing

Read Trust Code § 115.011(a).

A person must have standing to bring an action to enforce a trust. Beneficiaries and trustees have typically have standing because they hold title to trust property. In *Moon v. Lesikar*, 230 S.W.3d 800 (Tex. App.— Houston [14th Dist.] 2007, pet. denied), the court acknowledged that normally a beneficiary is an interested person who would have standing to bring an action. However in this case, the settlor's daughter, a mere contingent beneficiary, was complaining about a transaction made by the settlor of a revocable trust. The court recognized that this was a matter of first impression in Texas and thus examined cases from other jurisdictions. The court concluded that since her father was both the settlor and the trustee and had full power to revoke the trust, the vesting of his daughter's contingent interest was subject to the father's discretion until his death and thus she lacked standing to complain about an alleged improper sale of trust property.

Normally, persons other than the settlor or beneficiaries lack the ability to meddle in trust affairs because they have no legally recognized basis to support their actions. Even the settlor may lack standing because the settlor has conveyed away all title to the property. The settlor may, however, have standing in some other capacity such as by retaining the power to revoke, serving as a trustee, or being named as a beneficiary.

Some states permit individuals who do not hold title to trust property to enforce a trust. These jurisdictions grant standing to "interested persons" and then define interested persons broadly. For example, the Texas definition in Trust Code § 111.004(7) provides that "whether a person [other than a beneficiary or trustee] is an interested person may vary from time to time and must be determined according to the particular purposes of and matter involved."

The Texas attorney general has standing to enforce a charitable trust. The attorney general's involvement in charitable trusts is covered later in this chapter.

2.   Parties

Read Trust Code § 115.011(b).

Notes and Questions

1.   Who are the necessary parties to a trust action?

2.   A suit against a trust must be brought against the trustee, that is, the legal representative of the trust. Accordingly, for a judgment to be rendered against a trust, "its trustee must be properly before the trial court as a result of service, acceptance, or waiver of process, or an appearance. * * * Stated differently, for relief to be granted against a trust, the trust—through its trustee—must be made a party to the action." *In re Ashton*, 266 S.W.3d 602, 604 (Tex. App.—Dallas 2008, no pet.) (explaining that the fact that the trustee in his individual capacity was a party to the lawsuit did not cure the defect).

3.   In *In re Estate of Webb*, 266 S.W.3d 544 (Tex. App.—Fort Worth 2008, pet. denied), will and testamentary trust beneficiaries reached a settlement with respect to various will and trust matters. The beneficiaries then sought to modify the trust under Trust Code § 112.054 to bring it into compliance with their settlement. The trustee objected claiming that he was not a party to the settlement. The trial court held that the trustee was not a necessary party to the modification action and granted the beneficiaries' motion to strike the trustee's intervention in the case.

The appellate court reversed. The court determined that the trustee was a necessary party to the settlement as well as a necessary party to any action to modify the trust. Trust Code § 115.011 provides that the trustee is a necessary party if the "trustee is serving at the time the action is filed." The court explained that under Probate Code § 37 [recodified as Estates Code § 101.001, title to property vests in the beneficiary immediately upon a testator's death unless the will provides otherwise. The testator's will did not provide otherwise and thus when the testator died, the trustee, as a beneficiary of the property albeit it trust, had title to the property. Thereafter, the trustee accepted the trust and thus he was serving as a trustee making him a necessary party to the action. Likewise, because the trustee was a beneficiary of the will, a family settlement agreement would not be binding upon him without his consent.

3. Jurisdiction

Read Trust Code § 115.001.

Jurisdiction over trust matters is typically in the district court. *See* Trust Code § 115.001(a). However, if the county also has a statutory probate court, the statutory probate court also has jurisdiction. *See* Trust Code § 115.001(d) & Est. Code §§ 32.006 & 32.007.

Section 115.001(a) provides an extensive list of actions over which the court has jurisdiction. Although the list is not exhaustive, it would be difficult to come up with a trust issue that would not fit into one of the statutory categories. A district court has jurisdiction over any proceeding by or against a trustee and any proceeding concerning a trust even if the type of action is not included in the enumerated list. Trust Code § 115.001(a-1).

Of particular importance is § 115.001(a)(8), the ultimate escape clause. The court has the ability to relieve a trustee from any duty, limitation, or restriction which is imposed by the trust instrument or the Trust Code. Thus, a trustee in breach of trust who has an equitable argument that the breach should be forgiven, may "beg" the court for "mercy."

Subsection (b) provides that the court has all of the powers of a court of equity such as the ability to apply cy pres, issue injunctions, and appoint receivers.

The court does not have continuing supervision over the trust unless the court order expressly so provides. See Trust Code § 115.001(c).

4. Venue

Read Trust Code § 115.002.

NOTES AND QUESTIONS

1. Where is venue proper if there is one (and only one) trustee and that trustee is not a corporation?

2. Where is venue proper if either (1) any trustee is a corporation or (2) more than one individual trustee is serving?

3.   When may a court transfer a case from one county of proper venue to another county of proper venue?

4.   When may a court transfer a case upon agreement of the parties?

5.   Rules of Procedure

Read Trust Code § 115.012.

Unless the Trust Code provides otherwise, the Texas Rules of Civil Procedure apply.

6.   Virtual Representation

Read Trust Code § 115.013.

Section 115.013 provides for virtual representation under specified circumstances so that a court order may bind beneficiaries who did not actually agree because, for example, they are minors, unborn, or unascertained.

7.   Guardians and Attorneys ad Litem

Read Trust Code § 115.014.

The court may appoint a guardian ad litem to represent the interest of a minor, incapacitated, unborn, unascertained, etc., beneficiary. *See* Trust Code § 115.014(a). "At any point in a proceeding a court may appoint an attorney ad litem to represent any interest that the court considers necessary." *See* Trust Code 115.014(b). The guardians and attorneys ad litem are entitled to reasonable compensation for their services. *See* Trust Code § 115.014(d) & (e).

B.   REMEDIES AGAINST THE TRUSTEE

The trustee's job, I think, does not afford him such a happy lot.
In return for modest fees, he's subject to a constant squeeze.
And written in the trustee's bible is the rule: "You're always liable."
In view of his how can it be, that anyone would be trustee?[1]

---

[1]Daniel M. Schuyler, 56 Nw. U.L. Rev. 177, 189 (1961).

1.   Money Damages

Read Trust Code § 114.001.

A trustee is accountable for any profit made by the trustee through or arising out of the administration of the trust even though the profit does not result from a breach of trust. *See* Trust Code § 114.001(a). For example, if the trustee obtains knowledge of a good investment while working for the trust and then makes the investment for the trustee individually, the trustee will be responsible for any profit the trustee makes. In all other cases, however, the trustee must breach the trust before liability attaches. *See* Trust Code § 114.001(b).

See Examples & Explanations § 21.2.1.

a. Lost Value

The court may award the loss or depreciation in value to the trust property caused by the breach. The plaintiff must be able to demonstrate that the trustee's breach caused the loss but does not need to show that the trustee personally benefited from the breach. *See* Trust Code § 114.001(c)(1).

b. Profit Made by Trustee

The trustee is responsible for any profit the trustee gained by being a trustee, except for the trustee's compensation. The trustee is liable for the profit even if the trust did not suffer a loss because of the breach. *See* Trust Code § 114.001(c)(2).

c. Lost Profits

The court may hold the trustee liable for the profits the trust would have earned had the trustee not breached the trustee's fiduciary duties. These damages are more difficult to prove because of their speculative nature. *See* Trust Code § 114.001(c)(3).

d. Punitive Damages

An intentional breach of duty by the trustee is considered a tort. Consequently, the court may be able to justify an award of punitive damages. *See Interfirst Bank Dallas, N.A. v. Risser*, 739 S.W.2d 882 (Tex. App. — Texarkana 1987, no writ).

2.   Removal of Trustee

Read Trust Code § 113.082.

Section 113.082 explains the circumstances under which a trustee may be removed from office. Despite the use of the word "may," Texas courts have held that they must remove a trustee for the specific reasons enumerated in the statute such as for materially violating the trust or becoming insolvent. *See Akin v. Dahl*, 661 S.W.2d 911 (Tex. 1983). The 2003 Texas Legislature changed the statute by adding the phrase "in its discretion" after the term "may" to make it clear that whether or not to remove a trustee is always a discretionary decision of the court.

The court has broad discretion to remove a trustee "for other cause." However, courts are reluctant to remove a trustee because of dissent between the trustee and the beneficiaries, especially when the settlor appointed the trustee (as compared to a court-appointed trustee). For example, the settlor may have anticipated the beneficiaries' greed and wanted the trustee to stand firm against their demands.

See Examples & Explanations § 21.1.2.

DITTA v. CONTE

Texas Supreme Court 2009
52 Tex. Sup. Ct. J. 823

Justice Willett delivered the opinion of the Court.

The court of appeals held that this trustee-removal suit was barred by the four-year statute of limitations applicable to breach-of-fiduciary-duty suits. We disagree and hold that no statutory limitations period restricts a court's discretion to remove a trustee. A limitations period, while applicable to suits seeking damages for breach of fiduciary duty, has no place in suits that seek removal rather than recovery. Accordingly, we reverse the court of appeals' judgment that the case was time-barred and remand to that court for further proceedings.

I. Background

In 1987, Joseph and Doris Conte created the Joseph P. Conte Family Trust, an inter vivos trust. The Trust agreement named Joseph the original trustee. Upon Joseph's death in 1993, Doris began serving as co-trustee along with her two children, Susan and Joseph Jr. The co-trustees were obliged to create and fund three separate trusts for the primary benefit of Doris. The co-trustees were to distribute quarterly income from a management trust to Doris, as well as principal amounts requested by Doris for "her comfort, health, support and maintenance, in order to maintain" the equivalent lifestyle to which Doris was accustomed at the time of Joseph's death.

Initially, Joseph Jr. managed the Trust's day-to-day affairs. About two years later, Susan and Doris discovered that Joseph Jr. was not administering the Trust in accordance with its terms. This discovery heralded a proliferation of litigation, including eight separate lawsuits between Susan and Joseph Jr. In the course of one of these suits, Doris was declared mentally incapacitated. Susan was made guardian of Doris' person, and Louis Ditta, the petitioner in this case and an attorney, was eventually made guardian of Doris' estate. Due to the declaration of incapacity, Doris was removed as a trustee of the Trust.

In August 1998, Ditta sought appointment of a receiver to take over the Trust, claiming that the discord between Joseph Jr. and Susan was materially injuring the Trust assets. Instead of appointing a receiver, the probate court appointed a temporary successor trustee, Paula Miller. At that time, the trustee powers of both Susan and Joseph Jr. were temporarily suspended. In June 2000, Miller filed an accounting for the Trust with the court that covered March 8, 1993 (the date of Joseph's death) to December 31, 1999. The accounting revealed that both Susan and Joseph Jr. had become significantly indebted to the Trust by using Trust assets for personal expenses.

Susan contested the accounting, but eventually the parties entered into an agreed judgment in January 2001. The agreed judgment approved Miller's accounting of more than $400,000 that Susan owed to the Trust and a similar debt owed by Joseph Jr. The agreed judgment provided that collection of the amounts owed by Susan and Joseph Jr. would be deferred during Doris' lifetime, unless the probate court later found that Doris' "financial needs" required earlier repayment.

In January 2003, Ditta persuaded the probate court to remove Joseph Jr. as trustee based on his violations of the Trust agreement. Thereafter, only Susan (whose trustee powers were suspended) and Miller (the temporary successor trustee) remained as trustees. On April 5, 2004, Ditta filed this suit, seeking Susan's removal as trustee. On both April 27 and November 3 of that same year, Susan and Joseph Jr., in their capacity as beneficiaries of the Trust, signed documents, pursuant to the terms of the Trust, to reappoint Susan as trustee if she were removed by the court in the removal proceeding initiated by Ditta.

Following a bench trial, the probate court removed Susan as trustee, modified the terms of the Trust regarding trustee succession, and appointed Frost Bank as successor trustee. Susan appealed and the court of appeals reversed, holding that Ditta's removal action was barred by the four-year statute of limitations governing breach-of-fiduciary-duty claims. The court of appeals reasoned that because "Susan's alleged breach of fiduciary duty formed the underlying basis for Ditta's removal action," and "both parties .

. . briefed the instant appeal as one to which a four-year statute of limitations applies," Ditta was required to bring his removal action no later than four years after the cause of action for removal accrued. The court of appeals also held that the probate court erred in modifying the terms of the Trust and appointing a successor trustee because it took those actions based on a time-barred petition.

II. Preservation of Error

In a post-submission brief, Susan asserts that Ditta has waived the argument that no limitations period should apply to the removal action. While Ditta did not make that precise argument, his entire brief to this Court assiduously detailed numerous reasons why the statute of limitations should not apply to his action. We have held that "[w]hen . . . the only issue is the law question of which statute of limitations applies, the court of appeals should apply the correct limitations statute even if the appellee does not file any brief." Further, a question is properly before this Court if it is subsidiary to, and fairly included within, an issue raised in a litigant's petition for review. This requirement is to be applied "reasonably, yet liberally," so that an appellate court can reach the merits of an appeal whenever it is "reasonably possible" to do so. In order to see that "a just, fair[,] and equitable adjudication of the rights of the litigants" is obtained, we broadly construe Ditta's issues to encompass the core question of whether a statute of limitations should be applied at all.

III. Timeliness of Trustee-Removal Claim

Ditta sought removal of Susan as trustee and reformation of the Trust to appoint a successor trustee. He asserted no cause of action giving rise to a claim for monetary damages such as breach of fiduciary duty. Therefore, we limit our analysis to the question of what, if any, statute of limitations should apply to a claim solely for removal of a trustee.

Neither the Texas limitations statutes nor Texas caselaw (save for the court of appeals' decision in this case) address what, if any, limitations period applies to a trustee-removal cause of action. Scant caselaw exists elsewhere on the issue.

The court of appeals applied the four-year statute of limitations applicable to suits for breach of fiduciary duty. Susan's removal as trustee, however, was not based solely on discrete breaches of fiduciary duty that occurred in the past. The probate court gave three reasons for removing Susan: (1) her indebtedness to the Trust and concurrent responsibility to collect on that debt if Doris needed the funds created an inherent and continuing conflict of interest; (2) Susan's prior use of Trust funds to pay off personal debts materially violated the terms of the Trust; and (3) Susan's tenuous relationship with Joseph Jr. impaired the performance of her trustee duties. Susan does not persuade us that any of these three reasons could not be considered by the probate court as grounds for her removal as trustee. The Trust Code provides courts wide latitude in deciding whether to remove a trustee:

> A trustee may be removed in accordance with the terms of the trust instrument, or, on the petition of an interested person and after hearing, a court may, in its discretion, remove a trustee . . . if: (1) the trustee materially violated or attempted to violate the terms of the trust and the violation or attempted violation results in a material financial loss to the trust; (2) the trustee becomes incapacitated or insolvent; (3) the trustee fails to make [a required] accounting . . . ; or (4) the court finds *other cause* for removal.

More fundamentally, even if the probate court's removal of Susan had been based solely on a conclusion that she committed a discrete breach of fiduciary duty, we conclude that the court's discretion to remove a trustee for such a breach is not subject to a statutory limitations period running from a specified period after the breach. Instead, the removal decision turns on the special status of the trustee as a fiduciary and the ongoing relationship between trustee and beneficiary, not on any particular or discrete act of the trustee.

A trust is not a legal entity; rather it is a "fiduciary relationship with respect to property." High fiduciary standards are imposed upon trustees, who must handle trust property solely for the beneficiaries' benefit. A fiduciary "occupies a position of peculiar confidence towards another." Accordingly, a trustee's association with the trust is that of a relationship or a status. Because a trustee's fiduciary role is a status, courts acting within their explicit statutory discretion should be authorized to terminate the trustee's relationship with the trust at any time, without the application of a limitations period.

By analogy, the marital relationship between spouses is a fiduciary relationship. That special relationship is of course more than the sum of discrete actions taken by one spouse toward another. If, for example, cruelty and adultery are recognized grounds for divorce, a spouse suing for divorce on those grounds should not be tasked to sue for divorce within a specific statutory limitations period. The effect of that conduct on the special relationship of trust and confidence between spouses may continue and change over time. And indeed, Texas law recognizes marriage as a status, and there is no statutory limitations provision expressly directed at divorce actions.

A trustee-removal action can also be analogized to a real-property action to remove a cloud on title. We have held that as long as an injury clouding the title remains, so too does an equitable action to remove the cloud; therefore, a suit to remove the cloud is not time-barred. As we recently noted in *Ford v. Exxon Mobil Chemical Co.*, if removal of the cloud depends on a tort or contract claim, it must be brought within the applicable limitations period. But if a cloud on title is void or has expired by its own terms, there is no limitations period on the equitable claim to declare the existing status.

Here, the probate court found that Susan, in her role as trustee, committed a breach of trust, and that her role as trustee was compromised due to her indebtedness to the Trust and her tenuous relationship with Joseph Jr. and Doris. These findings indicate that the potential for injury to the Trust would remain as long as Susan continued in her role as trustee; therefore, we hold that Ditta's claim for Susan's removal was not time-barred. Unlike *Ford*, Ditta is not merely attempting to recast a potentially time-barred claim (breach of fiduciary duty) as a claim for equitable relief (removal of Susan as trustee). The remedy Ditta seeks in this action is removal of Susan as trustee, not monetary or other relief. While removal actions are sometimes premised on a trustee's prior behavior, they exist to prevent the trustee from engaging in further behavior that could potentially harm the trust. Any prior breaches or conflicts on the part of the trustee indicate that the trustee could repeat her behavior and harm the trust in the future. At the very least, such prior conduct might lead a court to conclude that the special relationship of trust and confidence remains compromised. Like cloud-on-title cases, as long as potential harm to the trust remains, an action to remove the trustee should be allowed to proceed.

We therefore hold that a trustee removal action, regardless of the underlying grounds on which it is brought, is not subject to a limitations analysis. However, limitations periods continue to dictate when claims for fiduciary breaches must be brought. While the four-year limitations period proscribes whether an interested person can obtain monetary recovery from a trustee's fiduciary breach, it does not affect whether the interested person can seek that trustee's removal. To hold otherwise would allow trustees who previously harmed the trust relationship to remain in their fiduciary roles, regardless of their past transgressions.

IV. Conclusion

No statute of limitations period applies in a trustee-removal suit. Trusts are fiduciary relationships, and as such, their nature and character often change throughout the years of administration, as the Trust here did. Because the court of appeals decided this case on the limitations issue, it did not reach issues relating to the merits of Ditta's removal action, the reformation of the Trust, or the appointment of Frost Bank as successor trustee. Accordingly, we reverse the court of appeals' judgment and remand the case to that court for consideration of those issues.

3. Decree to Carry Out the Trust

Read Trust Code § 115.001.

The beneficiaries could sue the trustee to obtain a court order forcing the trustee to carry out the trustee's duties under the terms of the trust instrument or applicable trust law. This remedy is particularly effective if a trustee has not yet breached the trust but appears to be in danger of breaching because of inattention to trust matters.

4. Injunction

Read Trust Code § 115.001(b).

If a breach of trust appears imminent, a beneficiary or co-trustee may obtain an injunction or restraining order to prevent the trustee from performing the improper act. The court can hold the trustee in contempt if the trustee fails to comply.

5. Receivership

Read Trust Code § 115.001(b).

A court may appoint a receiver who can quickly swoop in and take possession of the trust property if the court fears that the trustee will not obey an injunction. Generally, a court is reluctant to appoint a receiver unless it is clear that the property would be lost, destroyed, or materially injured unless a receiver is appointed and that recovery by the complaining party is probable. "Receivership is an extraordinary harsh remedy and one that courts are particularly loathe to utilize." *Krumnow v. Krumnow*, 174 S.W.3d 820 (Tex. App.—Waco 2005, pet. denied). *See also Elliott v. Weatherman*, 396 S.W.3d 224, 228 (Tex. App.—Austin 2013, no pet.) ("Even if a specific statutory provision authorizes a receivership, a trial court should not appoint a receiver if another remedy exists at law or in equity that is adequate and complete.").

After resolution of the issue, the court will either appoint a new trustee or, if the trustee turns out to have been administering the trust properly, return the property to the trustee.

In *Alpert v. Gerstner*, 232 S.W.3d 117 (Tex. App.—Houston [1st Dist.] 2006, pet. denied), the probate court appointed a receiver to take possession of all trust property and to manage it under the terms of the trust. Later, the beneficiaries sued the receiver alleging that she breached her fiduciary duties. For example, they asserted that she did not manage the property prudently which caused a stock portfolio to decline in value from $600,000 to $13,000. The trial court agreed with the receiver that the beneficiaries' claims were barred by judicial immunity. The beneficiaries appealed.

The appellate court reversed. The court recognized that whether a court-appointed receiver is entitled to judicial immunity is an issue of first impression in Texas. The court then engaged in a comprehensive discussion of when "derived" judicial immunity is proper, that is, when the judge's immunity passes along to a person, like the receiver, to whom the court delegates duties. The court explained that immunity is proper if the person is intimately associated with the judicial process and is exercising discretionary judgment comparable to that of a judge.

After reviewing analogous Texas cases, the court held that the receiver was entitled to derived judicial immunity to the extent that she was authorized to take charge and keep possession of the trust property, prepare an inventory of trust property, and assist the court in determining who should be the trust of the trusts. "These functions are intimately associated with the judicial process and involve the exercise of discretionary judgment comparable to that of a judge." *Id.* at 130. However, the receiver is *not* entitled to derived judicial immunity for the alleged breaches of fiduciary duties to the beneficiaries in failing to exercise good faith or ordinary care in managing trust property. At this point, the receiver was acting as a representative of the interests of the beneficiaries, not as an agent of the court.

6.   Require or Increase Bond

Read Trust Code § 113.058(d).

The court may require a bond in cases where the settlor waived bond or increase the amount of an existing bond. This remedy is appropriate when the value of the trust property has increased significantly and additional bond is needed to provide beneficiaries with adequate protection.

7.   Declaratory Judgment

Read Trust Code § 115.001 & Civil Practices & Remedies Code § 37.005.

The trustee or a beneficiary may ask the court for a declaratory judgment to determine whether a contemplated action would be a breach of trust. In this way, the trustee does not run the risk of having a court later determine that a particular action was in breach. However, courts are leery about granting instructions unless there is an immediate and genuine legal problem. Otherwise, the courts would be flooded with petitions by timid or overcautious trustees who wish to obtain free legal advice.

8. Award of Attorney Fees

Read Trust Code § 114.064.

The court may award costs and attorneys' fees to *any* party (not just the winning party) in a trust action. Thus, all parties should request fees so the court may make an equitable and just award.

9. Criminal Sanctions

Read Penal Code § 32.45.

Section 32.45 provides criminal penalties when a fiduciary such as an executor, administrator, trustee, or guardian misapplies property, that is, deals with the property contrary to the terms of the instrument (trust, will, etc.) or any law prescribing the custody or disposition of the property (Probate Code, Property Code, etc.). Note that the fiduciary's conduct must be intentional, knowing, or reckless. Mere negligent conduct will not give rise to a criminal offense although it may subject the fiduciary to civil liability. No actual loss to the property or gain to the fiduciary is necessary. All that must occur is that the property be handled in a manner that involves substantial risk of loss.

10. Liability of Successor Trustee for Breach by Predecessor Trustee

Read Trust Code § 114.002.

C. REMEDIES AGAINST THE BENEFICIARY

Read Trust Code § 114.031.

A beneficiary is generally not in a position to breach the trust and is not liable for breaches of trust committed by the trustee. Under the circumstances listed in § 114.031, however, a beneficiary may be liable for a loss to the trust.

See Examples & Explanations § 21.4.

D. REMEDIES INVOLVING TRUST PROPERTY

1. Tracing

Tracing permits the beneficiary to recover the actual trust property or its proceeds from the trustee or a third party for the benefit of the trust. The beneficiary follows the trail of the misappropriated property and once located, can recover that property unless it is in the hands of a bona fide purchaser.

The tremendous benefit of this remedy is that the beneficiary has priority over the asset vis-à-vis the trustee's other creditors. The traced asset actually belongs to the trust and is thus not included among the trustee's personal assets which are subject to the claims of creditors. The beneficiary may have to elect between (1) tracing to the trust property or its proceeds and (2) recovering monetary damages; double recovery is not allowed.

Notes and Questions

1. Settlor's will left all of Settlor's property to a testamentary trust. Trustee took various items of Settlor's estate and appropriated them for Trustee's own purposes. When Beneficiary discovered what Trustee had done, Trustee was wearing some of Settlor's jewelry and had the other items sitting around Trustee's home. Trustee's creditors have levied on all of Trustee's property. Who is entitled to the property Trustee took from the trust?

2. Trustee embezzled $300 from the trust and deposited those funds into Trustee's personal bank account which prior to this deposit had a balance of $500. Trustee then withdrew $400 from this account to pay for a weekend at a ski resort. Later, Trustee withdrew an additional $300 to pay for a weekend at a beach resort. Trustee then received Trustee's income tax refund and deposited the $600 check in the account. To how much could Beneficiary trace after each of these transactions?

3. *See* Examples & Explanations § 21.3.1.

2. Subrogation

Subrogation may be useful if the beneficiary cannot recover the trust property through tracing because the trustee used trust property to pay a personal debt. The court may subrogate the beneficiary to the rights of the creditor who was paid. Thus, the beneficiaries "step into the shoes," that is, have the same position as, the creditor who was paid. If this creditor had a special right, such as a mortgage, Article 9 security interest, or a priority position in bankruptcy, the beneficiaries may use those rights against the trustee and other creditors.

NOTES AND QUESTIONS

1.   Trustee embezzled $15,000 from a trust. Trustee used $2,000 to pay a credit card debt and $13,000 to pay off the note on Trustee's car. A personal injury creditor has levied on all of Trustee's property. What rights to Trustee's property may Beneficiary be able to obtain?

2.   *See* Examples & Explanations § 21.3.2.

3.   Marshalling

A beneficiary who has a claim against the trustee may be able to force the trustee's other creditors to marshal their claims. Marshalling is an appropriate remedy when a creditor has a right to recover out of more than one fund or asset and another creditor, such as a trust beneficiary, has recourse to only one of those funds or assets. The creditor must first resort to the fund or asset which will not interfere with the rights of the beneficiary to preserve as much of that fund or asset as possible for the beneficiary. Of course, if both funds are needed for the creditor and the creditor has priority as to both, then the marshalling remedy will not help the beneficiary.

Notes and Questions

1.   Creditor has a $10,000 priority claim against Trustee's only two valuable assets. Asset A is worth $10,000 and Asset B is worth $6,000. Beneficiary obtained a $5,000 right to Asset A through subrogation but that right is junior to Creditor's right. How should the claims of these claimants be resolved?

2.   *See* Examples & Explanations § 21.3.3.

4.   Bona Fide Purchasers

Read Trust Code §§ 101.002, 114.081, 114.0821, & 114.082.

Under the common law, a person became a bona fide purchaser (BFP) of trust property by (1) paying value for the property and (2) being without actual or constructive notice of the existence of the trust and the concomitant equitable interest of the beneficiary. A BFP takes free of the beneficiary's interest and may retain and transfer the property without subsequent question by the beneficiary or someone claiming through the beneficiary. Because BFP status was denied to purchasers who knew they were buying trust property or were dealing with a trustee, purchasers were prone to pay less than fair market value for trust property because of the increased risk associated with the purchase.

To alleviate this problem, § 101.001 and its counterpart § 114.082, modify the common law rule and permit a purchaser, as well as donees, to achieve protected status even if the grantee is on notice that the grantee is dealing with a trustee or buying trust property (e.g., the conveyance to the trustee reads "Tom Smith, trustee"). This modern approach permits people to deal with trustees with relative safety and permits trustees to negotiate for higher sale prices. However, the purchaser or donee will not be protected under this section if the conveyance to the trustee either (1) identifies the trust (e.g., "to Tom Smith, trustee of the Windfall Trust"), or (2) discloses the name of any beneficiary "(e.g., "to Tom Smith, trustee for Benny Fishery"). The transferee, however may still be protected by § 114.081 as discussed below.

Section 101.001 is not actually in the Trust Code which begins with § 111.001. The reason for this section to be outside of the Trust Code which has a virtually identical provision (§ 114.082) is that § 101.001 applies even if there is no actual trust but rather just a designation of a person as trustee (a possible resulting trust). Section 101.001 applies when the conveyance is "to a person *designated* as a trustee" (emphasis added) while § 114.082 applies when the conveyance is "to a trustee."

The 2007 Legislature made a major overhaul of the provisions which provide protection to third parties who deal with trustees by amending Trust Code § 114.081.

- *Third party who provides value to the trust* – A person who deals with a trustee is not liable to the trustee or the beneficiaries if the trustee exceeded the scope of the trustee's authority in dealing with the person if the person (1) deals with the trustee in good faith and (2) the trust receives fair value. Trust Code § 114.081(a).

- *Third party who deals with the trust* – A non-beneficiary who deals with the trustee is not required to inquire into the extent of the trustee's powers or the propriety of the trustee's exercise of those powers if the person (1) deals with the trustee in good faith and (2) obtains either a copy of the trust instrument or a "certification of trust" as described in Trust Code § 116.086. Trust Code § 114.081(b).

- *Trustee's use of property* – A person who delivers money or other assets to a trustee is not required to make certain that the trustee properly uses the money or other assets as long as the person made the payment or delivery in good faith. Trust Code § 114.081(d).

- ***Dealing with ex-trustee*** – A non-beneficiary who assists an ex-trustee or for value deals with an ex-trustee is protected from liability as described above just as if the ex-trustee were still in office as long as the person is (1) in good faith and (2) without knowledge that the ex-trustee is no longer a trustee. Trust Code § 114.081(d).

- ***Correlation with other protections*** – "Comparable protective provisions of other laws relating to commercial transactions or transfer of securities by fiduciaries prevail" over the protections described above. Trust Code § 114.081(e).

E. CAUSES OF ACTION AGAINST THIRD PARTIES

Third parties may also be liable to the trust. For example, a third party who contracts with the trust and subsequently breaches that contract is liable. Additionally, a person is liable for torts which cause damage or loss to trust property. If the trustee does not bring these actions, the beneficiaries may be able to move forward with them on behalf of the trust. Alternatively, the beneficiaries can seek to have the trustee removed and replaced with a trustee who is willing to pursue these trust claims. Beneficiaries may also recover from third parties who assist a trustee to commit a breach of trust.

F. ENFORCEMENT OF CHARITABLE TRUSTS

1. Settlor

LOKEY v. TEXAS METHODIST FOUNDATION

Supreme Court of Texas, 1972
479 S.W.2d 260

STEAKLEY, Justice

This suit involves a charitable trust known as the K & L Trust, with an original res of $100,000, and an additional fund of $40,000, identified as the K & L—"A" Trust. The suit was instituted by Clarence W. Lokey, petitioner, against the Texas Methodist Foundation and the Attorney General of Texas. The primary relief sought is the removal of the Texas

Methodist Foundation as trustee over the funds, and the transfer of the funds in the K & L Trust to the trustees of Southwestern University in Georgetown, Texas, and the transfer of the funds in the K & L—"A" Trust to what is identified as the "Lokey Trust." Alternatively, petitioner sought declaratory judgment relief pertaining to the trusts. The National Division of the Board of Missions of the United Methodist Church intervened. It sued petitioner and the Foundation for cancellation of the trust agreements between them and a declaration that the trust funds are held for its sole use.

The trial court ruled in response to pleas raising the issues that petitioner did not have standing to bring the suit but that the intervenor National Division did have standing. The court ordered a dismissal of petitioner's suit and sustained the motion for summary judgment of the National Division. The summary judgment record includes, in addition to the pleadings and motions of the parties, depositions of the various principals. In granting the motion of the intervenor National Division for summary judgment, the court declared the trusts null and void and that the Foundation is holding the trust res for the National Division. Only petitioner appealed from this judgment. The Court of Civil Appeals dismissed petitioner's appeal, holding that he had no standing to institute and prosecute the suit, citing Coffee v. William Marsh Rice University, 403 S.W.2d 340 (Tex. 1966); and Carroll v. City of Beaumont, 18 S.W.2d 813 (Tex. Civ. App., 1929, writ ref'd) 468 S.W.2d 945. The intermediate court did not rule on petitioner's points which asserted error of the trial court in overruling his plea that the National Division did not have standing to intervene, and in granting its motion for summary judgment. It is also to be noted that the Attorney General filed an answer in the nature of a general denial but makes common cause with the other respondents in their claim that petitioner does not have standing.

We draw these facts from the summary judgment record. Petitioner is an ordained Methodist minister attached to the Texas Annual Conference of the United Methodist Church. The respondent and intervenor National Division is one of the three divisions of the Board of Missions of the United Methodist Church. In 1944, petitioner was released to work for the National Division and from 1948 held the title of Superintendent of Spanish-speaking Missions. He served the National Division in this capacity until his retirement in 1966. His salary and operating expenses were paid either by the National Division or out of funds raised by petitioner for the National Division. He was appointed by and worked closely with Methodist Bishop A. Frank Smith, who was President of the Board of Missions, until his death in 1962. Thereafter, petitioner's appointment was renewed annually by the presiding Bishop. The Rio Grande Conference includes local churches in Texas and New Mexico staffed by Spanish-speaking ministers. A primary objective of the National

Division is the strengthening of the work of the Rio Grande Conference by financial assistance. One of petitioner's duties for the National Division was the raising of money.

The initial trust agreement was in writing and was dated January 8, 1963; however, it was not executed by petitioner and respondent, the Texas Methodist Foundation, until sometime in the following year. By its terms, petitioner was identified as Settlor and the Foundation as Trustee. The instrument recited the transfer in cash to the Trustee by the Settlor of $100,000. This sum was represented by a check dated January 4, 1963, and drawn on an account with the Tyler Bank & Trust Company in the name of "The Methodist Church Spanish Speaking Missions, Clarence W. Lokey, Superintendent." This account was opened under date of November 23, 1955. The source of funds deposited in the account from time to time included checks from the Division of National Missions, and checks variously payable to the order of petitioner, to the order of the Treasurer of the Board of Spanish Speaking Missions, and to the order of the Division of National Missions.

The powers of the Foundation as Trustee were limited in the trust agreement as follows:

"While The Texas Methodist Foundation is appointed herein as Trustee for the purpose of investing the funds comprising the trust estate of this trust, the distribution of the funds shall be at the direction of the following persons:

"(a) Dr. C. W. Lokey, and such direct descendant of his as he may designate, either during his lifetime or in his Will.

"(b) Dr. Monroe Vivion, or, if he shall fail or refuse to serve or to continue to serve in the capacity appointed herein, then to his successor as Executive Director of The Texas Methodist Foundation; and

"(c) One other person named by the above two.

"It is intended that the three persons who will function as described above shall pass on their offices in the manner indicated above. A majority of such persons shall be able to act on behalf of all and The Texas Methodist Foundation may rely upon the direction of any one of the above or his successor as appointed herein in making any distributions of trust assets."

The primary purpose of the trust was stated to be the stabilizing and strengthening of the ministry of the Methodist Church with regard to people of Mexican, South American or Central American backgrounds. Additionally, it was stated that the trust fund may be administered for needed support of retired preachers, their widows and dependent children, of the Rio Grande Conference. It was then stated that any funds not distributed for such purposes shall be distributed "(1) for a chair of International Studies at Southwestern University in Georgetown, Texas; (2) for international scholarships; and (3) for exchange international professorships, all at Southwestern University in Georgetown, Texas, in so far as the income from the trust will provide." The trust agreement recited that the trust was irrevocable; that the funds should never be used for other than religious, charitable, scientific, literary or educational purposes; that the proceeds of the trust should be paid to the Foundation if the trust terminated for any reason; and that if the Foundation should cease to exist, the funds should be distributed to Southwestern University or its successor.

Petitioner later delivered to the Foundation a check dated July 8, 1964, in the sum of $40,000 drawn on the same account as the original check in the sum of $100,000 and forming the res of the K & L-"A" Trust. This matter was handled informally by petitioner and Dr. Vivion, the Executive Secretary of the Foundation, and is part of the controversy between them.

It is not disputed that the funds in question were raised by petitioner during the period of, and in connection with, his assignment to the National Division of the Board of Missions. He says, however, "The donors gave him money to spend as he and Methodist Bishop A. Frank Smith deemed best, provided it did not go to the respondent Board." He stated that he maintained a common account composed of donated funds to be transmitted to the National Division and donated funds subject to his and Bishop Smith's control by donor restriction. He did not identify by the name of the donor, or by document, any gifts to him to be used by him and Bishop Smith but stated that the funds were given to be administered by them for purposes over and above and away from and not in "that framework," i.e., not as funds to be used by the Board of Missions. He had no separate records of these gifts and no one but he and Bishop Smith knew about the $100,000, and the later $40,000 subsequently transferred to the Foundation as Trustee. He stated that he personally gave some of the money but had no record or "clear recollection of" how much money he personally gave. The withholding from the National Division of the portion of the commingled funds ultimately forming the res of the trust was pursuant to "a decision" by petitioner and Bishop Smith that they would raise money over and beyond their commitment to the National Division, which money would not be handled through or revealed to the National Division, but would "stay in the area to serve the needs of the area." It is also to be noted that the judgment of the trial court recites that counsel for petitioner stipulated that he "did not claim individual ownership of either the $100,000 or the $40,000 but claimed to be a trustee of such money, made such by the donors thereof."

Taking this at full-face import, it would appear that contributions were made to petitioner and Bishop Smith for local use in fostering the missionary program of the Methodist Church among Spanish-speaking people; that petitioner considered these contributions to have amounted to the sums placed in the trusts; and that petitioner entered into the trust agreements with the Foundation for the purpose of applying the funds to the purposes for which they were donated.

The unusualness of the circumstances at hand is self-evident. There are reasons to believe that all the principals have acted in good faith. The common and primary purpose of all the parties has been the furtherance of the work of the Methodist Church among Spanish-speaking people, particularly in the Rio Grande Conference; and the caring for retired preachers of this Conference, and for their families. This was the purpose of the donations to petitioner; a portion of his deposition testimony in this respect is copied in the margin. [footnote omitted] The conflict which has arisen concerns where, and in what manner, and by whom, the trust funds will be used in furthering this common purpose; a portion of petitioner's deposition testimony as to this is also copied in the margin. [footnote omitted] Petitioner seeks by this suit to remove the Foundation as Trustee and to have the funds held in the K & L Trust transferred to Southwestern University, and those held in the K & L—"A" Trust transferred to the "Lokey Trust." The National Division by its intervention seeks to destroy the trust and to free the funds for its use and benefit, particularly in the Rio Grande Conference. The Foundation seeks to enforce the trust agreement as it understands its terms, but did not resist the intervention of the National Division or its motion for summary judgment, and did not appeal from the judgment in its favor. If petitioner has standing to bring this suit, he has standing to complain of the action of the trial court in overruling his plea against the standing of the intervenor, and in granting the motion of the intervenor for summary judgment. This latter action of the trial court was in error if the intervenor did not have standing, or, if so, if it nevertheless did not discharge its burden as the movant for summary judgment.

Article 7425b-24 of the Texas Trust Act invests the district court with original jurisdiction of matters affecting any trust instrument and provides that "actions hereunder may be brought by a trustee, beneficiary, or any person affected by or having an active interest in the administration of the trust estate." Article 7425b-39 authorizes the removal of trustees under certain conditions "on petition of any person actually interested." In our view, petitioner and the intervenor National Division meet these requirements and have standing to litigate the controversies which have arisen. Petitioner was the chief actor in raising and handling the funds in question and he is one of a committee of three charged with the duty and responsibility of directing the distribution of the $100,000 trust fund, upon any one of which the Foundation may rely in making distribution of trust assets. He and the Foundation are also in controversy as to the terms and conditions under which the fund of $40,000 was delivered and received, and as to the status of this fund under all the circumstances. The intervenor National Division claims the funds as its own in all events and sues to have them freed from the trusts for its use and benefit. It squares with a reasonable construction of the quoted provisions of the Texas Trust Act, and with the history of the funds and the precipitating factors to this unfortunate litigation, to recognize the right of these principals to their day in court as parties actively interested. They have a special interest not shared by the general public.

We did not rule in Coffee v. William Marsh Rice University, 403 S.W.2d 340 (Tex. 1966), that parties other than the Attorney General are precluded from instituting litigation involving a charitable trust. We pointed out that this question was not before us and the above noted provisions of the Texas Trust Act were not there considered. Even so, we recognized in *Rice University* that the Attorney General is not generally regarded as the only person who can bring a suit to enforce or attack a charitable trust, or to question its operation; but that any other person doing so must have some special interest in the performance of the trust different from that of the general public. We also emphasized that Article 4412a does not say that the Attorney General is the preclusive party in suits involving charitable trusts. The fact that it is the certain duty of the Attorney General to invoke the powers inherent in our courts to prevent an abuse of a charitable trust does not deny the power of a court in the exercise of its chancery powers from intervening when its jurisdiction is otherwise properly invoked. Cf. Boyd v. Frost National Bank, 145 Tex. 206, 196 S.W.2d 497 (1946); and Powers v. First National Bank of Corsicana, 138 Tex. 604, 161 S.W.2d 273 (1942). Carroll v. City of Beaumont, 18 S.W.2d 813 (Tex. Civ. App. 1929, writ ref'd), recognizes that jurisdiction of the courts may be invoked by parties other than the Attorney General, i.e., those having "peculiar or individual rights, distinct from those of the public at large," they being parties "legally concerned," as we have held is the case with petitioner and the intervenor National Division. * * *

The judgments below are reversed and the cause is remanded to the trial court for further proceedings in accordance with this opinion.

POPE, J., dissenting.

REAVLEY, J., not sitting.

2. Texas Attorney General

Read Property Code ch. 123.

The attorney general of Texas has standing to enforce charitable trusts. To increase the likelihood that the attorney general is aware of lawsuits involving charitable trusts, Chapter 123 requires that the party initiating the action give notice to the attorney general. This notice is by certified or registered mail within 30 days of filing but not less than 25 days before a hearing and must include a copy of the petition. See Property Code § 123.003. Section 123.001(3) provides an extensive list of proceedings to which the attorney general is entitled to notice.

If the attorney general does not receive notice, any judgment or settlement is voidable. In other words, the attorney general may set aside any judgment or settlement at any time. No grounds are required other than the fact that the attorney general did not receive notice. *See* Property Code § 123.004.

It is significant to note the broad definition given to the term "charitable trust" in § 123.001(2). The term encompasses any inter vivos or testamentary gift to a charitable entity in addition to traditional charitable trusts. An attorney perusing the statutes might read the caption to Chapter 123 which contains the term "charitable trusts" and not realize that the chapter applies to all charitable gifts, whether they be in trust or outright. Likewise, the term "charitable trusts" includes any charitable entity, even if not run as a trust.

G. BARRING OF JUDICIAL REMEDIES

1. Settlor's Approval in Trust Instrument

Read Trust Code § 111.0035.

Generally, the terms of the trust prevail over conflicting Trust Code provisions. Section 111.0035 which was added to the Trust Code in 2005 and modified by each subsequent legislature enumerates the growing list of non-waivable items and provides detailed rules with regard to the waiver of certain trustee duties.

a. Trust Purposes

The settlor may not change the restriction in Trust Code § 112.031 that a trust may not be created for an illegal purpose or require the trustee to commit a criminal or tortious act or an act that is contrary to public policy.

b. Trustee Exculpation

In another new section enacted in 2005, § 114.007, the rules regarding trustee exculpation are recodified and expanded. The settlor is prohibited from restricting the limitations on exculpation imposed by this section.

c. Statute of Limitations

The settlor may not shorten the periods of limitation for commencing a judicial proceeding regarding a trust.

d. Trustee's Duty to Account for Irrevocable Trusts

The settlor may not limit the duty of a trustee of an irrevocable trust to respond to a beneficiary's demand for an accounting under Trust Code § 113.151 provided that the beneficiary is either (1) entitled or permitted to receive trust distributions or (2) would receive a distribution from the trust if the trust terminated at the time of the demand.

Note the settlor may restrict the trustee's duty to account in other situations such as (1) if the trust is revocable or (2) if the beneficiaries of the irrevocable trust are remote, that is they are not eligible for current distributions or a distribution if the trust were to terminate.

e. Trustee's Duty of Good Faith

The settlor may not limit the trustee's duty to act in good faith and in accordance with the purposes of the trust.

f. Court's Power

The settlor may not restrict the power of a court to take action or exercise jurisdiction. The statute provides a non-exclusive list of powers included in this restriction:

- Modify, terminate, or take other action with regard to the trust under Trust Code § 112.054,

- Remove a trustee under Trust Code § 113.082,

- Exercise jurisdiction over the trust under Trust Code § 115.001,

- Determine matters related to the trustee's bond (e.g., require, dispense with, modify, or terminate the bond), and

- Adjust or deny compensation to a trustee who committed a breach of trust.

g. Forfeiture Clauses

The settlor may not trump the limitations on the enforceability of no-contest clauses imposed by Trust Code § 112.038. A forfeiture clause is presumed enforceable unless the party who wants the clause to be unenforceable establishes by a preponderance of the evidence that (1) just cause existed for bringing the action and (2) the action was brought and maintained in good faith.

h. Trustee's Duty to Inform Beneficiaries

The settlor may not limit the common law duty to keep the beneficiary informed except under the following conditions:

- The trust is revocable,

- The beneficiary is under age 25, or

- The beneficiary is neither eligible for current distributions nor a distribution if the trust were to terminate now.

2. Mandatory Arbitration

RACHAL v. REITZ

Supreme Court of Texas, 2013
403 S.W.3d 840

Justice GUZMAN delivered the opinion of the Court.

Federal and state policies favor arbitration for its efficient method of resolving disputes, and arbitration has become a mainstay of the dispute resolution process. Today we determine whether these policies render an arbitration provision contained in an inter vivos trust enforceable against the trust beneficiaries. The trust here contained a provision requiring all disputes regarding the trust and the trustee to proceed to arbitration. When a trust beneficiary sued the trustee, the trustee moved to compel arbitration. The trial court denied the motion. The court of appeals, sitting en banc, affirmed, concluding that the provision could not be enforced under the Texas Arbitration Act (TAA) because there was no agreement to arbitrate trust disputes. We conclude that the arbitration provision contained in the trust at issue is enforceable against the beneficiary for two reasons. First, the settlor determines the conditions attached to her gifts, and we enforce trust restrictions on the basis of the settlor's intent. The settlor's intent here was to arbitrate any disputes over the trust. Second, the TAA requires enforcement of written agreements to arbitrate, and an agreement requires mutual assent, which we have previously concluded may be manifested through the doctrine of direct benefits estoppel. Thus, the beneficiary's acceptance of the benefits of the trust and suit to enforce its terms constituted the assent required to form an enforceable agreement to arbitrate under the TAA. We reverse the judgment of the court of appeals and remand to the trial court to enter an order consistent with this opinion.

I. Background

Andrew Francis Reitz established the A.F. Reitz Trust in 2000, naming his sons, James and John, as sole beneficiaries and himself as trustee. The trust was revocable during Andrew's lifetime and irrevocable after his death. Upon Andrew's death, Hal Rachal, Jr., the attorney who drafted the trust, became the successor trustee.

In 2009, John Reitz sued Rachal individually and as successor trustee, alleging that Rachal had misappropriated trust assets and failed to provide an accounting to the beneficiaries as required by law. Reitz sought a temporary injunction, Rachal's removal as trustee, and damages.

Rachal generally denied the allegations and later moved to compel arbitration of the dispute under the TAA, relying on the trust's arbitration provision. That provision states:

> Arbitration. Despite anything herein to the contrary, I intend that as to any dispute of any kind involving this Trust or any of the parties or persons concerned herewith (e.g., beneficiaries, Trustees), arbitration as provided herein shall be the sole and exclusive remedy, and no legal proceedings shall be allowed or given effect except as they may relate to enforcing or implementing such arbitration in accordance herewith. Judgment on any arbitration award pursuant hereto shall be binding and enforceable on all said parties.

The trust further provided that "[t]his agreement shall extend to and be binding upon the Grantor, Trustees, and beneficiaries hereto and on their respective heirs, executors, administrators, legal representatives, and successors."

The trial court denied Rachal's motion to compel and Rachal filed this interlocutory appeal. See Tex. Civ. Prac. & Rem. Code § 171.098(a)(1) (authorizing interlocutory appeal for orders denying applications to compel arbitration). A divided court of appeals, sitting en banc, affirmed the trial court's order. 347 S.W.3d 305, 312. The court of appeals held that a binding arbitration provision must be the product of an enforceable contract between the parties, reasoning that such a contract does not exist in the trust context, in part because there is no consideration and in part because the trust beneficiaries have not consented to such a provision. Id. at 308, 310–11. The court further concluded that because there is no contractual agreement to arbitrate in this context, it is for the Legislature, rather than the courts, to decide "whether and to what extent the settlor of this type of a trust should have the power to bind the beneficiaries of the trust to arbitrate." Id. at 311–12.

The four dissenting Justices reasoned that further legislation is not necessarily required because a trust can be "a written agreement to arbitrate" within the meaning of the TAA even without the signatures of the beneficiaries and successor trustee. 347 S.W.3d at 312–13 (Murphy, J., dissenting) (quoting Tex. Civ. Prac. & Rem. Code § 171.001(a)). The dissent notes that the TAA does not require a formal contract to arbitrate but only a written agreement, a broader term that includes legal contracts but also less formal agreements. Id. The dissent concludes that, because the Legislature chose the broader term "agreement" in the TAA, rulings in other jurisdictions that arbitration provisions in trusts are unenforceable are inapplicable to arbitration provisions under the TAA. Id. at 313–14. We granted the trustee's petition to decide whether an arbitration provision under the TAA in an inter vivos trust is enforceable against trust beneficiaries.3

II. Discussion

A. Standard of Review

* * * We review de novo whether an arbitration agreement is enforceable. * * *

This case also requires us to construe a statute. Our primary goal in construing a statute is to give effect to the Legislature's intent. Texas Mut. Ins. Co. v. Ruttiger, 381 S.W.3d 430, 452 (Tex.2012); TGS–NOPEC Geophysical Co. v. Combs, 340 S.W.3d 432, 439 (Tex.2011). We defer to the plain meaning of a statute as the best indication of the Legislature's intent unless a different meaning is apparent from the context of the statute or the plain meaning would yield absurd results. Molinet v. Kimbrell, 356 S.W.3d 407, 411 (Tex.2011). Moreover, we determine legislative intent from the entire act, not merely from isolated portions. Ruttiger, 381 S.W.3d at 454; TGS–NOPEC, 340 S.W.3d at 439.

B. Trusts and the TAA

Rachal echoes the dissenting justices' view that the TAA does not require a formal contract but rather only an agreement to arbitrate future disputes. Reitz argues that even if the TAA requires only an agreement to arbitrate—as opposed to a formal contract—the trust instrument here does not meet that less exacting standard because it lacks mutual assent and unity in thought between its parties. We agree with Rachal.

1. Settlor's Intent

Generally, Texas courts endeavor to enforce trusts according to the settlor's intent, which we divine from the four corners of unambiguous trusts. * * * We enforce the settlor's intent as expressed in an unambiguous trust over the objections of beneficiaries that disagree with a trust's terms. * * *

Here, the settlor unequivocally stated his requirement that all disputes be arbitrated. He specified that, "[d]espite anything herein to the contrary," arbitration would be "the sole and exclusive remedy" for "any dispute of any kind involving this Trust or any of the parties or persons connected herewith (e.g., beneficiaries, Trustees)...." Because this language is unambiguous, we must enforce the settlor's intent and compel arbitration if the arbitration provision is valid and the underlying dispute is within the provision's scope. Meyer, 211 S.W.3d at 305.

2. The TAA

The TAA provides that a "written agreement to arbitrate is valid and enforceable if the agreement is to arbitrate a controversy that: (1) exists at the time of the agreement; or (2) arises between the parties after the date of the agreement." Tex. Civ. Prac. & Rem. Code § 171.001(a) (emphases added). The TAA further states that a "party may revoke the agreement only on a ground that exists at law or in equity for the revocation of a contract." Id. § 171.001(b) (emphasis added). The Legislature specifically chose to enforce "agreements" to arbitrate. Id. § 171.001(a). It knew how to enforce only "contracts;" it selected that term to specify the grounds for revoking an agreement to arbitrate. Id. § 171.001(b). The language of the TAA indicates legislative intent to enforce arbitration provisions in agreements. If the Legislature intended to only enforce arbitration provisions within a contract, it could have said so. * * *

Because the TAA does not define agreement, we must look to its generally accepted definition. TGS–NOPEC, 340 S.W.3d at 439. Black's Law Dictionary defines an agreement as "a manifestation of mutual assent by two or more persons." Black's Law Dictionary 78 (9th ed.2009). Contract treatises have made similar observations. Williston commented:

> An agreement, as the courts have said, "is nothing more than a manifestation of mutual assent by two or more legally competent persons to one another." In some respects, the term agreement is a broader term than contract, and even broader than the term bargain or promise. It covers executed sales, gifts, and other transfers of property.

1 Samuel Williston & Richard A. Lord, A Treatise on the Law of Contracts § 1:3, at 13–14 (4th ed.1990) (citations omitted) * * *

We therefore address whether the trust here was supported by the mutual assent required to render the trust an agreement and the arbitration provision valid. Typically, a party manifests its assent by signing an agreement. * * *

We expressly adopted the federal doctrine of direct benefits estoppel in the context of arbitration agreements under state law in In re Kellogg Brown & Root, Inc., where we held that a non-signatory who is seeking the benefits of a contract or seeking to enforce it "is estopped from simultaneously attempting to avoid the contract's burdens, such as the obligation to arbitrate disputes." 166 S.W.3d 732, 739 (Tex.2005). As the Fourth Circuit described it, "the doctrine recognizes that a party may be estopped from asserting that the lack of his signature on a written contract precludes enforcement of the contract's arbitration clause when he has consistently maintained that other provisions of the same contract should be enforced to benefit him." Int'l Paper Co. v. Schwabedissen Maschinen & Anlagen GMBH, 206 F.3d 411, 418 (4th Cir.2000) (quoted in Kellogg Brown & Root, 166 S.W.3d at 739). We noted in Kellogg Brown & Root that if the claims are based on the agreement, they must be arbitrated, but if the claims can stand independently of the agreement, they may be litigated. 166 S.W.3d at 739–40 * * *.

In Weekley Homes, we addressed the circumstances under which direct benefits estoppel binds parties for actions other than filing suit. 180 S.W.3d at 131–32. There, we stated that a "nonparty may be compelled to arbitrate if it deliberately seeks and obtains substantial benefits from the contract itself" during the performance of the agreement. Id. at 132–33. We likened the situation to promissory estoppel, where a promisor induces substantial action or forbearance by another and estoppel requires enforcing the promise to prevent injustice. Id. at 133. There, the plaintiff never signed the agreement to purchase the newly constructed home but claimed the authority of the agreement in directing the construction and repair of the home, submitted reimbursement claims for expenses incurred during repairs, and conducted settlement negotiations with the builder. Id. We held that these were sufficiently substantial actions demanding the builder comply with the contract to equitably estop the plaintiff from resisting the agreement's arbitration provision. Id.

We must examine here whether the direct benefits estoppel doctrine applies to an arbitration provision in a trust. A beneficiary may disclaim an interest in a trust. See Tex. Prop. Code § 112.010; see also Aberg v. First Nat'l Bank, 450 S.W.2d 403, 407 (Tex. App.–Dallas 1970, writ ref'd n.r.e.) (stating the well-settled rule that a trust beneficiary who has not manifested his acceptance of a beneficial interest may disclaim such interest). And a beneficiary is also free to challenge the validity of a trust: conduct that is incompatible with the idea that she has consented to the instrument. See Rapid Settlements, Ltd. v. SSC Settlements, LLC, 251 S.W.3d 129, 148 (Tex.App.–Tyler 2008, no pet.) (holding direct benefits estoppel inapplicable when a nonsignatory filed suit for a declaration that an arbitration agreement was not binding on it). Thus, beneficiaries have the opportunity to opt out of the arrangement proposed by the settlor.

On the other hand, a beneficiary who attempts to enforce rights that would not exist without the trust manifests her assent to the trust's arbitration clause. For example, a beneficiary who brings a claim for breach of fiduciary duty seeks to hold the trustee to her obligations under the instrument and thus has acquiesced to its other provisions, including its arbitration clause. In such circumstances, it would be incongruent to allow a beneficiary to hold a trustee to the terms of the trust but not hold the beneficiary to those same terms.

Here, Reitz both sought the benefits granted to him under the trust and sued to enforce the provisions of the trust. On the death of the settlor, Reitz did not disclaim an interest in the trust, and his suit directly seeks actual damages for any amounts inappropriately taken from the trust. See Tex. Prop. Code § 112.010 (presuming a beneficiary accepts an interest in a trust and establishing time period to disclaim that interest). Reitz also sued to enforce the trust's provisions against the trustee. The trust specifically prohibited the trustee from making "any distribution to or for the benefit of himself which is not subject to an ascertainable standard under the Code" and contained a number of other powers of and restrictions on the trustee. Reitz claimed Rachal "has materially violated the terms of the Trust and his fiduciary duty by failing to account to the beneficiary and ... has materially violated th[e] terms of the Trust by his conversion of the Trust assets which has resulted in material financial loss to the Trust." Reitz further claimed, among other things, he was "entitled to any profits that would accrue to the trust estate if there had been no breach of trust." In accepting the benefits of the trust and suing to enforce its terms against the trustee so as to recover damages, Reitz's conduct indicated acceptance of the terms and validity of the trust.6 In sum, we hold the doctrine of direct benefits estoppel applies to bar Reitz's claim that the arbitration provision in the trust is invalid. See Weekley Homes, 180 S.W.3d at 131–32; Kellogg Brown & Root, 166 S.W.3d at 739–40; FirstMerit Bank, 52 S.W.3d at 755–56.

Reitz argues, however, that direct benefits estoppel cannot apply here because there is no underlying contract. We have generally applied direct benefits estoppel when there is an underlying contract the claimant did not sign, but we have never held a formal contract is required for direct benefits estoppel to apply. * * * As equitable defensive theories, direct benefits estoppel and promissory estoppel promote fairness by holding a party to its position in the performance of an agreement or in bringing litigation. * * * A valid, underlying contract is not required under these theories, nor is it required here; thus, Reitz's argument is without merit. * * *

3. Other Jurisdictions

Reitz points to the holdings of two courts in sister states that support his view that arbitration provisions in trusts are unenforceable. There is a dearth of authority as to the validity of an arbitration provision in a trust, and the opinions Reitz relies on have been superseded. The two courts—both intermediate courts—that considered this precise issue declined to enforce mandatory arbitration provisions in trusts. See Diaz v. Bukey, 125 Cal.Rptr.3d 610, 615 (Ct.App.2011), pet. granted, 129 Cal.Rptr.3d 324, 257 P.3d 1129 (2011), remanded with directions, 148 Cal.Rptr.3d 495, 287 P.3d 67 (2012); Schoneberger v. Oelze, 208 Ariz. 591, 96 P.3d 1078, 1079 (Ct.App.2004), superseded by statute, Ariz. Rev. Stat. § 14–10205. These courts generally concluded that a trust's arbitration provision is not enforceable because a trust is not a contract between the grantor, trustee, and beneficiary and thus does not bind those who do no sign the instrument to arbitrate future trust disputes. This bright-line distinction between trusts and contracts was first discussed in Schoneberger, where an Arizona court of appeals explained:

> Arbitration rests on an exchange of promises. Parties to a contract may decide to exchange promises to substitute an arbitral for a judicial forum.... In contrast, a trust does not rest on an exchange of promises. A trust merely requires a trustor to transfer a beneficial interest in property to a trustee who, under the trust instrument ... holds that interest for the beneficiary. The undertaking between trustor and trustee does not stem from the premise of mutual assent to an exchange of promises and is not properly characterized as contractual.

96 P.3d at 1083 (internal citations and quotations omitted). A California intermediate court later adopted the Arizona court's explication. Diaz, 125 Cal.Rptr.3d at 615. The court of appeals here followed the analysis in Schoneberger. 347 S.W.3d at 310–11.

But the Arizona Legislature superseded Schoneberger and the California Supreme Court vacated Diaz. Unlike the TAA's requirement that the arbitration provision be in an "agreement," the Arizona statute at issue in Schoneberger required the arbitration provision to be "in a written contract."8 96 P.3d at 1082. The Arizona Legislature superseded Schoneberger, providing that: "A trust instrument may provide mandatory, exclusive and reasonable procedures to resolve issues between the trustee and interested persons or among interested persons with regard to the administration or distribution of the trust." Ariz. Rev. Stat. § 14–10205.9

A California appellate court followed Schoneberger in refusing to enforce an arbitration provision in a trust. Diaz, 125 Cal.Rptr.3d at 615. The California statute at issue, like the Texas statute, addresses arbitration provisions in "written agreements." Cal. Civ. Proc. Code § 1281.1 ("[A]ny request to arbitrate ... shall be considered as made pursuant to a written agreement to submit a controversy to arbitration."). The California Supreme Court instructed the court of appeals to vacate its decision and reconsider the case in light of Pinnacle Museum Tower Association v. Pinnacle Market Development (US), LLC, 55 Cal.4th 223, 145 Cal.Rptr.3d 514, 282 P.3d 1217 (2012). Diaz v. Bukey, 148 Cal.Rptr.3d 495, 287 P.3d 67, 67 (2012). In Pinnacle, a condominium developer included a mandatory arbitration provision in the recorded declaration of restrictions, which also provided for the creation of an owners' association. Id. at 1221–22. The association sued the developer for construction defects, and the developer moved to compel arbitration based on the provision in the declaration of restrictions. Id. at 1223. The California Supreme Court held that the Federal Arbitration Act applied to the provision in question, which refers to arbitration provisions "in ... a contract." Id. (quoting 9 U.S.C. § 2). The court held that the recorded declaration was contractual in nature, despite the fact that the individual owners—not the owners' association— agreed to be bound by the declaration, and that enforcing the arbitration provision against the owners' association was not unconscionable. Id. at 1228–29, 1233–34. The court of appeals has yet to issue its new opinion in light of Pinnacle.

We note that other courts, while not addressing the precise issue raised here, have nonetheless favorably viewed arbitration provisions in trusts. * * *

C. Scope

Having determined the arbitration provision at issue is enforceable against Reitz, Rachal must also establish that the dispute is within the scope of the agreement. Meyer, 211 S.W.3d at 305. Once a valid arbitration agreement is established, a "strong presumption favoring arbitration arises" and we resolve doubts as to the agreement's scope in favor of arbitration. Ellis v. Schlimmer, 337 S.W.3d 860, 862 (Tex.2011). Reitz asserts that his lawsuit falls outside the scope of the agreement because the trust's terms indicate the settlor's intent to exempt trustee misconduct claims from the scope of the arbitration provision. We disagree.

When determining whether claims fall within the scope of the arbitration agreement, we look to the factual allegations, not the legal claims. FirstMerit Bank, 52 S.W.3d at 754. The arbitration provision here requires that:

Despite anything herein to the contrary, I intend that as to any dispute of any kind involving this Trust or any of the parties or persons concerned herewith (e.g., beneficiaries, Trustees), arbitration as provided herein shall be the sole and exclusive remedy, and no legal proceedings shall be allowed or given effect except as they may relate to enforcing or implementing such arbitration in accordance herewith.

Reitz's suit against Rachal to enforce the trust's restrictions qualifies as "any dispute of any kind involving this Trust or any of the parties or persons connected herewith."

Reitz nonetheless argues that a subsequent provision in the trust regarding exoneration of trustees indicates an intent to allow for litigation of disputes with the trustee. The provision Reitz relies on refers to a trustee's liability for unintentional misconduct and permits the trustee to fund litigation or dispute related costs from the trust, providing that a beneficiary who initiates the proceedings without good faith shall have the defense costs deducted from his share of the trust income and assets. This provision does not defeat the arbitration requirement for two reasons. First, to the extent the two provisions conflict, the arbitration provision—by its own terms—prevails over "anything herein to the contrary." Second, the trustee exoneration provision, when read in conjunction with the arbitration provision, still has meaning. Even if the arbitration provision requires that all disputes over the trust be resolved in arbitration, the trustee exoneration provision is effective in at least two situations: (1) when a claim filed in court is then sent to arbitration, and (2) when a claim is filed in, and stays in, court because direct benefits estoppel or another doctrine that would compel arbitration does not apply. Under the first scenario, the trustee exoneration provision simply acknowledges that some claims that belong in arbitration will be initiated in court and determines how these defense costs are paid. Under the second scenario, not all claims initiated in court can be compelled to arbitration. We previously noted that the doctrine of direct benefits estoppel will not provide the mutual assent necessary to compel arbitration in all circumstances. One who does not accept benefits under a trust and contests its validity could not be compelled to arbitrate the trust dispute under the doctrine of direct benefits estoppel. In such a case, the trustee exoneration provision determines how these defense costs are paid. Our construction of the arbitration and trustee exoneration privileges gives meaning to both provisions. Universal C.I.T. Credit Corp. v. Daniel, 150 Tex. 513, 243 S.W.2d 154, 158 (1951). In sum, Rachal demonstrated the existence of a valid arbitration agreement that covers the claims at issue.

III. Conclusion

Beneficiary Reitz sued trustee Rachal to require him to comply with the terms of the trust at issue, which contains an arbitration provision. The TAA requires arbitration provisions to be in written agreements. Reitz's assent to the trust is reflected in his acceptance of the benefits of the trust and his suit to compel the trustee to comply with the trust's terms. Reitz's claims that Rachal violated the terms of the trust are within the scope of the arbitration provision, which requires the arbitration of "any dispute of any kind involving this Trust." Thus, Rachal carried his burden of demonstrating that the trust contains a valid arbitration agreement that covers Reitz's claims. We reverse the judgment of the court of appeals and remand to the trial court to enter an order consistent with this opinion.

Notes and Questions

1.   Although this was a trusts case, it would seem likely the court would reach the same result if the arbitration provision was contained in a will.

2.   Do you think this decision is correct? Although beneficiaries do have the ability to disclaim before accepting benefits, it is unlikely that beneficiaries read the trust and seek legal advice about the consequences of accepting benefits. Instead, beneficiaries just collect the benefits and study the trust instrument in detail only when something goes wrong. If a settlor really wanted to mandate arbitration, the settlor could include a provision requiring the trustee to obtain the beneficiary's written consent to arbitrate as a condition precedent to receiving trust distributions.

3.   The court does not discuss how to handle the situation where the beneficiaries are minors or incompetent individuals.

4.   Arbitration provisions may become boilerplate so that the justification that the settlor intentionally imposed the requirement may be problematic.

3.   Release by Beneficiaries

Read Trust Code §§ 114.005 & 114.032.

A beneficiary may give prior approval to the trustee for actions that would otherwise be in breach of trust. Likewise, the beneficiary may ratify breaches of trust which have already occurred.

Section 114.032 provides for limited virtual representation so that a release may bind beneficiaries who did not actually agree because, for example, they are minors, unborn, or unascertained. Note that this provision may not be used to modify or terminate the trust. *Compare* Trust Code § 115.013 (judicial virtual representation).

Notes and Questions

1. What are the requirements for a beneficiary release?

2. What liabilities may a beneficiary release?

3. Under what circumstances may a beneficiary virtually represent another beneficiary?

4. *See* Examples & Explanations § 21.6.2.

4. Court Decree

Read Trust Code § 115.001(a)(8).

This section is the ultimate escape clause. The court has the ability to relieve a trustee from any duty, limitation, or restriction which is imposed by the trust instrument or the Trust Code. Thus, a trustee in breach of trust who has an equitable argument that the breach should be forgiven, may "beg" the court for "mercy."

See Examples & Explanations § 21.6.3.

5. Statute of Limitations

Read Civil Practice & Remedies Code § 16.051 (residual limitations period of "four years after the day the cause of action accrues").

The statute of limitations does not begin to run against the beneficiary until the beneficiary has notice that the trustee has repudiated the trust. The beneficiary does not have a duty to investigate until the beneficiary has knowledge of facts which are sufficient to trigger a reasonable person to inquire. In other words, the statute of limitations does not run from the date of the trustee's breach but rather from when that breach is, or should have been, discovered. *See Courseview, Inc. v. Phillips Petroleum Co.*, 312 S.W.2d 197 (Tex. 1957).

WRIGHT v. GREENBERG

Court of Appeals of Texas – Houston [14th Dist.] 1999
2 S.W.3d 666
pet. denied

MAURICE E. AMIDEI, Justice.

Karon Rosenfield Wright (Karon), individually and as trustee of two testamentary trusts, appeals from two summary judgments for Joyce Z. Greenberg (Joyce), independent executrix of her deceased husband's (Jacob's) estate and trustee of a trust established by him prior to his death. In three issues, Karon contends the trial court erred in granting summary judgments in favor of Joyce because (1) there is no evidence that Jacob exercised the power of appointment in his will, and Jacob was estopped to exercise the power of appointment, (2) Joyce was estopped to assert the statute of limitations or other affirmative defenses, and (3) Joyce failed to negate the discovery rule by proving Karon discovered or should have discovered Jacob's alleged breach of trust. We affirm.

I. FACTUAL AND PROCEDURAL BACKGROUND.

Lurine Karon Greenberg (Lurine) was Jacob's first wife, and she died in 1975. Karon is Jacob's and Lurine's daughter, and is the same person known as Abby Greenberg Rosenfield. In her will, Lurine left all of her residuary estate to Jacob in trust, and directed him to divide the trust estate equally between the "Jacob Greenberg Trust" and the "Abby Greenberg Rosenfield Trust." By the terms of her will, Lurine named Jacob the trustee and beneficiary of the Jacob Greenberg Trust (Jacob's Trust), and named Jacob the trustee of the Abby Greenberg Rosenfield Trust (Karon's Trust). Jacob was given the discretionary power to distribute the trust income and corpus of Karon's Trust to Karon in such amounts as he believed "for the best interests" of Karon. Upon the death of Jacob, Lurine's will appointed Karon as successor trustee of Karon's Trust. Lurine's will gave Jacob "the power to appoint the entire remaining principal of Jacob's Trust, free of the trust, by will, irrespective of the time of his death, in favor of his estate." Should Jacob fail to exercise that power, Lurine's will provided that the remaining principal of Jacob's Trust passed to Karon's Trust with Karon as successor trustee.

Jacob died in 1995 and his will named his second wife, Joyce, the independent executrix of his will. That will provided:

By this Will, I intend to dispose of all my property (that owned by me and that over which I have any power of disposition), real, personal and mixed, of whatever kind and wherever situated, including any property over which I may have a power of appointment (emphasis added).

In the residuary clause of Jacob's will, he left all of the "rest, residue and remainder" of his estate to the trustee or successor trustee of the Jacob Greenberg Family Trust created in 1988. After Jacob died, and his will was admitted to probate, Karon sued Joyce for an accounting of both trusts, damages for Jacob's alleged mishandling the trusts, a declaratory judgment that Jacob's will was not a valid exercise of the power of appointment in Lurine's will, and an order that the corpus of Jacob's Trust be turned over to Karon as successor trustee to the two testamentary trusts established by Lurine's will.

Joyce filed a motion for partial summary judgment, alleging that Jacob's will effectively exercised the power of appointment given to him under Lurine's will as a matter of law. Karon responded alleging that Jacob's will did not specifically refer to the power of appointment in Lurine's will, nor did Jacob's will refer to the property subject to the power of appointment. Furthermore, Karon contended Jacob's will did not dispose of the property over which he had a power of appointment, but only stated his "intention" to dispose of property over which he had a power. Thereafter, Karon filed her second amended original petition alleging additionally that Jacob was estopped to exercise the power of appointment, and Joyce was estopped to assert the statute of limitations and all other affirmative defenses to Karon's actions for accounting, breach of trust, and claims for damages. By her second amended original answer, following Karon's amended petition, Joyce contended Karon's claims for an accounting are barred by the four-year statute of limitations, and Karon knew or should have known of Jacob's alleged mishandling of the trust within the four-years from the alleged breach of trust. Joyce filed a second motion for summary judgment further contending she was not estopped from asserting any and all defenses, and that Karon's actions regarding the funding, distribution or administration of Karon's Trust were time barred. The trial court granted Joyce's first motion for partial summary judgment on the ground that she established as a matter of law that Jacob's will exercised his testamentary power of appointment over the assets of Jacob's Trust under Lurine's will. The trial court also granted Joyce's second motion for partial summary judgment without stating any grounds. Both summary judgments were made final and severed from the remaining part of the case for purposes of this appeal.

[discussion of summary judgment, and power of appointment issues omitted]

C. ESTOPPEL

* * *

2. Estoppel to assert the statute of limitations and affirmative defenses.

Joyce contends Karon's actions for accountings for both trusts are barred by the residual four-year statute of limitations. TEX. CIV. PRAC. & REM. CODE ANN. § 16.051 (Vernon 1997 & Supp. 1999). In issue two, Karon contends Joyce is estopped to assert the statute of limitations and all other affirmative defenses.

Karon argues that her affidavit establishes her claim of equitable estoppel against Joyce to assert limitations and other affirmative defenses. She argues that her testimony in her affidavit shows that Jacob's conduct precluded inquiry into his dealings with Lurine's trusts. She claims she had "no other choice" than to show respect to her father and rely on what information he saw fit to provide to her.

The only summary judgment proof attached to Karon's response was her affidavit. The only statements in Karon's affidavit relating to a claim of estoppel were:

6. "From before my mother's death until his death, my father bragged about his financial success and frequently complained about the amount of tax he had to pay. After his marriage to Joyce Z. Greenberg, my father travelled [sic] and entertained to an extent and in a style far in excess of the standard to which he had been accustomed while my mother was alive.

7. "My father told me a number of times that I would be "a very rich girl." I understood this to mean that I would receive at least the assets of the Jacob Greenberg Trust. I relied on this statement in not making further inquiry about both the Jacob Greenberg Trust and the Abby Greenberg Rosenfield Trust. Only after my father's death did I learn that my father had purported to terminate the Jacob Greenberg Trust before his death.

8. "From my mother's death until his death, my father provided me with only such information as he saw fit concerning my mother's estate and the Abby Greenberg Rosenfield Trust and no information about the Jacob Greenberg Trust. Any requests for information were met with angry tirades by my father. I felt I could not make inquiries of him without jeopardizing what positive relationship I and my sons did have with my father. Despite our problems, I felt I had no choice but to show respect for my father and rely on such information as he did provide me."

Joyce replied to Karon's response and objected that these statements were hearsay, inadmissible character evidence, and in violation of the Dead Man's statute (rule 601(b), Texas Rules of Evidence). There is no order sustaining or overruling these objections, and nothing in the judgment indicates the trial court considered these objections. Therefore, the objected to evidence remains a part of the summary judgment evidence. * * * On appeal, Karon contends her evidence raised a material fact issue and the trial court erred in granting Joyce's second motion for summary judgment.

To constitute an equitable estoppel, there must exist: (1) a false representation or concealment of material facts; (2) made with actual or constructive knowledge of the facts; (3) to a party without knowledge or the means of acquiring knowledge of the real facts; (4) made with the intention that it should be acted on; and (5) the party to whom it was made must have relied on or acted on it to his prejudice. * * *

In this case, Karon's affidavit fails to show any misrepresentation or concealment of material facts. The statement that Jacob told her she would be "a very rich girl," upon which she relied in not making any further inquiry about the trusts, is nothing more than an opinion and cannot be the basis of an equitable estoppel. To create an estoppel, the representation relied on must be a statement of material fact, and not a mere expression of opinion. * * * The affidavit does not set forth facts to establish any element of equitable estoppel. The affidavit consists of conclusory statements concerning Karon's relationship with Jacob and what he did or did not do in general terms. Affidavits containing conclusory statements unsupported by facts are not competent summary judgment proof. * * * More importantly, there is nothing in Karon's statement indicating she was prejudiced by Jacob's actions or inactions. Her statement provides no insight as to any detriment, loss, or injury she suffered by Jacob's actions or inactions. * * * We find that Karon has not raised a material fact issue on any element of equitable estoppel.

Karon further argues that Jacob's "position, conduct and relationship effectively precluded inquiry into his dealings with" Lurine's trusts. A defendant is estopped from relying on limitations as an affirmative defense when the defendant is under a duty to make a disclosure but fraudulently conceals the existence of the cause of action from the party to whom it belongs. * * * The estoppel effect ends when the party learns of facts or circumstances that would lead a reasonably prudent person to inquire and thereby discover the concealed cause of action. * * * As we indicated in our discussion above, Karon's affidavit is not summary judgment evidence of any element of equitable estoppel. Her conclusions that she had to rely on Jacob and respect his dealings with the trusts are not evidence of a concealment of a cause of action such as to create a fact issue of estoppel. Furthermore, Joyce attached documents to her second motion for summary judgment demonstrating that Jacob had notified Karon, in writing, that he was resigning as trustee of Karon's trust effective March 1, 1990. He remained the trustee of Jacob's trust until his death, and when his will was probated, whatever remained in Jacob's trust went to Joyce. Karon filed her original petition against Joyce on March 25, 1996, six years after she had been notified that Jacob resigned as trustee. Her affidavit does not controvert the fact that more than four years passed from the time she was notified of Jacob's resignation as trustee until suit was filed. We find Joyce was not estopped to assert her claim of the statute of limitations or any affirmative defenses. Karon's contention in issue two that Joyce was so estopped is overruled.

D. STATUTE OF LIMITATIONS.

In her third issue, Karon contends her claim with respect to Karon's trust is not barred by limitations. Karon relies on S.V. v. R.V., 933 S.W.2d 1, 8 (Tex. 1996), for the proposition that a breach of fiduciary duty is inherently undiscoverable because "a person to whom a fiduciary duty is owed is either unable to inquire into the fiduciary's actions or unaware of the need to do so." Id.

In the recent case of KPMG Peat Marwick v. HCH, the supreme court set forth the standard of review for motions for summary judgment on the affirmative defense of limitations, as follows:

A defendant moving for summary judgment on the affirmative defense of limitations has the burden to conclusively establish that defense [citation omitted]. Thus, the defendant must (1) conclusively prove when the cause of action accrued, and (2) negate the discovery rule, if it applies and has been pleaded or otherwise raised, by proving as a matter of law that there is no genuine issue of material fact about when the plaintiff discovered, or in the exercise of reasonable diligence should have discovered the nature of its injury [citations omitted]. If the movant establishes that the statute of limitations bars the action, the nonmovant must then adduce summary judgment proof raising a fact issue in avoidance of the statute of limitations [citation omitted].

KPMG Peat Marwick v. Harrison County Housing, 988 S.W.2d 746, 748 (Tex. 1999).

1. Did Joyce conclusively prove when the cause of action accrued?

In her first amended original petition and counterclaim, Joyce pleaded that Karon's demand for an accounting and other claims were barred by the residual four-year statute of limitations, > section 16.051, Texas Civil Practices and Remedies Code. In her second motion for partial summary judgment, Joyce alleged that any action for an accounting or for a breach of trust regarding the Abby Greenberg Rosenfield Trust accrued no later than March 1, 1990, the date of Jacob Greenberg's resignation as trustee. In support of that motion, Joyce attached copies of a letter from Jacob to Karon, dated April 16, 1981, stating he had set up the trusts pursuant to Lurine's will, and setting out in detail the sums of money she would receive. He asked Karon to sign the duplicate copy of that letter and the accounting which was attached to it to indicate her approval. In her handwritten letter to Jacob, Karon acknowledged receipt of the correspondence but stated: "I have decided not to sign the letter which you recently sent." Copies of Jacob's letters to Karon dated February 27, 1990, resigning as trustee of Karon's trust and appointing Karon's sons, Alan and Thomas as successor co-trustees, were attached. Jacob's resignation became effective as of March 1, 1990. Alan and Thomas signed the appointments as successor trustees to Karon's trust.

In her response, Karon objected to Joyce's summary judgment proof but never obtained a ruling on her objections from the trial court. Therefore, all Joyce's summary judgment proof remains a part of the summary judgment evidence. See Giese v. NCNB Texas Forney Banking Center, 881 S.W.2d 776, 782 (Tex. App.-Dallas 1994, no writ).

The only summary judgment proof offered in response to Joyce's summary judgment motion was Karon's conclusory affidavit discussed above under her estoppel claims. As we indicated, her affidavit raises no fact issues because it is conclusory. In her brief, Karon now asserts that the discovery rule is applicable and S.V. v. R.V. makes a fiduciary's misconduct "inherently undiscoverable." S.V. v. R.V., 933 S.W.2d at 8. She contends the burden is on Joyce to negate the discovery rule by proving as a matter of law that no issue of material fact exists concerning when Karon discovered or should have discovered the breach of trust.

We find that Joyce conclusively proved that this cause of action accrued no later than March 1, 1990, by Jacob's resignation as trustee of Karon's trust. Karon does not dispute that she received this notice. On appeal, Karon contends Joyce had to negate the discovery rule by proving there is no fact issue concerning when Karon discovered or should have discovered the harm. In KPMG Peat Marwick, the supreme court considered a similar contention. KPMG Peat Marwick, 988 S.W.2d at 749-50. In that case, Peat Marwick's summary judgment evidence conclusively established that the two-year statute of limitations had accrued more than two years prior to HCH filing its lawsuit. Id. at 749. HCH asserted that Peat Marwick fraudulently concealed its wrongful conduct, and thus, limitations did not begin to run until HCH knew or should have known of its injury. Id. HCH also asserted that its pleading was sufficient summary judgment evidence of the affirmative defense of fraudulent concealment to defeat Peat Marwick's summary judgment motion. Id. HCH did not raise fraudulent concealment as an affirmative defense to the statute of limitations. Id. The supreme court held:

> First, a party asserting fraudulent concealment as an affirmative defense to the statute of limitations has the burden to raise it in

response to the summary judgment motion and to come forward with summary judgment evidence raising a fact issue on each element of the fraudulent concealment defense. A mere pleading does not satisfy either burden. Thus, even assuming that HCH pled fraudulent concealment as an affirmative defense to Peat Marwick's answer pleading limitations, HCH still had to respond to Peat Marwick's summary judgment motion. There is no such response in the record. Therefore, HCH did not carry its burden to both plead the defense and support it with summary judgment evidence.

KPMG Peat Marwick, 988 S.W.2d at 749-50.

In this case, Karon did not allege, plead nor otherwise raise the discovery rule in her response to Joyce's second motion for partial summary judgment. Karon raises the negation of the discovery rule for the first time on appeal. The supreme court in Peat Marwick stated that the defendant must "negate the discovery rule, if it applies and has been pleaded or otherwise raised ...." Id. at 748. Karon neither pleaded the discovery rule defense nor otherwise raised it with her summary judgment affidavit. Therefore, we find that Joyce conclusively proved when the cause of action accrued. We overrule Karon's contention in issue three that the statute of limitations does not apply to her claim, and we affirm the judgment of the trial court.

6. Laches

A beneficiary's right to recover may be barred by laches even if the statute of limitations has not yet run. It is unfair to expect the trustee to defend an action if the beneficiary unreasonably delays in asserting the beneficiary's rights and this delay makes it difficult for the trustee to make an adequate defense. For example, material witnesses could have died or become incompetent or relevant documents may have been lost or destroyed.

7. Bankruptcy of Trustee

A bankrupt trustee who breached fiduciary duties but not in an evil manner may be successful in getting a judgment based on that breach discharged. However, if the breach was otherwise, discharge may not b available.

For example, in *Bullock v. BankChampaign*, 133 S. Ct. 1754 (2013), the settlor created a trust for his children and named one of the children as the trustee. The trustee breached his fiduciary duties by borrowing funds from the trust and thus his siblings obtained a judgment against him for the benefits he received from his self-dealing. The trustee had previously repaid all borrowed funds with interest and the trial court determined that he had no malicious motive. The trustee later filed for bankruptcy and sought discharge of the judgment. The Bankruptcy Court held that the debt was not dischargeable under 11 U.S.C. § 523(a)(4), which provides that discharge is not available "for fraud or defalcation while acting in a fiduciary capacity." Both the Federal District Court and the Eleventh Circuit Court of Appeals agreed.

The Supreme Court of the United States in a unanimous opinion reversed. The Court explained that the debt could be discharged because the trustee was not (in this author's words) "evil." The Court held that for the debt to be non-dischargeable, the trustee must have acted with a culpable statement mind "involving knowledge of, or gross recklessness in respect to, the improper nature of the fiduciary behavior."

Chapter Five

OTHER "TRUSTS"

A. TRUST DEPOSITORY ACCOUNTS

1. Definition

A trust depository account is an account in the name of one or more parties as trustee for one or more beneficiaries where the relationship is established by the form of the account and the deposit agreement with the financial institution and there is no subject of the trust other than the sums on deposit in the account. *Read* Est. Code § 113.004). A written agreement signed by all of the trustees is required. *Read* Est. Code § 113.152. It is not essential that payment to the beneficiary be mentioned in the deposit agreement. *See Stogner v. Richeson*, 52 S.W.3d 903 (Tex. App.—Fort Worth 2001, pet. denied) (holding that the depositor's failure to check a box by trust account language or to name a beneficiary in the indicated box did not prevent the account from being deemed a trust account because the depositor had made his intention clear from other indications on the signature card such as by checking the box marked "other" and filling in the word "trust").

A trust account does not include a regular trust account under a testamentary trust or a trust agreement which has significance apart from the account, or a fiduciary account arising from a fiduciary relationship such as attorney-client.

Trust accounts, also called *Totten trusts, savings account trusts,* or *tentative trusts,* operate in much the same way as P.O.D. accounts, that is, upon the death of all trustees, the surviving beneficiaries divide the balance remaining in the account.

2. Historical Note

Despite their resemblance to P.O.D. accounts, trust accounts have a totally different history because they evolved from trust law rather than contract law. In the past, courts took several approaches to cope with trust accounts, most of which prevented the account from operating as the depositor intended. Some common examples included: (1) the depositor lacked the intent to create a real inter vivos trust and thus the court did not recognize the existence of a trust; (2) the depositor intended to create a trust, but the trust was invalid because the depositor retained complete control over the account and did not assume the fiduciary duties required of a trustee; and (3) the true purpose of the arrangement was to effectuate an at-death transfer of property and thus the account would not operate to do so because it did not comply with the formalities of a valid will.

On the other hand, some courts held that the depositor created a valid revocable trust. Thus, the depositor could make withdrawals at any time but, upon death, the balance would pass to the beneficiary. The landmark New York case of *In re Totten*, 71 N.E. 748 (1904), adopted this latter approach and thus trust accounts are often referred to as *Totten trusts*.

Texas, in accordance with modern law, has now stripped trust accounts of their trust law components. Trust accounts are treated as contractual arrangements providing for payment of the balance upon the death of all trustees to the surviving beneficiaries. Because of this tremendous similarity to P.O.D. accounts, many states (but not Texas) and the Uniform Probate Code have abandoned the distinction and now treat trust accounts just like P.O.D. accounts. *See* UPC § 6-201(8).

3. Effect During Lifetime

a. Ownership

All funds in a trust account belong beneficially to the trustee during the trustee's lifetime. *Read* Est. Code § 113.104. If there is more than one trustee, each owns the account funds in proportion to his or her net contributions. The trustees have the unrestricted right to withdraw all funds and close the account without approval of or notice to the beneficiaries.

Generally, the beneficiaries have no rights during the lifetime of the trustees. However, the deposit agreement or other clear and convincing evidence could demonstrate otherwise, e.g., the trustee physically delivered the passbook to the beneficiary. This rarely occurs as trust accounts are typically used in situations in which the depositor does not want the beneficiaries to have rights while the depositor is alive.

b. Right to Withdraw

During the lifetime of the trustee or trustees, a trust account may be paid, on request, to any trustee. *Read* Est. Code § 113.205. No notice to or consent of a beneficiary is required. The beneficiaries have no withdrawal rights while any trustee is alive.

4. Effect After Death

a. Ownership

A beneficiary has no rights until all trustees have died. A beneficiary must outlive all trustees to have any rights. *Read* Est. Code § 113.153. Upon the death of the sole or surviving trustee, the account is divided among the surviving beneficiaries.

If two or more beneficiaries survive the trustees, there is no right of survivorship in the event of death of any beneficiary thereafter, unless the instrument expressly provides for survivorship between them. *Read* Est. Code § 113.153.

b. Right to Withdraw

Payment may be made, on request, to the beneficiary upon presentation to the financial institution of proof of death showing that the beneficiary or beneficiaries survived all persons named as trustees. *Read* Est. Code § 113.205.

After the death of all trustees, and unless the financial institution has received written notice that the beneficiary has a vested interest not dependent upon the beneficiary surviving the trustee, payment may be made to the personal representative or heirs of a deceased trustee if proof of death is presented to the financial institution showing that the decedent was the survivor of all other persons named on the account either as trustee or beneficiary. *Read* Est. Code§ 113.205.

5. Benefits

a. Probate Avoidance

Funds remaining on deposit in the account are immediately available for the survivor without the necessity of wading through a protracted will contest action or a lengthy and costly estate administration.

b. Inexpensive Will Substitute

A trust account has been called a "poor person's will" because it is an inexpensive and simple method to provide for the disposition of account funds upon the depositor's death. A very common arrangement of parties is "Husband or Wife, with rights of survivorship, in trust for Children."

c. Depositor Gives Up No Control

The depositor gives up no control over the funds while alive. Thus, a trust account is much "safer" than a joint account with rights of survivorship because there is no risk that the P.O.D. payee will make unauthorized withdrawals or abscond with the funds.

d. Small Gifts in Complex Estate

A person who has already created a sophisticated estate plan may wish to add a nominal gift to a friend or long-time employee. This person may use a trust account to make this type of gift without the cost or inconvenience of redoing the will.

6. Disadvantages

a. Lack of Professional Management

A trust account does not secure professional management of the deposited funds as may be achieved by using other estate planning techniques such as a traditional trust.

b. No Tax Benefits

A trust account will not secure tax benefits for the depositor. The depositor will pay income tax on any interest earned by the account. The account will be included as part of the depositor's gross estate for federal estate tax purposes.

c. Client Confusion

A P.O.D. account is normally a better estate planning tool than a trust account because clients have an easier time understanding how a P.O.D. operates. A client may find it confusing that the word "trust" in the term "trust account" has a very different meaning from when the word is used in other contexts. For example, a trustee of a trust has fiduciary duties and cannot engage in self-dealing while a trustee of a trust account may in most cases withdraw the money at any time and for any (or no) reason.

7. Definition of "Account"

A wide-variety of arrangements are encompassed by the term "account" under Est. Code § 113.001 including, but not limited to, the following types of deposit contracts:

- Checking account,
- Savings account,
- Certificate of deposit, and
- Share account.

However, the following types of arrangements are specifically *excluded* from coverage by the multiple-party account provisions of the Est. Code under § 113.004:

- Business accounts (e.g., accounts for partnerships, joint ventures, associations, corporations, unincorporated associations, charitable or civic organizations, etc.)

- Account maintained by the trustee of a trust where the relationship is established other than by the deposit agreement, and

- Other fiduciary accounts (e.g., an attorney's trust account containing client funds).

8. Definition of "Financial Institution"

The term "financial institution" is broadly defined to include "an organization authorized to do business under state or federal laws relating to financial institutions." *Read* Est. Code § 113.001. Examples of financial institutions include, but are not limited to, the following organizations:

- Banks,
- Trust companies,
- Savings banks,
- Building and loan associations,
- Savings and loan companies/associations,
- Credit unions, and
- Brokerage firms that deal in the sales and purchases of stocks, bonds, and other types of securities.

9. Effect of Divorce

Under most circumstances, provisions of a trust account in favor of an ex-spouse or a relative of the ex-spouse who is not a relative of the deceased spouse will not be effective to transfer the funds to the ex-spouse or ex-spouse's relative. *Read* Est. Code § 123.151.

10. Conflicting Disposition by Will

It is unlikely that a will provision expressly gifting the trust account or account funds would be sufficient to alter the terms of an account contract providing for payment to a beneficiary. Wills control the disposition of property in a decedent's probate estate; the proceeds of a trust account never reach the estate but instead pass directly to the surviving beneficiaries.

11. Survival

The survival statute, Estates Code § 121.152, imposes a 120 hour survival period for joint owners. However, the statute is silent regarding situations where the person who receives the property is not an "owner," such as the beneficiary of a trust account. It thus appears that unless the account contract provides otherwise, there is no requirement beyond mere survival for the trust account beneficiary to be entitled to the account funds.

12. Effect of Depositor's Incapacity

When a depositor becomes incompetent, the depositor no longer has the ability to manage the depositor's property, including trust accounts. Management duties may then pass to a court appointed guardian of the estate or conservator. Assume that Depositor has two accounts: Account One in Depositor's name alone, and Account Two which has a beneficiary provision in favor of Payee. Guardian needs money to pay Depositor's expenses and thus starts spending the money in Account Two. What right, if any, does Payee have to complain and to force Guardian to use the funds in Account One first? There is no clear resolution of this issue. For a discussion of this issue, see Glenn M. Karisch, *Multi-Party Accounts in Texas* 25-28 (2003), available at http://www.texasprobate.com/articles/accounts.sa2003.PDF.

13. Rights of a Living Party's Creditors

Trust accounts are generally not an effective method of avoiding creditors. While the depositor is alive, the depositor's creditors may reach the account to the extent of the depositor's net contributions. Generally, however, creditors of a trust account beneficiary have no right to reach account funds.

14. Rights of Deceased Party's Creditors

a. General Creditors

Funds in a trust account are available to pay the debts of a deceased depositor but only as a last resort after all other estate assets are exhausted. *Read* Est. Code §§ 113.251-113.252. Trust accounts are not effective against the estate of a deceased party to transfer to the surviving party or parties sums needed to pay debts, taxes, and expenses of administration (including statutory allowances to the surviving spouse and minor children) if other assets of the estate are insufficient. Accordingly, the use of a trust account is not a total probate avoidance technique; probate will be avoided only if the estate is solvent without taking into consideration the amounts in the account to which the deceased party was beneficially entitled.

A party who receives payment from a trust account after the death of another party is liable to the deceased party's personal representative to the extent necessary to discharge the debts, taxes, and expenses of administration. No proceeding to assert this liability may be commenced unless the personal representative has received a written demand by a surviving spouse, a creditor, or one acting for a minor child of the deceased party. The statute of limitations for such an action is two years after the party's death. A financial institution will not be liable for making payment to a surviving party unless it received written notice from the personal representative before payment was made that such sums are needed to pay debts, taxes, or expenses of administration.

b. Secured Creditors

A trust account is not effective against the claim of a secured creditor who has a lien on the account. *Read* Est. Code §§ 113.251-113.252. Any trustee may use the account as collateral without the joinder of any of the other trustees. If the secured creditor is a financial institution, the creditor must give written notice sent by certified mail to the other trustees that the account was used as collateral within thirty days of perfection. However, notice need not be given to parties who have no current ownership rights such as trust account beneficiaries.

c. The Financial Institution

If the deceased party was indebted to the financial institution, the financial institution has a right of set-off against the trust account up to the amount to which the deceased party was beneficially entitled immediately before his or her death. In the absence of proof of net contributions, this amount will be deemed a pro rata share with all other parties having present rights of withdrawal. *Read* Est. Code § 113.210.

A bank may setoff claims against a deceased customer's deposits without the necessity of complying with the claims procedures established by the Probate Code. The bank's right to setoff mature debts owed to the bank by the customer survives the customer's death and continues against the decedent's personal representative. The bank's setoff right exists even when the customer's debt to the bank matures after the customer's death. The right to setoff an unmatured claim exists without regard to the solvency of the deceased's estate. It remains undecided whether a court could order a bank to release funds to satisfy a family allowance if the statutory preference for the family allowance conflicts with the bank's setoff right. See *Bandy v. First State Bank, Overton, Texas*, 835 S.W.2d 609, 617–19 (Tex. 1992).

15. "Stopping" Payment from a Trust Account

Normally, a financial institution is protected if it pays the account according to the statutory rules. The protection, however, "does not extend to payments made after a financial institution has received written notice from any party able to request present payment to the effect that withdrawals in accordance with the terms of the account should not be permitted." *Read* Est. Code § 113.209. Constructive notice is insufficient; the financial institution's protection is not affected by any other type of notice or any other information available to the financial institution. *See Mbank Corpus Christi, N.A. v. Shiner*, 840 S.W.2d 724 (Tex. App.— Corpus Christi 1992, no writ) (holding that the bank had the right to pay the entire balance of a non-survivorship account to the surviving party because the bank had not received the necessary notice not to pay) and *Bandy v. First State Bank, Overton, Texas*, 835 S.W.2d 609 (Tex. 1992) (holding that oral notice to the bank by party wishing to prevent the survivor of a non-survivorship account from making withdrawals was insufficient to comply with the statute).

16. "Old" Accounts

Chapter XI of the Probate Code took effect on August 27, 1979. What if the account in question was created before that date? The courts have held that the law in effect on the date of death is controlling; not the law when the account was opened and the account agreement signed. See *Sheffield v. Estate of Dozier*, 643 S.W.2d 197 (Tex. App.—El Paso, 1982, writ ref'd n.r.e.) (the joint account at issue was opened about three months before the effective date of the new provisions and the deceased party died over a year after the effective date).

Notes and Questions

What is the proper distribution of account funds in the following situations?

1.   "A in trust for B." A dies.

2.   "A in trust for B and C." A dies.

3.   "A in trust for B and C." B dies. Later, A dies.

4.   "A or B in trust for C." A dies.

5. "A or B as joint tenants with rights of survivorship in trust for C." A dies.

6. "A in trust for B and C." A dies. Neither B nor C make any withdrawals from the account. B dies.

B. RESULTING TRUSTS

A resulting trust arises by operation of law when the facts and circumstances show that a person had the intent to hold equitable title to property although legal title is in the hands of another. Unlike an express trust where the manifestation of the settlor's trust intent must be shown by written or spoken words, a resulting trust exists when the person's conduct demonstrates that the person anticipated holding a beneficial interest in the property. Accordingly, resulting trusts are sometimes called *implied trusts* because they are implied from a person's conduct and actions rather than arising after the person makes an express statement of intent.

Resulting trusts do not have actual trust terms and do not involve an ongoing fiduciary relationship. Instead, the holder of the legal title ("trustee") simply has the obligation to convey that legal title to the holder of the equitable title ("beneficiary"). The beneficiary of a resulting trust is the person who had the implied intent to hold equitable title and thus the beneficiary and the "settlor" are the same person. If the settlor has already died, the beneficiaries of a resulting trust are the settlor's successors in interest, that is, the settlor's heirs if the settlor died intestate or, if the settlor died testate, the beneficiaries of the settlor's will.

The Texas Trust Code does not apply to resulting trusts. *See* Trust Code § 111.003(1).

This section discuss the three common situations which give rise to resulting trusts.

1. Failure of Express Trust to Dispose of All Trust Property

A resulting trust arises if the settlor creates a valid trust but fails to dispose of all of the equitable title to the trust property. This can occur when an unanticipated set of circumstances arises or because the trust instrument was poorly drafted. The settlor's failure to convey all equitable title means that the settlor retained that title and is thus entitled to the return of the legal title to the remaining trust property.

Notes and Questions

1.   Settlor created a valid trust which had the following dispositive provision: "Trustee shall pay all income from the trust property to Beneficiary so long as Beneficiary is alive." Beneficiary has died and the trust does not contain any additional dispositive language. What should Trustee do with the remaining trust property?

2.   *See* Examples & Explanations § 22.2.

2.   Failure of Express Trust

Read Trust Code § 112.053.

A resulting trust may arise if the settlor attempts to create an express trust but that attempt fails because, for example, the settlor did not indicate a trust purpose, describe the beneficiaries specifically, or comply with the Rule Against Perpetuities. Although the would-be settlor may have been successful in transferring legal title to the property, the settlor is treated as retaining the equitable title if the would-be settlor's attempt to create a trust fails. In effect, the would-be settlor has an implied reversionary interest in the property.

See Examples & Explanations § 22.1.

BRELSFORD v. SCHELTZ

Texas Civil Appeals—Houston [1st Dist.] 1978
564 S.W.2d 404
writ ref'd n.r.e.

PEDEN, Justice.

Plaintiffs, Regina Brelsford and Kenyon Houchins, were denied partition of a tract of land, a portion of which defendant Allan Scheltz had conveyed to Mrs. Brelsford in payment for legal services. The court granted defendants' motion for judgment when the plaintiffs rested their case. Plaintiffs argue that they were joint tenants and had the right to have partitioned their undivided interest in the property. We affirm.

Mary Ida Scheltz, mother of Allan and Michael Scheltz, conveyed the land in question to "Michael Scheltz, Trustee," in 1972. No trust powers or terms were set out in this deed, but Michael Scheltz wrote to Allan Scheltz at the same time stating that he held an undivided one-half interest in the land as trustee for Allan. When Mary Ida Scheltz died in 1973, she devised all of her property equally to her two sons and appointed Michael Scheltz as independent executor. Her will has been admitted to probate and

Michael has qualified as executor. Allan Scheltz conveyed 8% of his purported one-half interest in the property in question to Regina Brelsford in 1975 for performing legal services, and she assigned half of that interest to Kenyon Houchins. It is upon this conveyance and assignment that Mrs. Brelsford and Mr. Houchins base their suit.

There are no findings of fact or conclusions of law.

To establish their right to have the tract partitioned, plaintiffs-appellants had the burden of proving joint ownership and an equal right to possession with the other joint owners. *Manchaca v. Martinez*, 148 S.W.2d 391 (Tex. 1941); 44 Tex. Jur. 2d 263, Partition § 17; Vernon's Texas Civil Statutes, Art. 6082. Appellants showed neither joint ownership nor present right to possession; they showed only that Allan Scheltz had an equitable interest, not an equitable title.

The interest of a beneficiary under an express trust is an equitable title, not a mere equitable right, but the deed from Mary Ida Scheltz to Michael Scheltz, Trustee, did not create a valid express trust under the Texas Trust Act, Art. 7425b-7, Vernon's Texas Civil Statutes. That act provides in part that

> "* * * a trust in relation to or consisting of real property shall be invalid, unless created, established, or declared:
>
> 1. By a written instrument subscribed by the trustor or by his agent thereunto duly authorized by writing;
>
> 2. By any other instrument under which the trustee claims the estate affected."

The mere use of the word "Trustee" does not of itself *create* a trust. *Costello v. Hillcrest State Bank*, 380 S.W.2d 780, 782 (Tex. Civ. App. 1964, no writ). In order to show an express trust, the controlling tests are that 1) the words of the settlor ought to be construed as imperative and thus imposing an obligation on the trustee, 2) the subject to which the obligation relates must be certain, and 3) the person intended to be the beneficiary must be certain. *Unthank v. Rippstein*, 386 S.W.2d 134, 136 (Tex. 1964). The missing terms of an express trust may not be established by parol evidence. *Best Investment Co. v. Hernandez*, 479 S.W.2d 759, 763 (Tex. Civ. App. 1972, writ ref. n.r.e.). The letter from Michael Scheltz to Allan Scheltz did not establish the terms of the trust since it is not subscribed by the trustor or her duly authorized agent.

When an express trust fails, the law implies a resulting trust with the beneficial title vested in the trustor or, in the case of the trustor's death, in her estate and devisees. *Morrison v. Parish*, 384 S.W.2d 764, 767 (Tex. Civ. App. 1964, writ dism'd); *Ray v. Fowler*, 144 S.W.2d 665, 669 (Tex.

Civ. App. 1940, writ dism'd, judgm. cor.); Bogert, Trust and Trustees 812 § 468 (2d ed. revised). In the case at bar, the property appears to be held in a resulting trust by Michael Scheltz for the benefit of the estate of Mary Ida Scheltz. When Allan Scheltz executed the conveyance to appellant Brelsford the only estate he owned was a beneficial interest as a devisee under his mother's will. There is in evidence a copy of a letter from Internal Revenue Service stating that taxes due on the estate of Mrs. Mary Scheltz on March 4, 1977 amounted to $39,469.97. Until Allan Scheltz receives an interest in the property under the division of his mother's estate or, possibly, by transfer from Michael Scheltz as trustee, Allan Scheltz has only a non-possessory equitable interest, not an equitable title, and neither he nor his assigns may maintain a suit for partition. *Cf. Smith v. Kountze*, 119 S.W.2d 721, 726 (Tex. Civ. App. 1938), rev'd on other grounds, 135 Tex. 543, 144 S.W.2d 261 (1940).

Another possible result of the failure of the express trust is that Michael Scheltz holds the property in a resulting trust for the benefit of himself and Allan. Parol evidence is admissible to show the circumstances under which a resulting trust arose. *Hidalgo County v. Pate*, 443 S.W.2d 80, 88 (Tex. Civ. App. 1969, writ ref., n.r.e.); *Miller v. Donald*, 235 S.W.2d 201, 205 (Tex. Civ. App. 1950, writ ref., n.r.e.), and the letter from Michael to Allan is evidence of the circumstances surrounding the attempt to create a trust.

> "But if, as in most cases, the conveyance in trust was voluntary, and *there is no express or implied gift of the property to the trustee or another* in the event of the failure of the trust, the court decrees a resulting trust for the settlor or his successors." Bogert, Trust and Trustees 812, § 468 (2d ed. revised) (emphasis added).

Even if the letter provides evidence of an implied gift from Mary Ida Scheltz to her two sons, Allan Scheltz still holds only a non-possessory beneficial interest in the resulting trust, so neither he nor his assigns may maintain a suit for partition. See *Smith v. Kountze*, supra. A trustee almost universally takes possession of the trust res. Bogert, Trusts and Trustees 219, § 583 (2d ed.). Only an owner of a possessory interest may compel partition. *Douglas v. Butcher*, 272 S.W.2d 553 (Tex. Civ. App. 1954, writ ref., n.r.e.).

Affirmed.

Note

In *Pickelner v. Adler*, 229 S.W.3d 516 (Tex. App.—Houston [1st Dist.] 2007, pet. denied), the testatrix's will provided that the residuary of her estate passed to the beneficiary (the attorney who drafted the will) "to be distributed in accordance with the specific instructions I have provided him." The testatrix provided these instructions verbally to the beneficiary and they were also found in her handwriting on the back of an envelope.

The trial court held that it could not give effect to these oral instructions and that the residuary gift was void. (No argument was made that the handwritten note was sufficient to be a codicil to her will.) The court explained that the handwritten note was not in existence at the time the testatrix signed her will and thus the note could not have been incorporated by reference into her will. The court also noted that it is against public policy for an attorney to draft a will for an unrelated person and to name himself as a beneficiary of that will. (This will was prepared before the effective date of Probate Code § 58b which automatically voids such gifts.) The court held that the testatrix lacked trust intent and that consequently this property passed to the testatrix's heirs by intestate succession. The intended recipient under her oral instructions appealed.

The appellate court affirmed the result. The court engaged in an extensive discussion of the types of trusts recognized by Texas law, express, resulting, and constructive, as well as the concepts of the "secret trust" and the "semi-secret trust." Unlike the trial court, the appellate court held that it was clear that the testatrix intended to create a trust and that the beneficiary was to receive only legal title to property. Because the trust lacked essential terms (the names of the beneficiaries), it was a semi-secret trust, that is, a resulting trust, so Beneficiary holds the property for the testatrix's successors in interest (her heirs).

3. Purchase-Money Resulting Trust

In the typical purchase of property, the seller gives title to the purchased property to the buyer. Even if the buyer intends to use the property as a present for a relative or friend, the buyer first receives the item and then transfers it to the donee on the appropriate occasion. A purchase-money resulting trust (PMRT) may arise if the person who pays the purchase price for property does not receive the title to that property but instead directs the seller to transfer the property to another person. Because of the highly unusual nature of this type of transaction, the court may conclude that the person who paid the purchase-money actually intended to obtain an equitable interest in the property even though the seller conveyed legal title to someone else. Note that a few states do not recognize PMRTs and thus a court may determine that the person who paid the purchase-money has no interest in the property.

If you are confronted with a fact pattern involving the purchase of property by one person with title to that property being taken by another person, the result is not necessarily a PMRT. The transaction could actually be an outright gift or a loan.

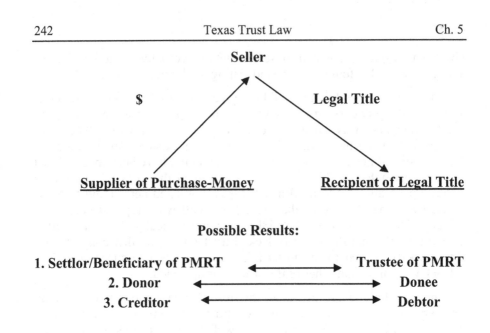

Possible Results:

1. Settlor/Beneficiary of PMRT   ⟷   Trustee of PMRT
2. Donor   ⟵————————————⟶   Donee
3. Creditor   ⟵————————————⟶   Debtor

Notes and Questions

1.   Parent gave $100,000 to Seller for the purchase of a home and had Seller place title to the land in the name of Child who had recently graduated from college and got married. Several years later, Parent and Child had a big argument during which many hurtful words were exchanged. Parent then demanded that Child convey the home to Parent. How should a court rule on Parent's request?

2.   Use the same facts as Note 1, except this time assume that the purchaser is Aunt and that Seller placed title in Nephew's name.

3.   *See Smith v. Deneve*, 285 S.W.3d 904, 912 (Tex. App.—Dallas 2009, no pet.) ("The trust arises out of the transaction and must arise at the time title passes.").

4.   Buyer gave $150,000 to Seller and had title to the property placed in Daniel's name. Daniel agreed to pay back the money but has failed to do so. Will Buyer be successful in obtaining a PMRT over this property?

5.   In *In re Estate of LaValle*, 218 S.W.3d 834 (Tex. App.—Beaumont 2007, pet. denied), both the trial and appellate courts agreed that the decedent made an irrevocable inter vivos gift to his son and that a purchase-money resulting trust did not arise. The widow asserted that her deceased husband had placed title in his son's name only to avoid claims which could have been made by the decedent's prior spouse. When the transferee is the child of the person who purchased the property, a rebuttable presumption arises that the transfer was a gift. Despite evidence

tending to rebut the presumption that the decedent had donative intent, the court explained that "it is not abuse of discretion to deny the remedy if the transfer was made for the purpose of defrauding creditors." *Id.* at 836. Although the decedent's prior spouse (the defrauded creditor) may have been able to claim successfully that a PMRT existed, the parties to the transfer (or their successors in interest) lack the ability to set aside the transfer.

    6.   *See* Examples & Explanations § 22.3.

C. CONSTRUCTIVE TRUSTS

    A constructive trust is an equitable remedy which a court imposes to prevent unjust enrichment. Constructive trusts do not arise because of the expressed or implied intent of the parties. Instead, the court adapts the split of title attribute of a trust to create a remedy when a person acquired title to property in an unconscionable manner. The court decides that the person with apparent full ownership of the property actually holds only the legal title because it would be unfair for that person to retain the beneficial interest in that property. The judgment of the court then acts to transfer legal title from the evil property owner ("trustee") to the person who would have owned the property but for the property owner's inappropriate conduct ("beneficiary").

    The Trust Code does not apply to constructive trusts. *Read* Trust Code § 111.003(2).

    "A party seeking imposition of a constructive trust must strictly prove: (1) breach of a special trust, fiduciary relationship, or actual fraud; (2) unjust enrichment of the wrongdoer; and (3) tracing to an identifiable res." *Flournoy v. Wilz*, 201 S.W.3d 833 (Tex. App.—Waco 2006, rev'd on other grounds, *Wilz v. Flournoy*, 228 S.W.3d 674 (Tex. 2007).

Notes and Questions

    1.   Defendant stole $10,000 from Plaintiff and used the money to take an exotic vacation to Tahiti. Defendant owns a variety of valuable assets such as automobiles, a home, and corporate securities. May Plaintiff obtain a constructive trust over any of this property?

    2.   Defendant purchased Plaintiff's home. Shortly thereafter, Defendant paid $80,000 on the mortgage and made valuable improvements by building a three room addition and a swimming pool. Plaintiff proves to the satisfaction of the court that Defendant's conduct during the sale was fraudulent and convinces the court that a constructive trust remedy is

proper. Is Defendant entitled to compensation for the mortgage payment and the improvements?

3.   A person asserting a constructive trust must strictly prove the elements of a constructive trust including the unconscionable conduct, the person in whose favor the constructive trust should be imposed, and the assets to be covered by the constructive trust. Mere proof of conduct justifying a constructive trust is insufficient. The evidence must permit the court to enter an order imposing the constructive trust and defining its terms.

For example, in *Medford v. Medford*, 68 S.W.3d 242 (Tex. App.—Fort Worth 2002, no pet.), Father devised a life estate in a house to Mother with the remainder passing to Son One and Son Two. Son One killed Mother and was convicted of causing serious bodily injury to an elderly person. Son Two rented the house. Son One sued to recover one-half of the rental income based on his status as a tenant in common. The trial court granted a take nothing summary judgment in favor of Son Two. Son One appealed.

The appellate court reversed. The court cited the Article I, § 21 of the Texas Constitution and Probate Code § 41(d) which provides that a conviction does not cause a corruption of the blood or forfeiture of property. Thus, the only way Son Two could prevent Son One from receiving the rental income was to demonstrate that a constructive trust should be imposed on Son One's share of the house because he caused the death of the life tenant. Despite the criminal conviction of Son One, the appellate court held that the conviction alone was not sufficient to support the trial court's imposition of a constructive trust. Son Two failed to present evidence regarding why he should be the beneficiary of the constructive trust and exactly what property over which the constructive trust should be imposed. The court also concluded that the trial court's take nothing judgment could not be read as imposing a constructive trust.

Courts are reluctant to enumerate a list of the types of wrongs for which a constructive trust remedy may be appropriate. Judges like to keep this equitable remedy flexible so that they can apply it in as many situations as possible. Nonetheless, the types of conduct giving rise to a constructive trust fall into three basic categories: (1) fraudulent conduct, (2) abuse of confidential relationships, and (3) unperformed promises made in contemplation of death.

1. Fraudulent Conduct

The property a person procures through fraudulent means may be subject to a constructive trust remedy. In this context, the term fraud is used broadly to refer to any type of wrongdoing, that is "all the multifarious means which human ingenuity can devise and are resorted to by one individual to get an advantage over another by false suggestions or by the suppression of the truth. No definite and invariable rule can be laid down as a general proposition defining fraud, as it includes all surprise, trick, cunning, dissembling, and any unfair way by which another is cheated." *Johnson v. McDonald*, 39 P.2d 150, 150 (Okla. 1934) (defining fraud although not in constructive trust situation). *See* GEORGE T. BOGERT, TRUSTS § 77, at 287 (6th ed. 1987) (fraud in constructive trust context as referring to "any kind of wrongdoing").

See Examples & Explanations § 23.1.

POPE v. GARRETT

Texas Supreme Court, 1948
147 Tex. 18, 211 S.W.2d 559

SMEDLEY, Justice.

This suit is by Claytonia Garrett against James Pope and others, the heirs of Carrie Simons, a Negro woman, to impress a trust upon property that passed to the heirs on the death of Carrie Simons intestate, after she, during her last illness, had been forcibly prevented by two of the heirs from executing a will devising the property to Claytonia Garrett.

Following trial before a jury the district court rendered judgment awarding to the plaintiff, Claytonia Garrett, the beneficial title to the whole of the property. The Court of Civil Appeals affirmed the trial court's judgment in part and reversed and rendered it in part, holding that a trust should not be impressed upon the interests of those of the heirs who had not participated in the wrongful act. . . .

On October 31, 1944, Thomas J. Green, a neighbor and friend of Carrie Simons, brought to her to be executed a will prepared by him at her request, by the terms of which all of her property was devised to plaintiff, Claytonia Garrett, who was not related to Carrie Simons. Present in the room at the time, besides Claytonia Garrett and Green, were the Reverend Preacher and Jewel Benson, a friend of plaintiff, who had been requested to come as witnesses of the will, and Lillie Clay Smith, sister of Carrie Simons, Mary Jones and Evelyn Jones, nieces of Carrie Simons, and Alberta Justus. The jury made the following findings: That Carrie Simons, some days before her death, requested Thomas Green to prepare a will for her leaving all of her property to Claytonia Garrett; that the will so prepared by Green was read by him to Carrie Simons; that after having heard the instrument read to her, Carrie Simons, in the presence of Reverend Preacher, Jewel Benson and others, declared it to be her last will; that Carrie Simons prepared to sign her name to the will but the defendants, Evelyn Jones and Lillie Clay Smith, by physical force or by creating a disturbance, prevented her from carrying out her intention to execute the will; that Carrie Simons was of sound mind at the time and was not in an unconscious condition; and that shortly after this incident she suffered a severe hemorrhage, lapsed into a semi-comatose condition and remained in that condition continuously until her death, which was on November 3, 1944. There is no proof that any of the heirs of Carrie Simons other than those above named were present or were in any way connected with the violence that prevented the execution of the will.

Two questions are presented by the two applications for writs of error that have been granted. First, should a trust be impressed in favor of Claytonia Garrett upon the property described in the will? And, second, if so, should the trust be impressed upon the interests inherited by all of the heirs or only upon the interests inherited by those who participated in the acts of violence that prevented the execution of the will?

We find no difficulty in approving the conclusion reached both by the trial court and by the Court of Civil Appeals as to the interests of the heirs who were guilty of the wrongful acts, that when they acquired, by the inheritance, the legal title to interests in the property, they became constructive trustees for Claytonia Garrett. According to the facts found by the jury, title undoubtedly would have passed to her under Carrie Simons' will but for the acts of violence. The case is a typical one for the intervention of equity to prevent a wrongdoer, who by his fraudulent or otherwise wrongful act has acquired title to property, from retaining and enjoying the beneficial interest therein, by impressing a constructive trust on the property in favor of the one who is truly and equitably entitled to the same. In Binford v. Snyder, 144 Tex. 134, 138, 189 S.W.2d 471, 472, the court quoted with approval the general rule as to the use of the constructive trust thus stated in the Ruling Case Law:

"It is a well settled general rule that if one person obtains the legal title to property, not only by fraud, or by violation of confidence of fiduciary relations, but in any other unconscientious manner, so that he cannot equitably retain the property which really belongs to another, equity carries out its theory of a double ownership, equitable and legal, by impressing a constructive trust upon the property in favor of the one who is in good conscience entitled to it, and who is considered in equity as the beneficial owner." . . .

It has been said that "The specific instances in which equity impresses a constructive trust are numberless,—as numberless as the modes by which property may be obtained through bad faith and unconscientious acts." Pomeroy's Equity Jurisprudence, 5th Ed., Vol. 4, p. 97, Sec. 1045 * * *

Citing Hutchins v. Hutchins, 7 Hill, N.Y., 104, the defendants, Pope et al., make the contention that plaintiff, Claytonia Garrett, is not entitled to any relief because she had no existing right in the property of Carrie Simons and thus was deprived by the acts of the defendants of nothing but an expectancy or hope to become a devisee. That case was an action at law for damages, the plaintiff alleging that the defendants, by false and fraudulent representations, induced his father to revoke a will in his favor and to execute a new one by which he was excluded from all participation in his father's estate. It was held that the plaintiff had no cause of action for damages because, according to the allegations of his declaration, he had no interest in the property beyond a mere naked possibility. Mr. Scott, citing the Hutchins case and two other like decisions and several decisions to the contrary, recognizes the conflict of authority on the question whether an action at law will lie against the heir for tort, but expresses his opinion that clearly a court of equity should prevent the heir from keeping the property which he has acquired by the result of his wrongful conduct and that the heir should be compelled to surrender the property to the intended legatee, since but for the wrong he would have received the property, and this even though the intended legatee had no interest in the property of the testator but only an expectancy. Scott on Trusts, Vol. 3, pp. 2371, 2372, Sec. 489.4. . . .

The argument is often made that the imposition of the constructive trust in a case like this contravenes or circumvents the statute of descent and distribution, the statute of wills, the statute of frauds, or particularly a statute which prohibits the creation of a trust unless it is declared by an instrument in writing. It is generally held, however, that the constructive trust is not within such statutes or is an exception to them. It is the creature of equity. It does not arise out of the parol agreement of the parties. It is imposed irrespective of and even contrary to the intention of the parties. Resort is had to it in order that a statute enacted for the purpose of preventing fraud may not be used as an instrument for perpetrating or protecting a fraud. . . .

In this case Claytonia Garrett does not acquire title through the will. The trust does not owe its validity to the will. The statute of descent and distribution is untouched. The legal title passed to the heirs of Carrie Simons when she died intestate, but equity deals with the holder of the legal title for the wrong done in preventing the execution of the will and impresses a trust on the property in favor of the one who is in good conscience entitled to it.

The second question is more difficult. Shall the trust in favor of Claytonia Garrett extend to the interests of the heirs who had no part in the wrongful acts? From the viewpoint of those heirs, it seems that they should be permitted to retain and enjoy the interests that vested in them as heirs, no will having been executed, and they not being responsible for the failure of Carrie Simons to execute it. On the other hand, from the viewpoint of Claytonia Garrett, it appears that a court of equity should extend the trust to all of the interests in the property in order that complete relief may be afforded her and that none of the heirs may profit as the result of the wrongful acts . . . .

The policy against unjust enrichment argues in favor of the judgment rendered herein by the district court rather than that of the Court of Civil Appeals. But for the wrongful acts the innocent defendants would not have inherited interests in the property. Dean Roscoe Pound speaks of the constructive trust as a remedial institution and says that it is sometimes used "to develop a new field of equitable interposition, as in what we have come to think the typical case of constructive trust, namely, specific restitution of a received benefit in order to prevent unjust enrichment." 33 Harvard Law Review, pp. 420, 421 * * *. Further and in the same trend, it has been said that equity is never wanting in power to do complete justice. Hill v. Stampfli, Tex. Com. App., 290 S.W. 522, 524.

We realize that a constructive trust does not arise on every moral wrong and that it cannot correct every injustice. . . . It must be used with caution, especially where as here proof of the wrongful act rests in parol, in order that it may not defeat the purposes of the statute of wills, the statute of descent and distribution, or the statute of frauds.

In the instant case the findings of the jury are well supported by the testimony of four disinterested, unimpeached witnesses, although their testimony is contradicted by that of two of the defendants. The will devising the property to the plaintiff, Claytonia Garrett, which Carrie Simons was prevented from executing, was introduced in evidence. In view of the authorities and equitable principles which have been cited and discussed, it is our opinion that the judgment of the district court should be affirmed in order that complete justice may be done.

The judgment of the Court of Civil Appeals is reversed and the judgment of the district court is affirmed.

2. Abuse of Confidential Relationship

Constructive trusts also arise if a transfer of property occurs because of an abuse of a confidential relationship which exists between the parties. The courts treat a wide variety of family, personal, social, and business relationships as being confidential if the complaining party was justified in relying on the other party to the transaction to be fair, honest, and to fully disclose all relevant facts. In other words, the relationship is confidential if the person's guard was down and was not treating the other person as if they were in an arms-length transaction. "However, not every relationship involving a high degree of trust and confidence rises to the stature of a fiduciary relationship. * * * Texas courts do not create such a duty lightly." *Moneyhon v. Moneyhon*, 278 S.W.3d 874, 878 n. 3 (Tex. App.— Houston [14th Dist.] 2009, no pet).

Notes and Questions

1.   George and Leo had been good friends for twenty years. Leo decided to open a new business and convinced George to transfer some of his property to the business. Although Leo's conduct did not amount to fraud, he knew that the business was risky and that George would have difficulty regaining his property. George could easily have discovered these facts if he had done even a cursory investigation but due to their long friendship, George did not believe that it was necessary. May George obtain an constructive trust and force Leo to return the property?

2.   *See* Examples & Explanations § 23.2.

3.   Unperformed Promises Made in Contemplation of Death

A constructive trust may arise if one person induces the transfer of property by promising the transferor to do something with that property at a later time and then fails to perform the promise. For example, assume that Donor gave property to Donee based on Donee's oral promise to execute a will leaving that property to Donor's child. If Donee fails to make a will containing the promised bequest, the court may impose a constructive trust on the property in favor of Donor's child regardless of who receives title to the property under Donee's will or, if Donee did not have a will, via intestacy.

Notes and Questions

1.   Testator executed a will containing the following dispositive provision: "I leave my home to Beneficiary." After Testator died, Victor claims that Testator and Beneficiary had an oral agreement that Beneficiary would hold the home in trust for Victor's benefit. How should a court rule on Victor's claim?

2.   *See* Examples & Explanations § 23.3.

SAMPLE WILL WITH TESTAMENTARY TRUST FORM

The first time you are asked to draft a will, an application for probate, or other estate planning document, you may initially panic wondering where to start. Although you know the legal rules, it is often quite a different experience to actually draft the documents. Do not despair. There are many form books available to start you on the right track. Always remember, of course, that no form should be used blindly and that no form will exactly fit your needs. Use a form as a guideline and be sure to make all appropriate changes. Never leave language in a document from a form without being sure you understand it and intend for it to be included.

Below is a list of some commonly used form books:

- 24 W. Dorsaneo & L. Larson, Probate Code Litigation (Texas Litigation Guide, most recent edition).
- 11, 11A, & 11B, Donald J. Malouf & Henry J. Lischer, Jr., Estate Planning (West's Texas Forms, most recent edition).
- State Bar of Texas, Texas Probate System (most recent edition).
- Texas Forms ch. 24 (Bancroft-Whitney, most recent edition).
- 12, 12A, & 12B Aloysius A. Leopold & Gerry W. Beyer, Probate and Administration of Estates (West's Texas Forms, most recent edition).

Computer programs are being used on an increasingly frequent basis to assist will preparation. Many attorneys prepare and store forms in computer usable formats. Commercial publishers also market computer programs which assist in form preparation. Some programs supply only the text of forms much like traditional form books. Other programs prompt the user to enter relevant information and then use that data to select and print a suitable form, inserting individualized information at the appropriate locations. Most of these programs are designed for use by attorneys but others are targeted at the lay community.

The form which follows may be used as a starting point for drafting a simple will.

LAST WILL OF [CLIENT]¹

I, [Client],[2] a resident of [City], Texas, [County] County, declare that this is my last will and I revoke all prior wills and codicils.

ARTICLE I
DESCRIPTION OF FAMILY

A. Marital Status

[if never married] I am not married and I have never been married.

[if single but previously married] I am not married. I was formerly married to [Ex-Spouse]. [We were divorced] [[Ex-Spouse] died] on [date].[3]

---

[1]Draft of January 2, 2017.

This sample will is designed to help you prepare Client's will. Please remember that this form, like any form, is just a guide; do not use it without considering the ramifications of each clause. The provisions must be individualized to fit the particular needs of Client.

Before attempting to use this form, you must familiarize yourself with the Texas Estates Code.

A will is only one part of an estate plan. You should be sure to plan for Client's potential disability with a durable power of attorney for property management (statutory form located in Estates Code § 752.051), a medical power of attorney (statutory form located in Health & Safety Code §§ 166.163 & 166.164), and a self-designation of guardian (statutory form located in Estates Code § 1104.204). You should also discuss whether Client wishes to express instructions regarding end-of-life decisions such as (1) the use of artificial life sustaining procedures with a directive to physicians ("living will") (statutory form located in Health & Safety Code § 166.033) or an out-of-hospital do-not-resuscitate order (see Health & Safety Code § 166.083), (2) anatomical gifts (see Health & Safety Code § 692.003), and (3) body disposition instructions (statutory appointment of agent form located in Health & Safety Code § 711.002).

Please note the following features of this form which are designed to reduce the likelihood of unauthorized page substitution. (1) Spaces on the bottom of each page for the initials of Client and the witnesses. (2) Use of *ex toto* pagination in the header.

[2]If Client has been known by other names (e.g., nickname, name prior to marriage, name used during previous marriage, etc.), they should be listed here. For example, "I [Client], also known as * * * or "I have also been known as * * * "

[3]Continue in a similar manner if Client has been divorced more than once.

| [Client] | [Witness One] | [Witness Two] |

[if currently married for first time] I am married to [Spouse]. We were married on [date]. This is my only marriage.

[if remarried] I am married to [Spouse]. We were married on [date]. I was formerly married to [Ex-Spouse]. [We were divorced] [[Ex-Spouse] died] on [date].[4]

B. Descendants

[if no living descendants] I have no living descendants.[5]

[if living descendants] I have [number] child[ren] [and [number] grandchildren]. [description][6]

C. Parents

My parents are [Mother] and [Father].[7]

D. Siblings

[if no siblings] I have no siblings.

[if siblings] I have [number] siblings. [description][8]

E. Additional Family Description[9]

---

[4]Continue in a similar manner if Client has been divorced more than once.

[5]Include a description of deceased descendants, if any.

[6]Provide a description of each child and grandchild including identity of the other parent and date of birth. If any child was adopted, indicate this fact and the date of the adoption.

[7]Indicate whether living or deceased.

[8]Indicate names and whether living or deceased. If the family tree is relatively small, nieces and nephews may also be indicated.

[9]Additional description of family members may be necessary if Client has few living relatives.

[Client]	[Witness One]	[Witness Two]

Last Will of [Client]
Page 3 of 21

ARTICLE II
GENERAL PROVISIONS

A. Definitions[10]

B. Survival[11]

If any beneficiary dies within [number] days of my death, such person shall be deemed to have predeceased me. The phrase "survives me" and similar expressions used in this will refer to this [number] day survival requirement.

C. Express Disinheritance[12]

I expressly intend that my [description of relationship], [Name], take no property from my estate either under this will or by intestacy.

---

[10]Define any terms used in the will which may cause controversy if left undefined. For example, if Client makes a class gift to "children," you should carefully explain whether Client intends to include adopted children, children born out of wedlock, and children born as the result of assisted reproduction techniques. The same considerations arise if a class gift is made to "grandchildren." In addition, Client should specify the age by which an adopted grandchild needs to be adopted by Client's child to fall within the class.

[11]The statutory survival period is 120 hours. Estates Code § 121.101. Many clients will want to increase this period.

[12]If Client wishes to make certain an heir does not take any portion of the estate, even if by chance Client dies partially intestate, an express disinheritance provision is appropriate. Estates Code § 254.003. If Client fears that an as yet unknown person may claim paternity (such as occurred when Elvis "died"), you may include a statement such as, "I expressly disinherit any child of mine whom I have not expressly listed by name in Article [ ]."

[Client]   [Witness One]   [Witness Two]

Last Will of [Client]
Page 4 of 21

D. Pretermitted Children[13]

I intentionally make no provision for any child whom I may have or adopt after execution of this will.

E. Divorce[14]

If I am divorced from [Spouse] or [condition][15] at the time of death, all provisions in this will in favor of [Spouse] are to be given no effect. For purposes of this will, [Spouse] will then be treated as if [Spouse] predeceased me.

F. *In Terrorem* Provision[16]

If any beneficiary under this will [or the trust created herein] contests or challenges this will [or trust] or any of its [their] provisions in any manner, be it directly or indirectly (including the filing of a will contest action), all benefits given to the contesting or challenging beneficiary are revoked and those benefits pass as if the contesting beneficiary predeceased me without descendants.

---

[13]An after-born or after-adopted child may be entitled to a statutory forced share under Estates Code §§ 255.052-255.056. This provision precludes the application of the statute. However, this section is not appropriate if Client intends to have or adopt children and wants them to share in the estate. Instead, these after-born and after-adopted children should be included as beneficiaries, such as by the use of a class gift to "children."

[14]Provisions in favor on an ex-spouse (as well as other ex-relatives) are automatically revoked unless the will provides otherwise. Estates Code §§ 123.001-123.002. However, merely filing for divorce is not treated as a divorce and will not revoke any provisions of the will unless the will expressly so states.

[15]State any condition Client wishes to trigger a revocation of spousal provisions, e.g., a filed and pending divorce petition.

[16]This provision may prevent heirs who are also beneficiaries of the will (but who are not receiving as much as they would under intestacy) from contesting the will. Note that the clause may be unenforceable if the contestant has just cause for instituting the proceedings and brings them in good faith. Estates Code 254.005.

| [Client] | [Witness One] | [Witness Two] |

G. Satisfaction[17]

No gift of any kind that I make under this will shall be considered either fully or partially satisfied by any inter vivos gift that I hereafter make.

H. Not Contractual[18]

At approximately the same time, [Spouse] and I are executing similar wills. The wills are not, however, the result of any contract or agreement between us and either will may be revoked at the sole discretion of its maker.

I. Anatomical Gifts[19]

I hereby confirm my intent to make the following anatomical gifts: [description of gift].[20]

---

[17]This provision prevents a remainder beneficiary from claiming that inter vivos gifts to the beneficiary of a pecuniary gift reduce the amount to which that beneficiary is entitled from the estate. See Estates Code §§ 255.101-255.102.

[18]This provision is appropriate only if Client and Spouse are executing wills with parallel dispositive provisions. The execution of reciprocal wills does not by itself suffice as evidence of a contract. Estates Code § 254.004. This provision makes Client's intent clear.

[19]Although anatomical gifts may be made by will (Health & Safety Code § 692A.005(a)(2)), it is not prudent because Client's will may not be found and read until long after the time for making usable gifts has passed. Thus, a separate document or registration with the Donate Life Texas Registry is recommended. However, confirmation in a will may be helpful if the family is unsure about Client's intent reflected only by a less formal anatomical gift card.

[20]Typical gifts include (1) certain specified organs such as the heart, liver, or kidneys; (2) any needed organ; and (3) the entire body.

| [Client] | [Witness One] | [Witness Two] |

J. Body Disposition Instructions[21]

I request that I be given a simple funeral and that my remains be [buried] [cremated] in an economical manner. It is my desire that the greatest possible portion of my estate pass to the beneficiaries I have named in this will.

ARTICLE III
SETTLEMENT OF ESTATE OBLIGATIONS[22]

A. Exoneration[23]

[if no exoneration desired] All specific gifts made in this will pass subject to any mortgage, security interest, or other lien existing at the date of my death without right of exoneration.

[if exoneration desired] If any specific gift made in this will is subject to a mortgage, security interest, or other lien, I direct that my executor pay the debt from other property of my estate which is not specifically given.

---

[21]Although body disposition instructions may be stated in a will (Health & Safety Code § 711.002(g)), they will not be effective unless the will is found immediately after death. Thus, it is better practice to use a separate document or appoint an agent to control the disposition.

[22]If Client is satisfied with some or all of the presumptions on the issues covered in this section, you may omit this Article or integrate the remaining provisions into Article II.

[23]This clause addresses whether non-specific gifts abate to pay mortgages, security interests, and other liens on specific gifts, unless the will provides otherwise. Texas had long followed the doctrine of exoneration, that is, debts on specifically gifted property were paid from other estate assets so that the beneficiary receives the asset unencumbered, rather than just the testator's equity. See *Currie v. Scott*, 187 S.W.2d 551 (Tex. 1945).

The doctrine has been abolished for wills executed on or after September 1, 2005. A specific gift passes subject to each debt secured by the property that exists on the date of the testator's death under Estates Code § 255.301. However, the testator may expressly provide in the will for the debts against a specific gift to be exonerated. Estates Code § 255.302.

[Client]   [Witness One]   [Witness Two]

B. Abatement[24]

I direct the gifts made in this will abate in the following order: [order].

C. Apportionment[25]

I direct that any tax payable because of a transfer of property upon my death, such as the federal and state estate tax, be paid from the following property of my estate in the order listed. [list]

ARTICLE IV
DISTRIBUTION OF PROPERTY[26]

[Option 1 — by type of gift]

A. Specific Gifts

I leave my [item[27]] to [Beneficiary]. If [Beneficiary] does not survive me, I leave my [item] to [Alternate Beneficiary].[28] If [item] is not in my estate, [ademption instructions].[29]

---

[24]This provision is unnecessary if Client is satisfied with the abatement order contained in Estates Code § 355.109 which provides that intestate property is the first to abate followed by residuary gifts, general gifts, and lastly specific gifts with personal property in each category being used before that category's real property.

[25] Any tax burden is apportioned among the persons interested in the estate according to Estates Code Chapter 124, Subchapter A. Thus, this provision is needed only if the estate is anticipated to be large enough to cause estate tax liability and Client wants to specify the gifts which abate to pay these taxes.

[26]This form contains three popular distribution options. Do not feel bound by these suggestions; your goal is to provide for the distribution Client desires. You may find it useful to combine portions of each option.

[27]Each gift must be precisely described so that there will be no doubt as to the item referred to after Client dies.

| [Client] | [Witness One] | [Witness Two] |

B.   General Gifts

I leave [amount][30] to [Beneficiary]. If [Beneficiary] does not survive me, I leave [amount] to [Alternate Beneficiary].[31]

C.   Residuary Gift[32]

I leave the residue of my estate to [Beneficiary]. If [Beneficiary] does not survive me, I leave the residue to [Alternate Beneficiary].[33]

[Option 2 — by identity of survivors — spouse and children example]

A.   If Survived by [Spouse]

If I am survived by [Spouse], I leave [Spouse] all of my property.

---

[28]Naming an alternate beneficiary prevents the application of the anti-lapse statute even in cases where the family relationship is close enough to make the statute otherwise applicable. Estates Code § 255.153.

[29]Express instructions regarding ademption prevents the gift from failing if the Client wants Beneficiary to receive an alternate gift (e.g., another item or money) if the named item is no longer in the estate.

Continue in a similar manner for each specific gift. If several beneficiaries are to receive multiple items, consider drafting subsections titled with each beneficiary's name which list the gifts.

[30]The beneficiary of a pecuniary gift is entitled to interest at the legal rate if distribution is delayed more than one year after the testator's death. Property Code § 116.051(3)(A).

[31]See note 28.

[32]The distributions contained in Option 2 and Option 3 may be used in place of this outright gift.

[33]See note 28.

| [Client] | [Witness One] | [Witness Two] |

Last Will of [Client]
Page 9 of 21

B. If Not Survived by [Spouse][34]

If [Spouse] does not survive me, I leave all my property to [Children]. If any of my children predecease me survived by descendants who survive me, these surviving descendants receive the deceased child's share as in an intestacy distribution governed by Texas Estates Code § 201.101, as amended at the time of my death.[35]

C. If Not Survived by [Spouse] or Descendants

If I am survived by neither [Spouse] nor descendants, I leave all my property to [Beneficiary]. If [Beneficiary] does not survive me, I leave all my property to [Alternate Beneficiary].[36]

[Option 3 — conditional gifts — spouse and children example]

A. If Survived by [Spouse]

If I am survived by [Spouse], I leave [Spouse] all of my property.

B. If Not Survived by [Spouse] and My Youngest Child is At Least [Age] Years Old[37]

If I am not survived by [Spouse] and if my youngest surviving child is at least [age] years old, I leave all my property to my surviving children.

---

[34]If the children are minors, consider using Option 3 which triggers a trust for underage children.

[35]Revise this sentence if Client prefers surviving children to grandchildren, e.g., "If any of my children predecease me, the share which that child would have received had that child survived me shall be divided equally among my surviving children."

[36]See note 28.

[37]If Client desires to provide for children of deceased children (i.e., Client's grandchildren), this section needs to be revised appropriately.

_____   _____   _____
[Client]   [Witness One]   [Witness Two]

C. If Not Survived by [Spouse] and My Youngest Child is Under [Age] Years Old[38]

If I am not survived by [Spouse] and if my youngest surviving child is under [age] years old, I leave all my property to the trustee, in trust, of the [Name] Trust created in Article V of this will.[39]

D. If Not Survived by Spouse or Children

If I am survived by neither [Spouse] nor children, I leave all my property to [Beneficiary].[40] If [Beneficiary] does not survive me, I leave all my property to [Alternate Beneficiary].[41]

---

[38]See note 37.

[39]This provision assumes that Client's primary desire is to benefit the younger children. If Client's primary desire is to treat all children equally, this provision needs to be changed to give children over the stated age their shares outright with only shares for the younger children passing into the trust.

[40]If Client names grandchildren, consider whether these shares should be held in trust.

[41]See note 28.

Last Will of [Client]
Page 11 of 21

ARTICLE V
[NAME] TRUST[42]

A. Conditions of Creation

This trust is to be created upon the conditions stated in Article IV.

B. Governing Law

This trust is to be governed by Texas law unless this Article provides to the contrary.

C. Trustees

I appoint [Trustee] as Trustee of this trust. If [Trustee] is unwilling or unable to serve, I appoint [Alternate Trustee] as trustee.

A trustee may resign without the necessity of a court proceeding by giving at least a 30 day written notice to each of the adult beneficiaries and the guardian of each of the minor beneficiaries.

D. Bond

No bond shall be required of any trustee named in this Article.[43]

---

[42]This Article is appropriate if Client desires to create a testamentary trust. The example assumes that Client wishes to create the trust for the benefit of Client's children.

For a coordinated estate plan, consider having Client's life insurance and other death benefit contracts payable to this trust. For example, Client's spouse could be named as the primary beneficiary, the trust as the contingent beneficiary if the children are under the stated age, and the children outright if they are over the stated age or if for some reason this testamentary trust is not created.

This Article may also be used as a basic guide if you are preparing an inter vivos trust provided you address additional concerns such as the property Client wishes to transfer to the trust and whether or not Client may revoke the trust. Unless Client is creating the trust for tax purposes, Client probably wants to retain the power to revoke. Unlike the vast majority of states, Texas law presumes that Client retains the right to amend and revoke the trust. Prop. Code § 112.051.

    [Client]   [Witness One]   [Witness Two]

E. Trustee Compensation

[trustees to be compensated] [44]

The trustee shall be entitled to reasonable compensation from the trust for serving as trustee.

[trustees to be uncompensated][45]

No trustee shall be entitled to compensation for serving as trustee.

F. Beneficiaries of Trust

The beneficiaries of this trust are [Children].[46]

G. Distribution of Trust Property Until Youngest Beneficiary is At Least [Age] Years Old[47]

The trustee shall pay to or apply for the benefit of my children under [age] years old so much of the net income and so much of the principal, up to the whole thereof, of the trust property as the trustee in the trustee's sole discretion deems advisable for the beneficiary's proper care, support,

---

[43]Bond is required unless (1) Client waives bond or (2) the trustee is a corporation. Prop. Code § 113.058. If Client wishes to enhance beneficiary protection by requiring a bond, despite its cost, this provision should expressly state that the trustee must post bond.

[44]A trustee is presumed to be entitled to "reasonable compensation." Prop. Code § 114.061.

[45]A waiver of compensation may be appropriate if Client names a family member or close friend as the trustee. However, a corporate or other professional trustee will probably not accept the trust if Client prohibits compensation.

[46]Depending on Client's circumstances, you may wish to list the children by name or use a class designation.

[47]This provision assumes that Client's primary desire is to provide for the younger children. If Client's desire is to treat all children equally, this provision needs to provide for the trust property to be divided into shares, one for each child. Distributions for each child would then be limited to this share. As soon as a child reaches the stated age, the trustee would then distribute the balance of that child's share, if any, directly to the child.

| [Client] | [Witness One] | [Witness Two] |

Last Will of [Client]
Page 13 of 21

education, medical expenses, and maintenance.[48] The trustee [is] [is not] required to treat each child equally. The trustee [may] [must] [need not] consider the beneficiary's other resources and income in making distribution decisions.[49]

[if Client also wishes to provide benefits for older children]

If in the trustee's opinion the trust income and corpus will be sufficient to satisfy the needs of my children who are under [age] years old for the duration of this trust, the trustee may pay to or apply for the benefit of my children who are at least [age] years old so much of the income [and principal] as the trustee in the trustee's sole discretion deems advisable for the beneficiary's proper care, support, education, medical expenses, and maintenance. The trustee [is] [is not] required to treat each child equally. The trustee [may] [must] [need not] consider the beneficiary's other resources and income in making distribution decisions.[50]

H. Events Causing Termination of this Trust[51]

This trust terminates when the first of the following events occurs:

    1. The death of all the beneficiaries [my children], or

    2. My youngest child beneficiary becoming [age] years old.

I. Distribution of Property Upon Termination

    1. If this trust terminates because of the death of all the beneficiaries

---

[48]The use of the property should be adjusted, if necessary, to fit Client's wishes. For example, some clients may wish to impose additional conditions, e.g., academic and disciplinary good standing in school.

[49]Adjust this provision to carry out Client's intent, i.e., is the trust to provide a minimum level of support and anything the beneficiary has or acquires is irrelevant or is the trust to provide a safety net if the client's other resources and income are inadequate.

[50]See note 49.

[51]If Client wishes to provide for grandchildren, this provision needs to be revised accordingly. This is especially the case if any of the grandchildren are minors.

    [Client]   [Witness One]   [Witness Two]

[my children], the trustee shall deliver all remaining trust property to [Beneficiary].[52]   If [Beneficiary] is not living at the time of trust termination, the trustee shall deliver all remaining trust property to [Alternate Beneficiary].

2. If this trust terminates because my youngest child reaches [age] years of age, the trustee shall deliver all remaining trust property to my then surviving children in equal shares. [53]

J.   Spendthrift Provision[54]

This is a spendthrift trust, that is, to the fullest extent permitted by law, no interest in the income or principal of this trust may be voluntarily or involuntarily transferred by any beneficiary before payment or delivery of the interest by the trustee.

K.   Principal and Income[55]

The trustee shall have the discretion to credit a receipt or charge an expenditure to income or principal or partly to each in any manner which the trustee determines to be reasonable and equitable.

---

[52]Grandchildren, if any, are commonly named as remainder beneficiaries. Client may wish to have the shares of grandchildren held under the terms of the trust until they reach the stated age.

[53]If Client wishes to provide for grandchildren (i.e., children of deceased children), this provision needs to be revised accordingly, e.g., create one share for each surviving child and one share for each deceased child who left surviving descendants who are still alive and then give one share to each surviving child and distribute a share created for a deceased child to that child's descendants.

[54]Most clients will be excited about the possibility of preventing the beneficiaries from transferring their interest as well as protecting that interest from the beneficiaries' creditors. Prop. Code § 112.035.

[55]Property Code Chapter 116 governs the allocation of receipts and expenditures unless the trust instrument otherwise provides. Prop. Code § 116.004(a)(1). To make it easier for non-corporate trustees to administer the trust, it may be advisable to include this provision which grants the trustee discretion. This provision is rarely used if Client names a professional or corporate trustee because they have the expertise and bookkeeping systems to make the allocations.

[Client]	[Witness One]	[Witness Two]

Last Will of [Client]
Page 15 of 21

L. Trustee Powers[56]

[if Client is satisfied with default powers]

The trustee shall have all powers granted to trustees under Texas law.

[if Client wishes to alter default powers]

The trustee shall have the following powers in addition to the powers Texas law grants trustees: [description]

The trustee shall not have the following powers which are ordinarily accorded trustees under Texas law: [description]

M. Exculpatory Clause[57]

The trustee shall not be liable for any loss, cost, damage, or expense sustained through any error of judgment or in any other manner except for and as a result of a trustee's own bad faith or gross negligence.

N. Rule Against Perpetuities Savings Clause[58]

If a court of proper jurisdiction finds that this trust violates the Rule Against Perpetuities, the remaining trust property shall be distributed to [Beneficiary].

---

[56]Extensive trustee powers are provided by statute. Prop. Code §§ 113.001 through 113.030. If Client wishes the trustee to retain any particular item in the trust (e.g., a family heirloom or the family home) without regard to diversification or its wisdom as an investment, include an express provision permitting the retention.

[57]This provision will increase the likelihood that a trustee, especially a non-corporate one, will accept the trust. See Prop. Code § 114.007.

[58]If the will or trust has any provision that might violate the Rule Against Perpetuities, a savings provision should be included. Prop. Code § 112.036 (statement of rule) & § 5.043 (reformation to carry out Client's intent, including use of cy pres).

[Client]   [Witness One]   [Witness Two]

ARTICLE VI
ESTATE ADMINISTRATION

A. Appointment of Independent Executor

I appoint [Executor] as independent executor of this will. If [Executor] is unwilling or unable to serve, I appoint [Alternate Executor] as independent executor.[59]

B. Creation of Independent Administration[60]

To the extent permitted by law, no action shall be had in any court exercising probate jurisdiction in relation to the settlement of my estate other than the probating and recording of my will and return of any required inventory, appraisement, and list of claims of my estate.

C. Bond[61]

No bond shall be required of any executor named in this will.

D. Executor Compensation[62]

[executor to be compensated]

The executor shall be entitled to reasonable compensation for serving as the executor of my estate.

---

[59]The statutory order in absence of a nomination by will is found in Estates Code § 304.001.

[60]This provision tracks the language of Estates Code § 401.001.

[61]Bond is required unless (1) Client waives bond, (2) the personal representative is a corporation, or (3) the court waives bond in an independent administration. Estates Code §§ 305.101 & 401.005. If Client wishes to enhance beneficiary protection by requiring a bond, despite its cost, this provision should expressly state that the executor must post bond.

[62]In the absence of a provision waiving compensation, the executor is entitled to compensation computed under Estates Code § 352.002.

| [Client] | [Witness One] | [Witness Two] |

[executor to be uncompensated][63]

The executor shall not be entitled to compensation for serving as the executor of my estate.

E. Executor Powers[64]

I vest my independent executor with full power and authority to sell, lease, encumber, or otherwise dispose of or convert any or all of my estate in such a manner as my executor may see fit, it being my desire that, subject only to the terms of this will, my independent executor shall have full power and authority to do all things reasonably necessary for the settlement of my estate.

F. Digital Assets

My independent executor may exercise all powers that an absolute owner would have and any other powers appropriate to achieve the proper investment, management, and distribution of: (1) any kind of computing device of mine; (2) any kind of data storage device or medium of mine; (3) any electronically stored information of mine; (4) any user account of mine; and (5) any domain name of mine. My independent executor may obtain copies of any electronically stored information of mine from any person or entity that possesses, custodies, or controls that information. I hereby authorize any person or entity that possesses, custodies, or controls any electronically stored information of mine or that provides to me an electronic communication service or remote computing service, whether public or private, to divulge to my independent executor: (1) any electronically stored information of mine; (2) the contents of any communication that is in electronic storage by that service or that is carried or maintained on that service; (3) any record or other information pertaining to me with respect to that service. This authorization is to be

---

[63]A waiver of compensation may be appropriate if Client names a family member or close friend as the executor. However, a corporate or other professional executor will probably not agree to serve if Client prohibits compensation.

[64]This section provides a broad grant of powers. Revise this section as needed if Client wishes to restrict the executor's powers or to provide an unusual power.

[Client] [Witness One] [Witness Two]

construed to be my lawful consent under the Electronic Communications Privacy Act of 1986, as amended; the Computer Fraud and Abuse Act of 1986, as amended; and any other applicable federal or state data privacy law or criminal law. My independent executor may employ any consultants or agents to advise or assist in decrypting any encrypted electronically stored information of mine or in bypassing, resetting, or recovering any password or other kind of authentication or authorization, and I hereby authorize my independent executor to take any of these actions to access: (1) any kind of computing device of mine; (2) any kind of data storage device or medium of mine; (3) any electronically stored information of mine; and (4) any user account of mine. The terms used in this paragraph are to be construed as broadly as possible, and the term "user account" includes without limitation an established relationship between a user and a computing device or between a user and a provider of Internet or other network access, electronic communication services, or remote computing services, whether public or private.

G. Exculpatory Clause[65]

The executor shall not be liable for any loss, cost, damage, or expense sustained through any error of judgment or in any other manner except for and as a result of the executor's own bad faith or gross negligence.

---

[65]This provision will increase the likelihood that an executor, especially a non-corporate one, will accept the position.

_____   _____   _____
       [Client]   [Witness One]   [Witness Two]

ARTICLE VII

GUARDIANS OF MINOR CHILDREN AND
ADULT INCAPACITATED CHILDREN [66]

A. Guardian of Person

I appoint [guardian] as guardian of the person of any and all of my children who require a guardian because of his or her status as (1) a minor or (2) an adult incapacitated person.

If [guardian] is unwilling or unable to serve, I appoint [alternate guardian].

B. Guardian of Estate[67]

I request that the guardian of the person named in subsection A above also seek appointment as guardian of [Child's] estate.

---

[66]This Article is appropriate if Client (1) has a minor child or (2) is serving as guardian of an adult child who, because of a physical or mental condition, is substantially unable (a) to provide food, clothing, or shelter for the child's self, (b) to care for the child's own physical health, or (c) to manage the child's own financial affairs. Estates Code §§ 1104.053 & 1104.103.

Guardian appointments are effective upon the death of the surviving parent. Unless the court finds that the designated person is disqualified, dead, refuses to serve, or would not serve the best interests of the ward, the court is required to appoint that person in preference to the individuals who would normally be entitled to the position. Estates Code §§ 1104.053 & 1104.103.

Guardian appointments may also be made in a separate document. Estates Code § 1104.153 provides a statutory form for guardian appointment which must be executed according to formalities similar to those for a will.

[67]A person entitled to appointment as guardian of the person is, after complying with Probate Code requirements, entitled to be appointed as the estate guardian. Estates Code §§ 1104.053 & 1104.103.

[Client]   [Witness One]   [Witness Two]

Last Will of [Client]
Page 20 of 21

C. Waiver of Bond[68]

I direct that no bond or other security shall be required of any guardian appointed in my will.

SIMULTANEOUS EXECUTION, ATTESTATION, AND SELF-PROVING[69]

I, _____, as testator, after being duly sworn, declare to the undersigned witnesses and to the undersigned authority that this instrument is my will, that I willingly make and execute it in the presence of the undersigned witnesses, all of whom are present at the same time, as my free act and deed, and that I request each of the undersigned witnesses to sign this will in my presence and in the presence of each other. I now sign this will in the presence of the attesting witnesses and the undersigned authority on this _____ day of _____, 20___.

_____
                                  Testator

The undersigned, _____ and _____, each being at least fourteen years of age, after being duly sworn, declare to the testator and to the undersigned authority that the testator declared to us that this instrument is the testator's will and that the testator requested us to act as witnesses to the testator's will and signature. The testator then signed this will in our presence, all of us being present at the same time. The testator is eighteen years of age or over (or being under such age, is or has been lawfully married, or is a member of the armed forces of the United States or of an auxiliary of the armed forces of the United States or of the United States

---

[68]Client may waive bond for the guardian of the person. However, "[t]he court may not waive the requirement of a bond for the guardian of the estate of a ward, regardless of whether a surviving parent's will or written declaration directs the court to waive the bond." Estates Code § 1105.101.

[69] This form is based on Estates Code § 251.1045.

    _____   _____   _____
        [Client]   [Witness One]   [Witness Two]

Last Will of [Client]
Page 21 of 21

Maritime Service), and we believe the testator to be of sound mind. We now sign our names as attesting witnesses in the presence of the testator, each other, and the undersigned authority on this _____ day of _____, 20_____.

_____   _____
[Witness One]   [Witness Two]

_____   _____

_____   _____
[Address]   [Address]

Subscribed and sworn to before me by the said _____, testator, and by the said _____ and _____, witnesses, this _____ day of _____, 20___.

(SEAL)

_____
Signature

_____
Official Capacity of Officer

_____   _____   _____
[Client]   [Witness One]   [Witness Two]

INDEX

U

V

W

Printed in the United States
By Bookmasters